88863

Pictures assembled and edited by:
Milton Rugoff and Susan Rayfield
Design and Coordination by:
Massimo Vignelli and Gudrun Buettner

Drawings by Walter Hortens

A Chanticleer Press Edition

Butterflies

Their World, Their Life Cycle, Their Behavior

Photographs by:
Edward S. Ross
Larry West
E. R. Degginger
Thomas C. Emmel
Boyce A. Drummond III
Othmar Danesch
Keith M. Spencer
D. F. Owen
Robert Goodden
Thomas W. Davies
Maria Zorn
Kjell B. Sandved
Keith S. Brown, Jr.
James H. Carmichael, Jr.
H. Vannoy Davis
Hermann Eisenbeiss
and others

Text:
Thomas C. Emmel
Consulting Editor:
Edward S. Ross

Alfred A. Knopf, New York

1-10 The freshly laid eggs (1) of the Baltimore
checkerspot (Euphydryas phaeton) *soon turn dark*
purple as the larvae develop within the eggshells.
The young caterpillar (2) goes through four molts (3)
and overwinters in communal webs before maturity
(4). It then molts to the pupa stage (5), which soon
hatches (6,7) into the adult butterfly (8). Emerging
in late May and June, the checkerspots find mating
partners (9) and the females begin laying eggs (10)
to start the cycle again.

THIS IS A BORZOI BOOK, PUBLISHED BY
ALFRED A. KNOPF, INC.

Prepared and produced by Chanticleer Press, Inc.

Staff of this book:
Publisher: Paul Steiner
Editor-in-Chief: Milton Rugoff
Managing Editor: Gudrun Buettner
Project Editor: Susan Rayfield
Production: Emma Staffelbach
Art Associate: Roberta Savage
Design: Massimo Vignelli

Color reproductions by Fontana and Bonomi,
Milan, Italy

Printed and bound by Amilcare Pizzi, S.p.A.,
Milan, Italy
First Edition 1975
Library of Congress Catalog Card Number: 75-10407
ISBN: 0-394-49958-1

Contents

The Fascination of Butterflies 16

Foreword

Butterflies are so intensely and vividly alive that they have impressed themselves upon man's imagination from earliest times. For centuries, English farmers, Japanese artists and Chinese emperors alike have celebrated their freedom, beauty and fragility. Today, when people from every walk of life are taking an increasing interest in wildlife, butterflies are among the living things that most people want to know more about.

My own introduction to the world of butterflies came at the age of eight, when my father put a net in my hands during a summer outing. My interest was captured forever. It led me to the study of biology, eventually to research in butterflies, and what has turned out to be a lifetime of exploration, discovery and excitement.

In the pursuit of my interest I have climbed after butterflies on the slopes of 19,000-foot peaks in the Andes, collected in the rich mountain meadows of the Colorado Rockies, photographed translucent-winged beauties in the Ecuadorian rain forests, and found new swallowtail races in the deserts of southern California. I have studied butterfly biology in the remote Galapagos Islands and in the teeming savannas of East Africa.

In organizing this book it seemed to me most effective and helpful to begin, in Part One, by explaining the biology and behavior of butterflies and the various families into which they are classified. In Part Two, I discuss the major regions of the world in which butterflies are found—rain forests, deserts, temperate zone woodlands, mountain heights, Arctic tundra and oceanic islands. In Part Three, I describe the various ways, economic and scientific, in which butterflies have proved important to man. Finally, in several sections at the end of the book I have offered advice to those interested in collecting and photographing butterflies.

My hope is that all this, together with the superb photographs, will lead the reader to something like the unalloyed pleasure I have experienced in this pursuit.

I would like to take this opportunity to thank Dr. Edward S. Ross, of the California Academy of Sciences, and Susan Rayfield and Milton Rugoff of Chanticleer Press for their exceptional help and advice in preparing this book. John F. Emmel, Boyce A. Drummond, Keith M. Spencer, Paul R. Ehrlich, Larry E. Gilbert and many others have contributed much to the development of this work through our discussions of exciting discoveries in the world of butterflies.

Thomas C. Emmel
University of Florida
Gainesville, Florida

The Fascination of Butterflies

There is a place on the California coast called Pacific Grove where vast numbers of monarch butterflies pause each winter to take advantage of the equable climate of that sheltered spot. They festoon the branches and leaves of Monterey pine and cypress and other growth so densely that they sometimes seem to be one great, thousand-winged organism. When the sun comes out, they stir and spread their wings to the life-giving warmth.

And each year thousands of visitors come from far and wide to watch them. They watch, fascinated by these quivering, tissue-thin, gold and amber bits of life. They watch, beguiled by the mass of color, delicate form and flickering motion, by the paradox of a species that is so vulnerable and yet has endured for eons, by the mystery of so many living creatures all drawn irresistably into a thousand-mile journey that, a month or two later, will end in death for many of them.

What attracts the visitors has attracted men since time forgotten. It has made butterflies, even more than birds, the symbol of freedom, of spritely grace, of all that cannot be tethered, caged or tamed.

It is not only the butterfly that stirs us but the transformation of a crawling, earthbound caterpillar into a weightless creature of air. In this change alone there are metaphors beyond the reach of any poet. No wonder Aristotle was spellbound as he observed this metamorphosis in the caterpillars of the white butterflies riddling his cabbages. And no wonder that legends have grown up around them as messengers of good luck and as spirits of the dead. The ancient Greeks thought they were the departed souls of the dead and in their mythology the goddess Psyche, personification of the soul, was often depicted as a maiden with the wings of a butterfly. In some countries, the image of a butterfly is still placed on gravestones. Country folk in Rumania believed that butterflies originated from the tears of the Virgin Mary. The Slavs opened a door or window to permit the soul of a dead person, often shown in the form of a butterfly, to escape from the body. Hindu mythology tells us that Brahma, watching the devouring caterpillars in his vegetable garden turn into pupae and finally lovely butterflies, was filled with a great calm, and thereafter was sure of reaching his own perfection in a final incarnation.

The life and development of the butterfly has also touched the imagination of many of the sages and poets of the Far East. Chuang Tzu, most original of the Taoist philosophers, delighted in similes from the world of nature, and often used the butterfly in his allegories. He was even nicknamed the "Butterfly Philosopher" because he once dreamed that he had been transformed into a butterfly and had found great happiness in gloriously free flight and in sipping nectar from flower after flower.

The artists and poets of ancient China, Indochina, Korea, and Japan have always been fascinated by the vivid colors and intricate designs of the butterflies of the Far East. The insect has exactly fitted their modes of thinking, their sense of detail and delicacy. But in the Western world it was not until the Renaissance with its rediscovery of nature that the butterfly became a part of our symbolic imagination. The great English poets, including Shakespeare, Spenser, Shelley, Keats, and Wordsworth, celebrated the beauty of butterflies although they were acquainted only with the relatively uncolorful species of England.

There are also many charming references to butterflies in American prose and poetry, but perhaps the most evocative is the one by Walt Whitman in his *Specimen Days:*

"Over all flutter myriads of light-yellow butterflies, mostly skimming along the surface, dipping and oscillating, giving a curious animation to the scene. The beautiful, spiritual insects! Straw-color'd Psyches! Occasionally one of them leaves his mates, and mounts, perhaps spirally, perhaps in a straight line in the air, fluttering up, up, till literally out of sight. In the lane as I came along just now I noticed one spot, ten feet square or so, where more than a hundred had collected, holding a revel, a gyration-dance, or butterfly good-time, winding and circling, down and across, but always keeping within the limits."

The name "butterfly" probably comes from the rich yellows of the European brimstone butterflies, which reminded peasants of butter. The brimstones, moreover, are elegantly shaped creatures that hibernate as adults rather than in the egg or pupa; aroused by the first warm days of spring, they are annually among the earliest butterflies to appear in northern Europe.

Few of nature's transformations have excited so much wonder as that in which the crumpled lump of the pupa unfolds into a masterpiece of symmetrical design. Bizarre notions about this metamorphosis go back to antiquity. In the Middle Ages, the learned monk Albertus Magnus, teacher of the great Thomas Aquinas, thought that caterpillars laid eggs and were entirely unrelated to butterflies, which he called "winged worms of various color." As late as the seventeenth century, Izaak Walton, who wrote so perceptively about the joys of angling and loved to watch caterpillars and butterflies as he fished, relied more on ancient writers than on his own observations. Naively he accepted the conclusion of Pliny, Roman writer on natural history, that "many caterpillars have their birth, or being, from a dew that in the spring falls upon the leaves of trees."

Perhaps we should not be too hard on the ancients, for the changes that occur in a metamorphosis are almost incredible. Two nineteenth-century authors of a biology textbook, perhaps not so sophisticated as writers today, sum up these transformations: "Were a naturalist to announce to the world the discovery of an animal which first existed in the form of a serpent; which then . . . weaving a shroud of pure silk of the finest texture, contracted itself within this covering into a body without external mouth or limbs, and resembling, more than anything else, an Egyptian mummy and which, lastly, after remaining in this state without food and without motion . . . should at the end of that period burst its silken cerements, struggle through its earthly covering and start into day a winged bird—what think you would be the sensation excited by this strange piece of intelligence? After the first doubts of its truth were dispelled, what astonishment would succeed! Among the learned, what surmises!—what investigations! Even the most torpid would flock to the sight of such a prodigy!"

It is not only biologists who respond to butterflies with such enthusiasm. A notable number of eminent men have made these most appealing of all insects one of their major preoccupations. After World War II, Sir Winston Churchill planned a "butterfly garden" where butterflies and their larval food plants would be stocked abundantly enough to make it self-perpetuating. In our own time the famous novelist Vladimir Nabokov has all his life been a professional student of butterflies and writes about them with rare literary skill.

For those who are yet to have the pleasure of becoming acquainted with butterflies the pictures in these pages as well as the text should serve as an introduction to the wonder and mystery of these remarkable creatures. They may help such readers understand how the first sight of an unknown butterfly can stir much the same excitement as a new masterpiece in any of the arts.

Part One

Part One

Life History of the Butterfly

Among the ancients, butterflies and caterpillars were thought to be entirely different creatures. It took thousands of years for people to realize that a creeping caterpillar would some day become a winged beauty floating across the hillside.

In primitive insects, such as roaches and silverfish, the first form that hatches out is a miniature of the adult. These and other types of insects go through three stages of development before reaching maturity, but only the most advanced insects, including the butterflies and moths, undergo a unique process called complete metamorphosis (from a Greek word meaning "change of form"), in which an insect goes through four radically different stages: egg, wormlike larva (or caterpillar), mummy-like pupa (or chrysalis), and finally the winged adult.

The magic of this last transformation can best be appreciated through the technique of time-lapse photography, in which a process that may (in the case of a monarch) take eight to ten days can be condensed into minutes.

At first the caterpillar, almost two inches long, decorated with yellow, black, and white bands, hangs by its tail curled up in the shape of a "J." Slowly its skin becomes loose and crinkly. It begins splitting apart at the head and, once started, the skin quickly slithers up the body to the tail. The exposed pupa begins to wriggle and squirm until the old skin drops off.

The pupa, a greenish yellow jelly-like mass, continues to squirm and then, gradually, it hardens, begins to glisten and becomes a shiny green, gold-speckled casing.

Slowly the pupa shrinks a little. After about eight days it darkens until the orange butterfly nestling within is just visible. A few hours later the pupa turns almost black but remains transparent, like a sheath of celluloid film. The butterfly is clearly revealed inside.

On one side of the pupa there is a trapdoor equipped with seams like a zipper. After about five hours the butterfly thrusts itself through this trapdoor and crawls out, head down. It then rights itself. Its wings are crumpled together, but the tiny body begins to pump fluid into them and almost imperceptibly they open. Suddenly, after only a few minutes, a monarch is poised in all its white-spangled, black-and-mellow-amber glory.

Structure of an egg

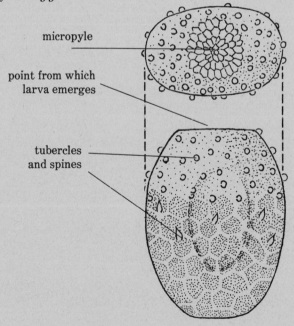

micropyle

point from which
larva emerges

tubercles
and spines

The Egg All butterflies begin life as eggs. Most are white, green, or yellow at first, but soon change color as the larva develops within them. The newly laid egg of the American wood nymph, for example, is yellowish. Within twenty-four hours, it changes to magenta-purple, and a day or two before hatching it looks like smoked cellophane, with the fully grown larva showing through the shell. The forms that eggs take

External structure of a caterpillar

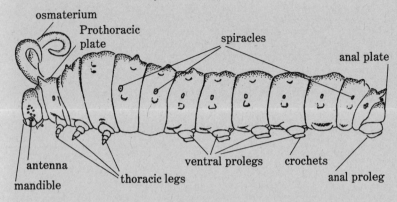

osmaterium
Prothoracic plate
spiracles
anal plate
antenna
mandible
thoracic legs
ventral prolegs
crochets
anal proleg

Internal structure of a caterpillar

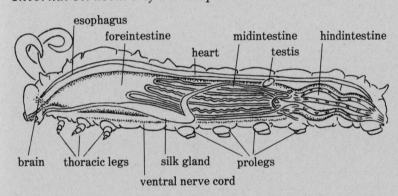

esophagus
foreintestine
heart
midintestine
testis
hindintestine
brain
thoracic legs
silk gland
prolegs
ventral nerve cord

vary according to the species: they may be conical, domed, round, or even shaped like a spindle, turban, or pincushion. Many have elaborately sculptured surfaces, from simple vertical ribs to deeply reticulated patterns of ridges intersected by spines, knobs, or other projections.

In spring or summer, females usually lay their eggs very deliberately on the leaves, stems, or flowers of plants that will later serve as food for the larva. Some butterflies, such as fritillaries in the genus *Speyeria*, drop their eggs at random, either during flight or while the female is settled near the food plant. When eggs are laid on the ground in this haphazard fashion, the larvae instinctively seek out the proper food source as soon as they hatch. But most butterflies glue their eggs to the surface of the food plant by a secretion which includes a fluid that quickly hardens the outside of each jelly-like egg into a thick shell, and this protects the egg from drying out or freezing.

Often the eggs are laid on the underside of a leaf where they are better protected from such enemies as parasitic wasps and predatory ants. But others are laid on blades of grass, branches, and even the mossy undersides of logs. Butterflies that lay eggs in the fall months usually deposit them on twigs and in cracks of tree bark, where they will pass the winter in relative safety. Depending upon the type of butterfly, the eggs are laid singly, in clusters, or in a large mass, sometimes several layers deep and in a pattern peculiar to each butterfly species. A female may deposit from several dozen to 1500 eggs during her lifetime. As Alexander Klots, one of America's leading entomologists, has put it: "The egg is a very valuable stage in the life cycle, being a small, compact unit of life that can be produced economically in large numbers, placed in a suitable environment and left to fend for itself."

The Caterpillar　The development of the larva within the eggshell can be completed in as little as three days after laying, as in some tropical species, or as long as a year, as in certain hairstreaks. When the young caterpillar is ready to hatch, it eats a hole in the side of the egg and pushes its way out. For most species, the caterpillar's first act is to eat the abandoned eggshell. Then it turns to the leaves or blossoms of the host plant. In some species, the young larva goes into a stage of suspended animation known as the diapause: without feeding, it crawls into a hiding place in bark or debris to pass a cold, unfavorable winter or a hot, dry summer.

Each caterpillar is primarily a food-processing machine; its sole aim is to eat enough for its own growth and also to store food in the form of fat to carry it through the nonfeeding pupa stage ahead. A caterpillar grows in spurts. As it ravenously devours food, its body swells until it can no longer be contained within its tight, unyielding outer skin. As the pressure increases, the skin finally splits, allowing a larger-bodied caterpillar to emerge. This process, called molting, occurs four or five times in the life-span of a typical caterpillar, the creature almost doubling in size each time. In the periods between molts, caterpillars are called instars, these stages being referred to as the first instar, the second instar, and so forth.

A typical caterpillar has a head and thirteen body segments. In most species, the head blends with the cylindrical body so that the caterpillar appears cigar-shaped. The heads of skipper larvae, however, seem to be separated from the rest of the body by a "neck." Caterpillars of blues, coppers, and hairstreaks are quite distinctive—short, flattened, and sluglike. A great many of these larvae have specialized honeydew glands which attract ants that in turn help defend the caterpillars against enemies.

The caterpillar's head consists of a pair of simple eyes, short antennae, and two strong, large jaws that form the sides of the mouth and have a razor-sharp cutting edge.

The first three pairs of the caterpillar's stumpy legs are used to grasp the leaf or other food as the larvae feeds. The remaining five pairs of legs end in stiff little hooks called crotchets, which help it to walk up vertical surfaces. When one of these legs is laid down on a smooth surface, the flat end is pressed down first, and its center then drawn up, creating a miniature suction cup. Aided by its legs, the caterpillar moves by contracting muscles that run from head to tail just beneath the skin. Beginning at the rear of the caterpillar, these contractions compress blood in the body cavity and force the front part of the body to arch upward and forward to a new position.

Inside the caterpillar, a large central tube that extends from the mouth to the tip of the abdomen forms the simple intestinal tract through which food passes. There are no veins or arteries in a caterpillar. Its green or yellow "blood," called hemolymph, completely fills the body cavity, continuously bathing all the internal organs. An open-ended pulsating tube running along the top of the caterpillar's body serves as the heart. In some smooth-skinned larvae, such as most of the satyrs, whites, and yellows, the heart tube can actually be seen through the skin.

Simple nerve connections run along the underside of the caterpillar, connecting the brain with other parts of the body. Caterpillars breathe through holes in their sides, called spiracles, which are connected to air tubes that radiate throughout the body.

The genital organs of the adult butterfly begin developing in the larval stage. Certain male caterpillars with transparent skin reveal a pair of testes visible as round or bean-shaped organs toward the end of their abdomen.

In many butterflies, the caterpillar is the longest stage of the entire life cycle, and the diversity of larval types is almost as great as that of the adults. Some caterpillars are green and have a skin so thin and transparent that the internal organs are visible. Others are more brightly marked—brilliant yellow, orange, red, or pink—with bold spots and stripes. Even within a single species, the appearance of the larva after each molt may vary tremendously. The newly hatched caterpillar bears a simple arrangement of hairs or bristles along its body, and has little elaboration of color or pattern. As it grows and periodically sheds its skin, each instar may display more complex surface patterns.

Many caterpillars have special adaptations for protection against predators. Long hairs screen out tiny parasitic wasps seeking to lay their eggs on the larva, and may also repel birds hunting for a tasty meal. Caterpillars that feed on poisonous plants, such as deadly nightshades, passionflowers, and milkweeds, incorporate the plant poisons into their tissues. Birds, lizards, toads, and small mammals learn to avoid the larvae of such butterflies, perhaps being warned by the larva's brightly colored stripes or other displays. The caterpillar of the swallowtail butterflies has an orange, fleshy, Y-shaped organ called the osmaterium, which it can thrust out from behind its head. This pulsating organ gives off a strong odor as it is waved about in the direction of the disturbance. When attacked, some swallowtail larvae will also rear up in a weaving, bobbing motion that looks like the threatening posture of a snake.

Other caterpillars, such as the spicebush swallowtail, display large eyespots on their backs that seem to frighten birds away. If disturbed by a predator some larvae feign death by curling into a tight ball and remaining motionless for several minutes. The caterpillars of many butterfly species, especially the satyrs, hide during the day and come out to feed only at night. Other caterpillar defenses range from camouflage, such as looking like a twig or leaf, to imitation of inedible objects like bird droppings. In some caterpillars, defensive signals change from molt to molt. For example, in California the anise swallowtail has a brilliant green-and-black-striped mature larva bearing bright orange spots, which probably serves as warning coloration, but the earlier four instars are mottled black and white, strongly resembling bird droppings.

The most remarkable caterpillar molt is the final one, when the fully grown larva is transformed into a pupa. In preparing to pupate, the larva first spins a silken pad. Caterpillars of some families also spin a silken girdle extending around their middle and thence to the adjacent surface; this holds them upright like the safety belt used by telephone linemen. Other butterflies have a hanging pupa and do not need a girdle. In either case, the larva grips its silken pad with special hooks at the tip of its abdomen and prepares to molt. The larva becomes dull and wrinkled as the old skin begins to separate from the new pupal shell forming beneath it. The skin splits by a wavelike series of muscular contractions and shrinks upward along the body toward the hooks.

The most difficult part of the process now takes place. The larva must withdraw an abdominal hook-studded structure called a cremaster out of the old larval skin and catch it in the silken pad outside. Then the cast-off skin can be discarded. The amazing fact about this complex aerial act is that very few caterpillars fail. This is fortunate, for if even the first attempt were not successful, the caterpillar would fall to the ground and die.

The Pupa

The third stage of the butterfly life cycle is the pupa, a term that comes from the Latin word for "doll," and describes this stage because it resembles a miniature infant in swaddling clothes. Like the egg, it is a nonfeeding stage during which major internal changes occur. Within the egg, the young embryo grew from a single fertilized cell into a caterpillar equipped with all the organs necessary for feeding and growing. Now, within the pupa, hormones trigger the crucial transformation of the larval tissues into those of the mature butterfly. At this stage, the pupa's content may be largely liquid. Essentially, all of the structures of the adult were already present in the caterpillar but were nonfunctioning rudiments called pads. During the pupal period, which may last, depending on the species, from a few days to several years, these pads develop into wings, legs, and the other organs found in the adult.

The outside surface of the pupa looks more like the adult butterfly than did the larva, for now the three adult body sections—head, thorax, and abdomen—are clearly sculptured. The large compound eyes protrude from the sides of the head, and the antennae sweep backward along the edges of the prominent cases that contain the wings. Often, a central, coiled tongue, or proboscis, coming out of the bottom of the head, and the three pairs of adult legs can also be recognized.

Like butterfly eggs and caterpillars, pupae vary considerably in size, color, and shape. Virtually all are camouflaged, looking like pebbles, leaves, twigs, flower buds, or even silvery rain or dewdrops. Horns, spines, and bizarre shapes further help to disguise them. Some caterpillars construct a small leafy tent in which to pupate, and this shelter helps to conceal the pupa from predators. During this resting stage, most pupae are immobile, capable only of twitching one or two body segments.

Structure of a pupa

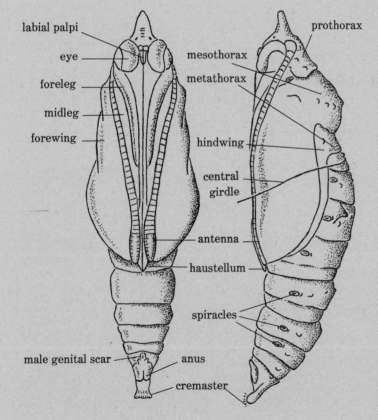

labial palpi
eye
foreleg
midleg
forewing
prothorax
mesothorax
metathorax
hindwing
central girdle
antenna
haustellum
spiracles
male genital scar
anus
cremaster

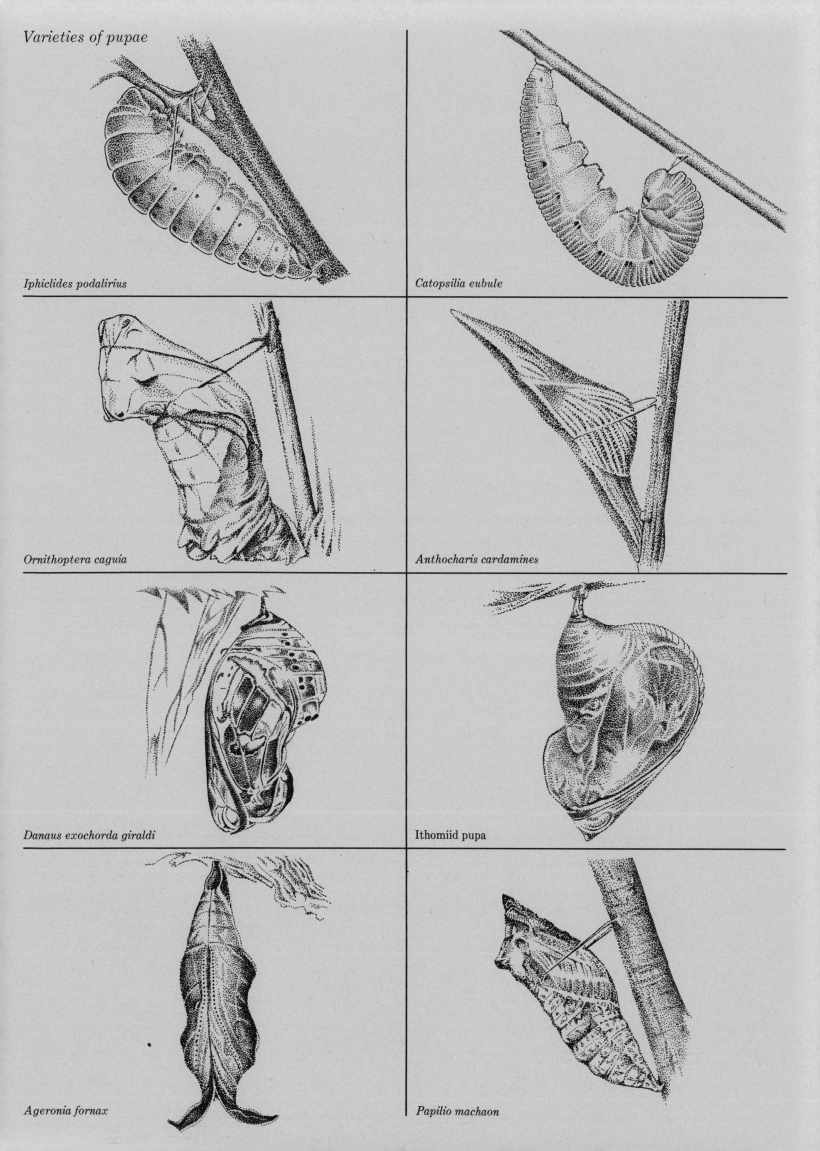

Varieties of pupae

Iphiclides podalirius

Catopsilia eubule

Ornithoptera caguia

Anthocharis cardamines

Danaus exochorda giraldi

Ithomiid pupa

Ageronia fornax

Papilio machaon

The Adult

The development of the adult butterfly inside the pupa is carried on in splendid isolation. Sealed within its impermeable casing, its only contact with the outside world is through its breathing holes, the spiracles. At this stage, no food is taken in and no wastes are excreted. The pupa depends upon its reserves of fat, built up in the caterpillar stage, and wastes are stored as liquid in the hind gut. During mass emergences of certain butterflies, these waste products, which often contain red pigments, are ejected, and the area may seem to be splattered with blood.

When the adult butterfly is fully formed inside its shell, the pupal skin splits, aided by the struggles of the adult to free itself. First the head and forepart of the body are thrust through, and then the antennae, legs, wings and other appendages are each withdrawn from their separate sheaths. Finally the adult pulls the end of its abdomen free. If it has emerged underground, for example in an ant nest, it crawls rapidly toward the light and the outside world. Wherever it emerges, the adult soon hangs suspended and pumps blood into the veins of its soft, crumpled wings, which rapidly expand and begin to harden. After an hour or more of rest, the butterfly is ready for its first flight.

The adult butterfly is a familiar sight to everyone. Its fragile sails dip and soar in garden, field and forest. However, the butterfly's flight is not just nature showing its whimsical side. This final stage of the life cycle is responsible for the vital functions of dispersal and reproduction, without which the species would soon become extinct.

The adult body is clearly divided into three sections: a head, a thorax, and an abdomen. Most of the butterfly's body and appendages are covered with a layer of flattened hairs called scales. These may be quite long, as on the main body, or very short and platelike, as on the surfaces of the wings. A few scales or hairs are found even on the eyes of many butterflies.

The large round compound eyes, with hundreds of smaller six-sided facets, are the most prominent features of the butterfly's head. The number of facets (and hence the size of the eye) is greater in the male than in the female, which may be related to his need for keen eyesight to seek out the female for courtship and mating. Up to 18,200 facets in each eye have been found in certain male swallowtails, and as few as 2,600 in some female lycaenids in Japan. Different theories persist regarding what the insect actually perceives. One theory holds that a mosaic image is formed with the limited view of each facet assembled into a single scene. Another theory proposes that an image is formed in each facet independently and the butterfly's brain sees the object as the total sum of information from all the facets. We do know that butterflies can perceive

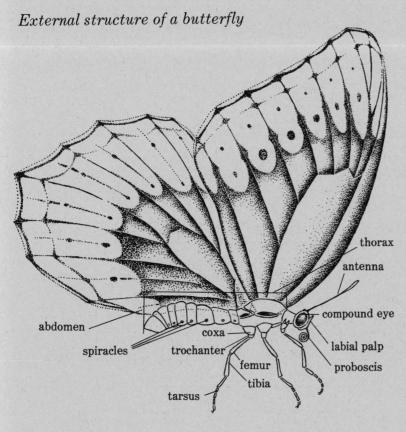

External structure of a butterfly

thorax

antenna

compound eye

labial palp

proboscis

abdomen

spiracles

coxa

trochanter

femur

tibia

tarsus

colors ranging from deep ultraviolet through blue and green to yellow, orange, and red. Many butterflies have ultraviolet patches on their wings that, while invisible to human beings, are brilliant iridescent signals to potential mates.

A pair of long antennae arises between the eyes, each shaft expanded toward its tip to form a club. The antennae carry receptors capable of detecting scents, touch, and probably sound.

The most prominent mouth part of the butterfly is the tightly coiled tongue, or proboscis, which is located on the underside of the head. This long, hollow sucking tube leads into the pharynx and acts as a suction bulb. Water, nectar, and other liquids are drawn up through the tongue when triggered by taste organs on the soles of the feet. Its tip has small chemical receptors and is often used for delicate probing by the hungry butterfly. In the laboratory, some butterflies seem to learn to associate other stimuli with feeding. Wood nymphs that are fed regularly early in the morning will begin uncoiling their tongues when the lights in their feeding room are turned on. Swallowtails will uncoil their tongues before being placed at a dish of sugar water.

The thorax is composed of three segments, each bearing a pair of legs. The second and third segments also carry the forewings and hindwings respectively. The wings of the butterfly consist essentially of two flattened membranes pressed close together. Running between them is a branching network of many hollow tubes or "veins," which serve as supporting struts. The pattern of these veins varies considerably from group to group and is often used in the classification of butterflies.

The wings are operated by internal muscles that change the shape of the thorax. When the thorax is flattened by the contraction of one set of muscles, the wings are raised. When it is narrowed by other muscles, the wings are lowered. Smaller muscles pulling directly on the bases of the wings adjust the position and angle of the wings during each stroke. When a butterfly is gliding along in leisurely fashion, it flaps its wings slowly and at only a slight angle from the horizontal plane. During cruising flight, used when the butterfly is passing from flower to flower or migrating, air presses against the underside of the wings, bending the front tips upward slightly and helping to increase the butterfly's forward speed to as much as twenty miles an hour. The wings pass through a vertical arc of 30 degrees. When the butterfly is alarmed, its wings beat rapidly and the tips almost touch at the top and bottom of each stroke.

Internal structure of a butterfly

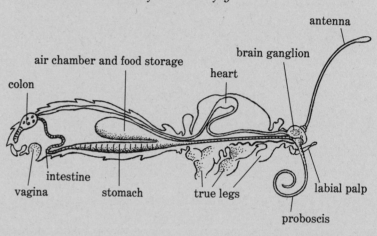

The vivid colors and patterns of a butterfly's wings never cease to astonish even the most casual observer. Both wing surfaces are densely covered with over-lapping scales arranged in rows like shingles on a

Wing Scales and Color

roof. Each represents the hardened wall of a single, greatly enlarged cell that arises from a socket on the wing. The scale contains air making it light in weight and an excellent insulator for temperature control.

Most commonly, the colors in a butterfly's wings are caused by pigments—chemical substances that absorb certain wavelengths of visible light and transmit the remainder, which are seen as color. Some of these pigments are created by the insect, while others are acquired from its food. Another kind of color results from the structure of the wing surface itself. Thin films project from the walls of each scale, their shapes and thickness changing the wavelengths of light hitting them and thus creating new colors. In the brilliant blue morphos and hairstreaks of South America, the light bouncing off the wings is in the blue end of the spectrum, and so appears as blue. The color white, too, is a structural effect, caused by the scattering of light across the scale surface. Luster and iridescence are also caused by structure. Overlapping transparent scales create many degrees of luster, from dull matte through velvet, satin, and mirror-like effects; these account for the bright metallic color of some coppers and the brilliant silvery spots on the wings of certain fritillaries. As light passes through films of various thicknesses and degrees of curvature around the scale, it bounces off at angles, creating iridescent colors such as the lovely purple in some African *Colotis* butterflies and the brilliant greens on the undersides of Mexican hairstreaks.

In the natural environment, these colors and patterns help conceal the butterfly from predators. A butterfly's bright green underside blends into the rich diversity of green foliage. Its pattern of zigzag lines matches surrounding grass blades and stems. Brilliant eyespots frighten enemies away. It is surprising how many butterflies with gaudy upper wings have very modestly colored undersides. The effect of a butterfly suddenly flashing up in a brilliant burst of color, then settling again and instantly blending into its background can confuse an enemy and often save the butterfly's life.

11, 12. A pearl-like egg (11) of the European swallowtail (Papilio machaon) *gleams on a leaf of one of its food plants in the carrot family. On the following spread (12) a pierid butterfly has laid its spindle-shaped egg next to the deeply sculptured, turban-shaped egg of a European skipper. Most butterfly eggs are pale when freshly laid, but they soon acquire the patterns and colors characteristic of each species.*

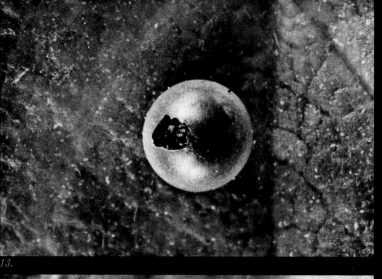

13.

14.

15.

13-15. *A new larva of the scarce swallowtail* (Iphiclides podalirius) *emerges from its eggshell. This is a critical time in the life of the butterfly, for the larva has energy for only a few minutes of effort to free itself from the crystalline walls of the shell. Many caterpillars do not make an exit hole in time, and are stillborn prisoners.*

16. *A close-up view of the head of a European swallowtail caterpillar reveals its strong jaws that can devour a leaf in minutes. Two semicircles of tiny simple eyes, the ocelli, and a pair of downward projecting mouth parts called palpi, can be seen at the sides of the triangular head shield. Clawed forelegs aid the caterpillar in holding its food.*

17-32. *The variety of caterpillars rivals the colorful diversity of the adults. Many have elaborate projections such as branched spines, forked tails, and fleshy lobes. Some use bluffing and aggressive behavior to ward off predators. Others, especially the lycaenids have "honeydew" secreting glands which attract ants that serve as guardians against enemies. Many display bizarre protective coloration such as imitating bird droppings or crumpled leaves to escape predation.*

33. *A group of caterpillars of the common grass yellow* (Eurema hecabe) *chew Cassia leaves in the rain forest at Wau, New Guinea. Most caterpillars are solitary feeders, particularly in the final molts, when their appetites are prodigious. Some even resort to cannibalism if another caterpillar gets in their way.*

17. Purple emperor (Apatura iris): *England*

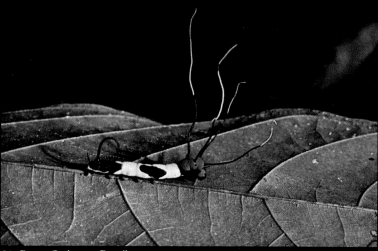
21. Butterfly larva: Brazil

18. Pipevine swallowtail (Battus philenor): *California*

22. Moss's hairstreak (Incisalia mossii): *California*

19. Ithomiïd (Mechanitis lysimnia elisa): *Ecuador*

23. Nymphalid (Charaxes *species): Tanzania*

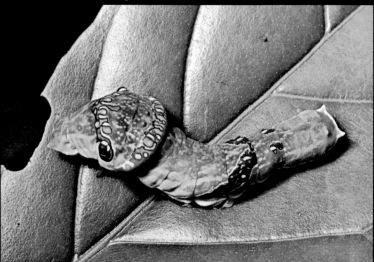
20. Swallowtail (Papilio helenus): *Thailand*

24. Foxy Charaxes (Charaxes jasius saturnus): *South Africa*

25. Nymphalid larva: Ecuador

29. Lorquin's admiral (Limenitis lorquini): *California*

26. Silver-spotted skipper (Epargyreus clarus): *Georgia*

30. Great copper (Lycaena xanthoides): *California*

27. Heliconian (Heliconius numata euphore): *South America*

31. Zebra heliconian (Heliconius charitonius): *Florida*

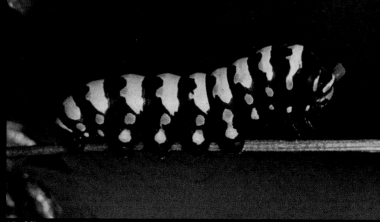

28. Minor's swallowtail (Papilio indra minori): *Colorado*

32. Swallowtail (Papilio demodocus): *Tanzania*

34. *A caterpillar of the citrus swallowtail* (Papilio demodocus) *from South Africa extends its bright red osmaterium when threatened, which emits a pungent odor. The larva thrusts its head upward and weaves from side to side to further intimidate the enemy.*

35-37. *The appearance of a caterpillar may change markedly from one molt to the next. The fifth and final instar of* Heliconius numata *from South America (36) becomes inactive and somewhat shrunken after it reaches full size, and may change color slightly as the pupa begins to form under the caterpillar skin. In the bottom figure (37) the larva has turned yellow and the old caterpillar skin begins to slip off the soft, newly formed pupa.*

35.

36.

37.

38, 39. At first, the pupa of the monarch butterfly (Danaus plexippus) *is a soft turquoise-green decorated with brilliant metallic gold spots. As it develops, the pupa turns darker green and then dark brown. Within a few hours of its emergence, the bright orange wings of the monarch with their characteristic black and white spots can be seen through the pupal skin. The butterfly hatches within nine to fifteen days, with a longer time needed in cooler climates.*

38.

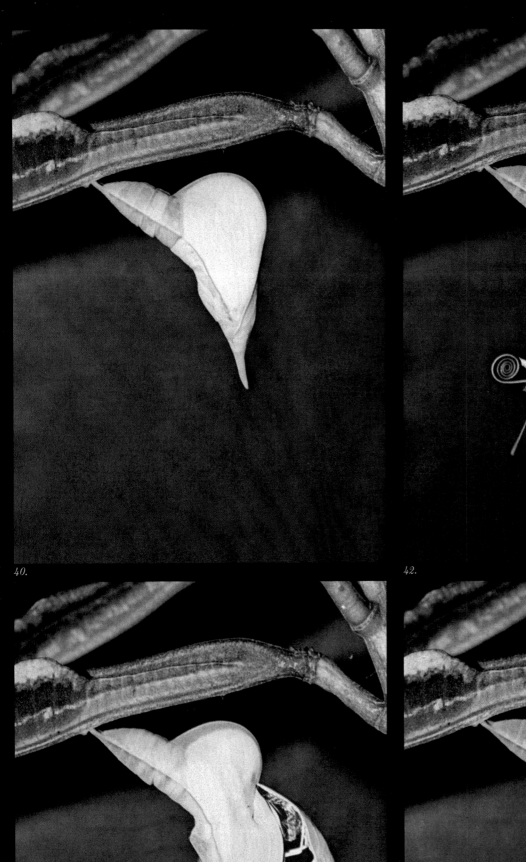

40.

41.

42.

43.

40-44. *When the transformation of larval structures into the complex organs of the adult is completed within the pupa, the last molt occurs and the butterfly emerges. Here a cloudless sulphur* (Phoebis sennae) *breaks out of its pupa on a* Cassia *tree in Louisiana. Butterfly pupae are exceedingly varied in shape. This pierid has a bowed wingcase which contains the developing wings, while the downcurving point beyond the head holds the palpi mouth parts. The first indication that the butterfly is about to emerge are splits in the pupal skin along certain fracture lines. The butterfly uses its legs to push its way clear and then hangs from the cast-off skin while waiting for its wrinkled wings to expand and dry.*

44.

45.

46.

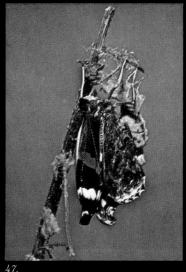

47.

48.

45-48. *The time taken for a butterfly to hatch
ranges from less than ninety seconds to five minutes.
A newly emerged adult such as this red admiral*
(Vanessa atalanta) *has small fleshy wings and a
rather plump abdomen. Its pulsating body pumps
clear green fluid through the wing veins and
between the upper and lower wing membranes.
Within ten to twenty minutes the wings reach their
maximum size and begin to harden, a process that
usually takes one to two hours. The butterfly is then
ready for its first flight.*

49-66. *Microscopic close-ups of wings reveal rows
of overlapping scales whose mosaic patterns form the
gorgeous colors and designs of the adult butterfly.
Colors are the result of either chemical pigments
within each scale or the surface structure of the
scale itself. Pigments absorb certain wavelengths of
light and transmit the remainder. Structural colors
are caused by light bouncing off minute films and
ridges on the scale surface. Thus, the "blue" scales
of the morpho butterfly change the wavelengths of
light into the dazzling blue color they emit. Among
the wing close-ups on the following pages, the
swallowtail* (Papilio rothschildi) *from the mountains
of New Guinea (49) and a* Papilio *from China (66)
combine both pigmental and structural colors in
their wings.*

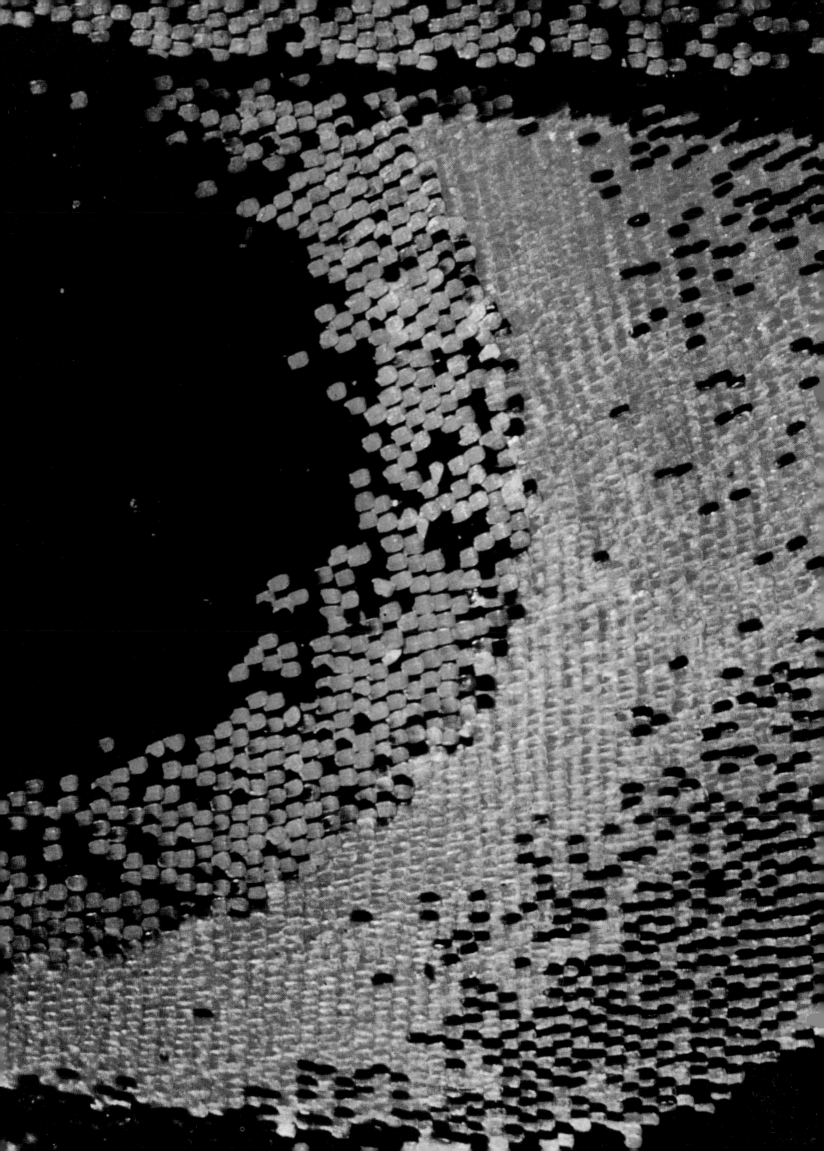

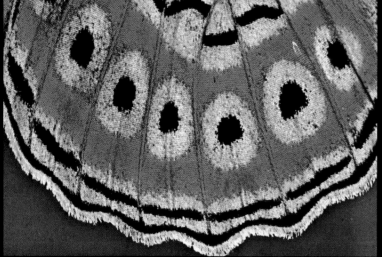

50. Asterope amulia: *Zaire*

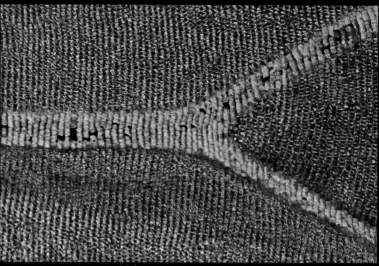

54. Troides amphrysus: *Malacca*

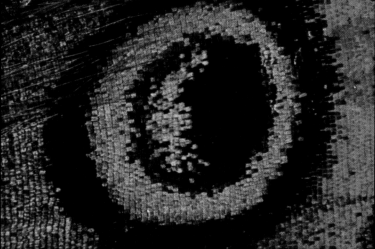

51. Junonia evarete: *Peru*

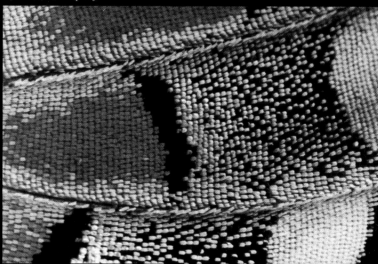

55. Papilio machaon: *Germany*

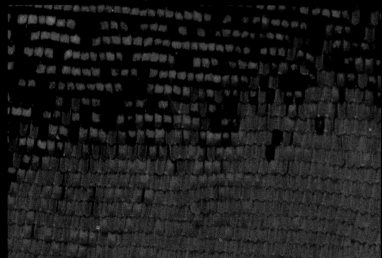

52. Nymphalid: *Peru*

56. Papilio ulysses: *New Guinea*

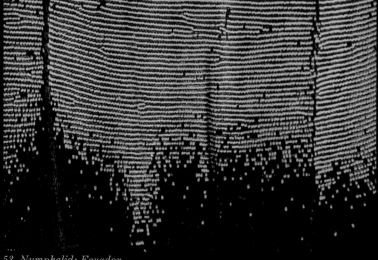

53. Nymphalid: *Ecuador*

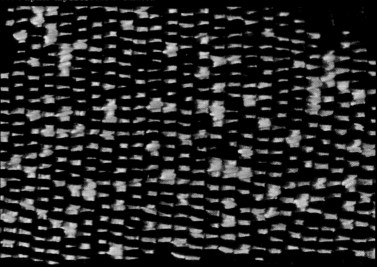

57. Papilio ulysses: *New Guinea*

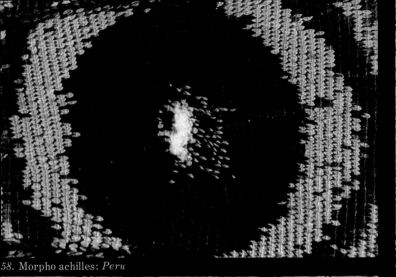
58. Morpho achilles: *Peru*

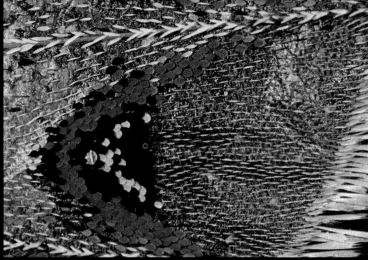
62. Archon apollinus: *Syria*

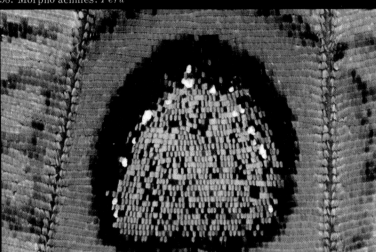
59. Morpho *species: Honduras*

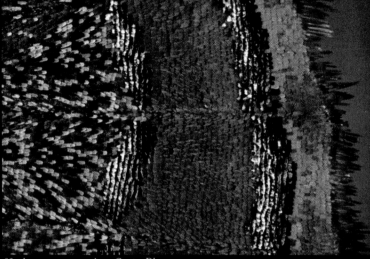
63. Anteros carausius: *Costa Rica*

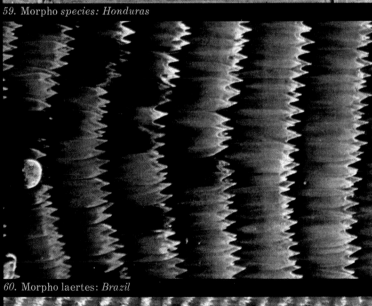
60. Morpho laertes: *Brazil*

64. Parnassius smintheus: *Montana*

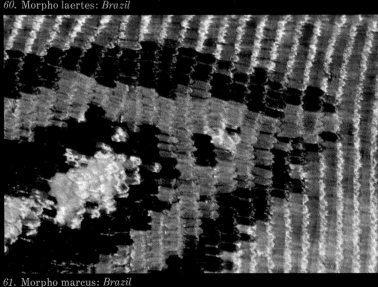
61. Morpho marcus: *Brazil*

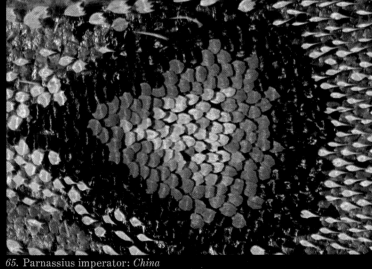
65. Parnassius imperator: *China*

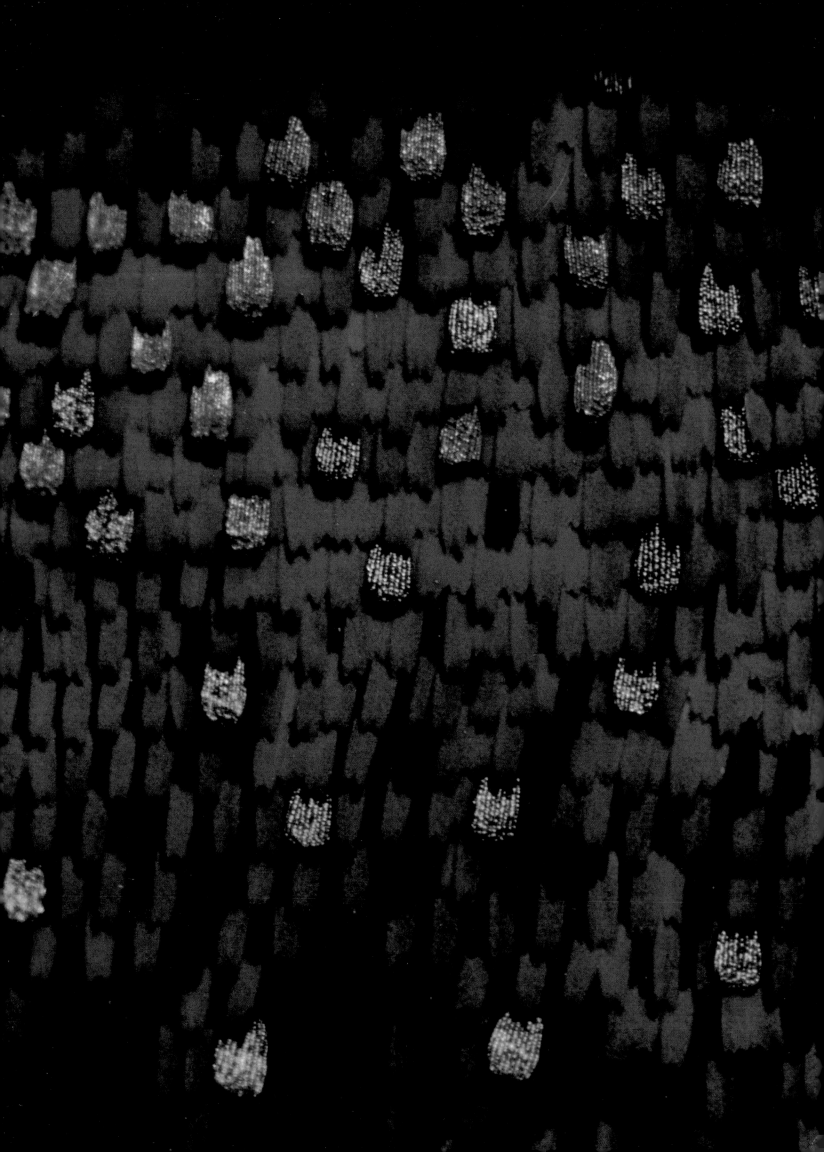

Butterfly Behavior

Butterflies are such a conspicuous part of the world of nature that it is hard to imagine anyone who has not seen them feeding at flowers or flying across a lawn or garden. Some aspects of butterfly behavior, however, are much less familiar.

In a quiet glen, a pair of butterflies act out a courtship display involving intricate aerial maneuvers, headlong chases, and delicate caresses as they stroke each other's antennae. From a flower along a roadside, a butterfly darts out to "challenge" an intruder invading his "territory"—be it dog, man, or another butterfly. Zipping off the bark of a tree, ten feet above the ground, another species pursues rival males while making strange, clicking sounds that can be heard more than 100 feet away.

Some butterflies maintain such a rigid schedule that they can be found at certain flowers at the same hour each day. In the evening, hundreds of others may fly in from all directions to pack tightly together at one sleeping roost, returning to the same spot each night for six months or longer.

Some butterflies are cannibals, others social parasites, and some contain such virulent poisons in their system that they can kill a lizard or a bird careless enough to eat them. They are insects of constant surprises.

Flight

A dew-covered butterfly clinging to a grass blade on a cold spring morning is temporarily earthbound, barely able to quiver its wings or move its legs until the warming sun raises its body temperature above 80°F. or more. Basking in the sun is more than an indulgence, it is an essential activity that tunes the butterfly's wing muscles and gives it the energy for flight.

In temperate climates, butterflies receive enough warmth from the sun to fly from spring to early fall. As the days shorten and temperatures drop, however, they become more sluggish and finally die or go into hibernation for the winter months. In the deserts, butterflies first become active a short time after dawn, when the air is already warm. Mountain or coastal species must wait until the mists clear later in the morning before they begin their day. Activity usually continues until the late afternoon, when lower light levels and cooling temperatures prompt the butterflies to seek shelter for the night. There are a few exceptions of course. The giant skippers of the American deserts are active mostly at dusk. Also, high mountain fogs or the heavy cloud cover of summer thunderstorms on alpine peaks will drive all butterflies to take temporary shelter under plants or rocks.

In tropical forests nearer the equator, the range of daily flight activity is far greater than in arctic or temperate climates, for the sultry heat enables butterflies to move about before sunrise and after

Wing positions of a butterfly in flight

sunset. Ithomiids such as *Mechanitis isthmia* visit flowers in clearings as early as 5:30 A.M. and by 8:30 A.M., the time that most other tropical butterflies become active, they are already moving into the forest shade. Later in the afternoon, when it often becomes dark and cool as rain clouds build to cover the sky, *Mechanitis* again leaves the forest to fly up into the tree canopy or out into clearings in search of nectar. Appropriately, almost all the flowers these butterflies visit are white and thus readily visible in the dim light.

The timing of these early morning and late afternoon visits to flowers by *Mechanitis* may be connected with the hours of courtship, which for most ithomiids are between 10:00 A.M. and 1:00 P.M. By flying earlier and later than most other butterflies, the shade-adapted ithomiids are thus freed for courtship and mating during the warmer middle part of the day. Other activities fit into this schedule as well. The emergence of new adults from pupae occurs from 9:00 to 10:00 A.M. Fertile females deposit their eggs during midday, usually from 10:30 A.M. to 1:30 P.M. This is the time of maximum radiation from the sun, and the females seem to need this extra energy for the rigorous activity of egg laying, which includes long, careful patrol flights around host plants in order to find the most suitable leaves on which to deposit their eggs. At that time they also seek out bird droppings and other sources of protein.

Not all tropical butterflies are on such a structured time schedule as the ithomiids, but investigations show that many have preferred times of maximum flight and even specific hours for their other activities.

At the height of their activity, butterflies, while not as fast as certain flies, can move along at a surprising speed. The giant skippers have been clocked at forty-two miles an hour. Most nymphalids, such as the daggerwing butterflies of Costa Rica, cruise at ten to twenty-five miles an hour in straightaway flight. Pierids and blues generally fly at speeds under five miles per hour.

Resting Positions

Many butterflies have characteristic resting positions, sometimes correlated with particular activities. A hairstreak, for example, distracts the attention of a predator by alighting on a leaf and holding its forewings firmly together over its body while rubbing first one hindwing and then the other back and forth. This helps focus the predator's attention on the tiny antennae-like hairs and eyespots at the outer margin of the hindwings rather than on the true head at the other end. Many skippers rest with forewings folded together over the back but with the hindwings held straight out to the side. This position probably represents an effort to increase body temperature through the absorption of solar heat. After a few minutes of sunbathing the temperature of its body rises and the skipper folds its wings above its back.

Certain butterflies, such as the arctics in the genus *Oeneis*, will alight on the ground, close their wings over their backs, and then walk in a tight circle until they face the sun directly, minimizing any shadow they might cast while resting—and also minimizing their visibility to a predator. They will even lean to one side or the other to reach this position. In the late afternoon in the temperate zone, buckeyes and red admirals are commonly observed with wings outspread in patches of sunlight on city driveways as well as on the forest floor. If disturbed, they fly up but promptly alight again, quickly facing away from the slanting afternoon sun and spreading their wings at the optimal angle to soak up the waning rays.

Sleeping Patterns

Toward evening, butterflies seek sheltered places such as the underside of a broad leaf or a branch to spend the night. Most butterflies roost alone; however, resting assemblages have been seen in a number of species. Tropical swallowtails in the tailless genus *Parides*, ithomiids, danaids, acraeines, and heliconians have all been observed in social nocturnal roosts. The daggerwing butterfly, *Marpesia berania*, also gathers in nightly roosts of as many as sixty-eight males and females. Even though the butterflies are widely scattered through the forest during the day, they return with remarkable fidelity to their "home" roost night after night for their entire life-spans, which in some heliconians may be as much as six months.

Communal roosts must give added protection or else predators would easily make mass kills. Among chemically protected species, it is believed that the distinctive odor given off by a group of poisonous butterflies better protects the individuals than if each roosted alone. After attacking one bitter-tasting individual in the group, local birds, lizards, or other predators will benefit from the experience and learn not to attack the others. Since the butterflies sleep in the same area nightly, only a limited number of local predators need to be educated before the group can roost in complete security. If the sleeping spot changed each night, the congregation would constantly be attacked by inexperienced predators.

In the case of the daggerwing butterflies in Costa Rica, an increased sensitivity to the approach of predators seems to give the butterflies an advantage in the struggle to survive. They bunch together on a leaf over an open area, all facing outward. If one is disturbed and flexes its wings, adjacent butterflies are touched and take up the wing-opening behavior, thus passing along an awareness of possible danger. If the butterflies are clustered over a clearing or river, orientation in one direction enables them to flee together when attacked, thus confusing and frightening a nocturnal predator and maximizing safe dispersal in all directions.

Adaptive Coloration and Mimicry

Batesian mimicry

edible *Limenitis archippus*

distasteful *Danaus plexippus*

Many species of butterflies have wing shapes and patterns which make them resemble leaves, bark, or gravel. This type of adaptive coloration is found from the tropics to the arctic and includes the tropical leaf butterflies in the family Nymphalidae as well as the arctic and alpine *Oeneis* satyrids. These insects use camouflage just as man does in warfare: to make a vulnerable object blend into its surroundings and escape observation. The portion of the wings exposed while the butterfly is resting, usually the underside, is mottled, and drab and often has special shading to reduce the sharpness of outline or break up the wing shape so that it blends with the constant play of light and shadows on the forest floor.

The most dramatic example of protective resemblance is the superb *Kallima* butterfly of southeastern Asia. While a *Kallima* is in flight, its gorgeous orange-and-blue-patched uppersides vividly advertise its presence, but it is a fast and evasive flier and usually manages to avoid being captured by birds. Upon settling, the *Kallima* seems to disappear magically. With its head upright, legs tightly clasped to a twig, and wings folded together over its back, its brownish undersurface makes the butterfly look like a decayed leaf still clinging to its stem. Although artists often portray the *Kallima* perched on twigs, one biologist maintains that it normally alights in leaf litter and lies on its side. If this is the case, its odd posture is fully as important in deceiving a predator as is its protective coloration.

Alfred Russel Wallace, the great and indefatigable British naturalist, followed this evasive insect through the jungles of the Malay archipelago in the 1800s. He describes how he tried again and again to capture it, but, though he spotted the exact place where the butterfly had settled, it would immediately disappear upon landing. Finally he discovered that its ability to resemble a dead leaf attached to a twig made it nearly invisible, even when it was right in front of him.

The American tropical biologist William Beebe came across several heliconiine butterflies in a South American jungle, asleep in undergrowth only three feet above ground. Their blackish brown wings, marked with solid and dotted bands of creamy buff, merged so perfectly with their background that all Beebe could see were the bands. They were "hanging in space," he writes, "mere continuation of the maze of pale, dead, angled twigs which stretched in every direction."

Certain butterflies elude their enemies by dazzling

and confusing them. These are usually robust-bodied species that have brightly colored areas on their wings and a rapid, zigzagging flight. Beebe observed such a butterfly in the Venezuelan Andes. Its wings were primarily dark brown, but in flight, when the forewings were suddenly spread and raised to reveal a great central splash of iridescent blue, they were bordered with galactic curves of eight hues, each surrounded by amber and made alive by a brilliant spark of iridescent green. The effect in sunlight was of a suddenly flashing electric light.

Many satyrs and lycaenid butterflies have eyespots on the rear margin of their hindwings. The hairstreaks have a perfect "dummy" head at that point, complete with false antennae. These extensions are often short and threadlike and may even have broadened whitish tips, perfectly resembling antennae with shiny end-bulbs. Some species, such as the East African *Hypolycaena* hairstreaks, have twisted, ribbon-like outgrowths several times longer than their body. Both types of false antennae tend to deceive a predator into attempting to seize the butterfly by the tail, its least vital area. The butterfly's behavior enhances the false-head effect: as soon as a hairstreak lands, it jerks its hindwings, causing its false antennae to move up and down. Meanwhile the true antennae remain motionless. To further increase the deception, *Thecla* hairstreaks turn around rapidly as they alight, so that the head is in the tail position, and *Deudoryx* hairstreaks even run backward a few steps.

Other butterflies rely on a showy appearance, displaying reds or oranges that attract the attention of predators. This aposematic, or warning, coloration is normally found in butterflies that are genuinely dangerous to predators because they contain poisonous alkaloids or other toxic compounds such as cardiac glycosides (heart poisons) that make animals ill. The butterflies advertise their virulence with easily remembered colors and patterns so that predators avoid them. Other edible butterflies in the same area mimic the brightly colored, inedible kinds, thus sharing their protection. This relationship has evolved through natural selection; individuals of a harmless species in which a mutation occurs that makes them look like a distasteful butterfly will be avoided by predators. These mimics tend to have more surviving offspring than those lacking the warning coloration.

There are hundreds of pairs of harmful models and edible mimics in the tropics. In many areas a number of unrelated species come to resemble each other in a mimicry complex, with perhaps one or several models and many mimics from various families of butterflies. One example of mimicry familiar to Americans is the monarch, a danaid model whose caterpillars feed on poisonous milkweeds and thus become poisonous themselves, and the viceroy, a harmless nymphalid whose caterpillars feed on nonpoisonous willows but resemble monarch larvae.

Several types of mimicry associations are known. If one species, the model, is distasteful and the other species is edible but mimics the model, the association is called Batesian mimicry. Henry Walter Bates discovered this phenomenon among butterflies of the Amazon Basin while he was exploring and collecting in that region from 1849 to 1860. On the other hand, a number of distasteful model species in an area may share a common color pattern. The phenomenon of a group of noxious butterflies all looking alike is termed Müllerian mimicry, a relationship named after Fritz Müller, a German zoologist who first identified it among Amazonian insects.

This latter type of mimicry does not at first seem to make much sense. Why should two inedible but unrelated species be similar in appearance? Müller argued in 1878 that a predator learns to recognize inedible prey only after he has tried them. If the inedible species all had different colors, the predator would have to learn to recognize each separately. As it is, he need learn to recognize only one type, and any other species that turns up with a similar appearance would almost automatically be protected. The greater the number of species using the same warning signals, the lower the losses of the individual species.

Batesian and Müllerian mimicry complexes occur around the world, but principally in the Old World and New World tropics. In both types of mimicry, a predator learns to avoid all butterflies of a particular color pattern after a repellent experience with a poisonous model. The British biologist E. B. Poulton characterized the difference between the two types of mimicry by saying that a Batesian mimic might be compared to an unscrupulous tradesman who copies the advertisement of a successful firm, whereas Müllerian mimicry was like an agreement between firms to adopt a common advertisement and share the expenses.

The poisonous alkaloids that many Batesian and Müllerian models absorb from larval food plants and that protect them from vertebrate enemies seem not to deter invertebrate predators. Many insects are known to eat poisonous butterflies without harmful effects. Yet laboratory experiments show that a single unpalatable danaid butterfly such as the monarch can produce violent vomiting in a bird as large as a blue jay and can even kill a small lizard. Relations with other animals have caused butterflies to evolve a great many specialized defenses. Concealing or warning color spines on caterpillars, unpleasant odors and noxious chemicals—all aid in the butterfly's never ceasing struggle for survival.

Predators and Parasites

Every class of vertebrates includes predators that attack butterflies. Of these, birds, lizards, shrews, moles, mice, bats, and monkeys are the most important, but frogs, toads, small snakes, and fish are also formidable enemies. The wings of many butterflies bear triangular rips or torn edges—the result of violent encounters with birds and other enemies. Invertebrates also attack every stage in the life cycle of butterflies. Spiders, scorpions, centipedes, assassin bugs, ambush bugs, dragonflies, praying mantids, robber flies, ants, beetles, and social and solitary wasps are important predators. In North America, the whitefaced hornets and their relatives catch even fast-flying butterflies like the American copper and pearl crescent.

Probably the greatest toll is taken of caterpillars. While birds eat many of these larvae, certain ants are their major enemies. In the tropics, not even the noxious ithomiid larvae, loaded with poisonous alkaloid chemicals, are safe from the rapacious jaws of raiding ants. Lacking spines, these caterpillars have little active defense when attacked, other than spewing out putrid drops of gut juices. In some ithomiid species, groups of caterpillars feeding on the underside of a leaf react in unison to ants walking directly overhead by dropping off, each suspending itself on a one-inch lifeline of silk.

Despite the abundance of predators on butterflies, most of these seemingly fragile creatures survive surprisingly well, an adequate number of offspring replacing their parents generation after generation. Barring major ecological catastrophes, their considerable reproductive capacity and numerous lines of defense insure survival against natural enemies.

Parasites are actually far more potent enemies of butterflies than predators. Parasitic insects lay their eggs in or near a suitable host, butterfly egg, caterpillar or pupa, and the parasite's larvae then live and grow inside the host, gradually destroying its tissues and causing its death. Practically all insect parasites are members of the orders Hymenoptera, including the ichneumon, braconid, and chalcid wasps, and Diptera which includes mostly tachinid and dexid flies. The females of the parasitic wasps have long, needle-like ovipositor tubes through which they lay their eggs inside their hosts. The flies usually deposit eggs on the caterpillar's skin or on its food plant, where the maggots hatch and, at their earliest opportunity, burrow into the caterpillar.

One of the most common of the braconid wasps is the tiny *Apanteles*, found in both the Old World and the New World. The female wasp often lays more than 100 eggs in a single caterpillar. The wasp larvae feed on the internal tissues of the caterpillar and reach maturity before the caterpillar is ready to pupate. Emerging through the skin of the caterpillar's ravaged body, the *Apanteles* larvae spin a mass of yellow silk cocoons that completely cover the remains of the host.

Bright red mites, small relatives of the more familiar blood-sucking ticks, live on butterfly adults, especially the satyrs. Small heliid flies also feed on butterflies from which they apparently suck hemo-lymph. They are often found firmly attached to the wing veins. The legs of an adult butterfly sometimes have several mites on them, apparently merely along for the ride. Bacteria and viruses also have been known to take a heavy toll of larvae of some butterfly species, especially the whites and sulphurs and the *Papilio machaon* group of swallowtails.

Feeding

One of the most familiar sights is that of a butterfly delicately balanced on a blossom sipping nectar with its long tongue. Nectar is not only a prime source of energy for most species, but also the attractant for pollination of many plants. Some flowers, such as a *Maxillaria* orchid of eastern Ecuador, have convoluted floral tubes that can be entered only by the long tongues of certain skippers. The flower supplies the butterfly with sugar-rich nectar and at the same time the head or feet of the skipper visitor are coated with sticky packets of pollen grains, which the butterfly carries on to the next bloom. In addition to a remarkable variety of flowers, many also need other food sources to complete their diet.

Sap oozing from scarred trees, as well as the juices of rotting and fermenting fruits, attract forest nymphalids. Experienced collectors frequently use fruit and sugarcane to lure rare species in the tropics. Some butterflies sip honeydew from such insects as scales and aphids, and rotting cattle entrails and similar evil-smelling carrion are like manna to many species. Dung and feces from a variety of animals, including monkeys, leopards, and elephants, draw butterflies by the hundreds. Bird droppings on jungle foliage lure many species, and urine-soaked ground is peculiarly attractive to swallowtails, pierids, metalmarks, and skippers. Even decaying fungus may bring certain butterflies streaming in to eat. These unusual sources appear to give the butterflies amino acids—the building blocks of proteins—and other essential nitrogen-containing substances.

In addition to these food sources, many adults drink a lot of water, often sucking drops of dew from leaf surfaces. Clouds of butterflies cluster around mud puddles on a hot summer day, drinking soil moisture. In the tropics and sometimes in the northern temperate zones, huge assemblages gather along muddy stream banks or on damp earth after a rain.

Naturalists have also often noted that some butter-flies stay in these mud puddle clubs for hours and pump so much liquid through their bodies that drops regularly exude from the tips of their abdomens.

This cannot be explained by simple thirst. Scientists at Cornell University recently discovered that the eastern tiger swallowtail extracts dissolved sodium salts from the water, which probably explains why some butterflies will land on sweat-soaked clothes, or even one's hands and face, to suck up perspiration through their uncoiled tongues.

The density of butterflies around feeding sources sometimes reaches extraordinary proportions. Alexander Klots has reported seeing hundreds of different kinds of butterflies gathered on the decomposing remains of a small crocodile on the banks of a tributary of the Amazon. I have seen as many as 200 American tiger swallowtails closely packed on a manure pile measuring less than half a square yard. Many of these aggregations seem to be composed of young unmated bachelor males. Such congregations are temporary, however, the participants rarely returning to the same spot a second day. It is well known that certain species, especially swallowtails and pierids, form mud puddle swarms of 100 to 200 individuals. Since the females usually emerge several days later than the males, these assemblies may serve to prevent young, recently emerged males from vainly seeking females at this time and from scattering too far from the population area. Also, avid drinking allows them to achieve a proper water balance in their bodies in preparation for intensive searching flights for females and the subsequent courtship activities. Chinese collectors in Taiwan as well as South American lepidopterists often put out dead decoy butterflies at patches of mud, which attract many specimens.

The highly organized nature of flight behavior in some species that drink in groups has led to the belief that there may be other as yet unknown explanations for butterfly feeding associations. George B. Longstaff, British author of *Butterfly-Hunting in Many Lands*, describes such a case in Ceylon, involving the pierid *Appias paulina:*

"Soon after mid-day large numbers of the males were seen flying down the bed of the stream, sometimes in ones and twos, but often three, four, or five together in strings . . . as though tied together by an invisible thread. . . . When disturbed they would quickly come back to the favoured spots, as many as five to seven together, in strings, all conforming to the movements of their leader like wild geese."

Butterflies That Live with Ants Caterpillars of several butterfly families have intimate associations with certain types of ants. Some pierid caterpillars have tubular hairs with spreading spines at the tip, which hold minute drops of what is presumably a honeydew attractive to ants. The metalmark *Anatole rossi,* in the pine-forested mountains of Veracruz, Mexico, is associated with ants on and around its *Croton* food plants. During the day, the ants guard the caterpillar against parasitic wasps and other enemies as it feeds, and in turn the ants are allowed to eat drops of honeydew secreted by glands on the caterpillar's back. In the evening and during the dry season, the ants carry the caterpillar down the stem to the base of the plant, where they imprison it in a small chamber dug in the soil. This protects the caterpillar from nocturnal predatory ants and from the grass fires that frequently sweep through the dry pine forests.

Similarly, the caterpillars of a great many blues, hairstreaks, and coppers secrete honeydew that brings ants to attend them. In Europe, four species of blues in the genus *Maculinea* have special associations with ant species of the genus *Myrmica*. During their first three instars the caterpillars eat the flowers of thyme, and larger caterpillars frequently cannibalize the younger and smaller ones. After their second molt, a honey gland becomes functional. Ants then attend them, stroking the caterpillars with their legs and antennae, which causes the larvae to secrete droplets of sweet fluid greatly relished by the ants. After the fourth and final molt, the caterpillars are carried into the ant nest. There they live as social parasites, acquiring the ant nest's odor and eating the ant's young while being fed by the adult ants. In the fourth instar, the caterpillars resemble the ant's own larvae in size and skin texture, and use begging behavior similar to that of the ant's young, which triggers the feeding response in the worker ants. The ants obtain some nectar but only a minute amount of actual food which is more than counterbalanced by the number of ant larvae that the caterpillars eat. This mutual relationship between caterpillar and ant is essential for the butterfly since it apparently cannot survive without the ants.

Sounds and Hearing

Unlike most moths, butterflies do not have complex hearing organs capable of sensing airborne vibrations. They do respond to sounds, however, which are probably sensed by sacs at the base of the wings in the nymphs, and by leg bristles and organs on the abdomen in other butterflies. Caterpillars are also known to react to a range of sound vibrations from 32 to 1024 cycles a second. This may be compared with the capacity of some moths to receive sounds of more than 100,000 cycles per second, or man's ability to register sounds in a range of 16 to 20,000 cycles per second.

Relatively few butterflies are able to produce sounds or at least not any in human auditory range. Skipper caterpillars can make a grating noise by scraping their jaws sideways over the surface of a leaf. Lycaenid and metalmark pupae create squeaking sounds by rapidly rubbing the edges of two abdominal segments together. One edge is like a file containing numerous teeth, which is dragged across the irregular surface of a plate on the next segment. At least six lycaenid butterflies can "hammer" their pupal bodies against the floor of their pupation chambers and the pupa of the monarch makes a very audible clicking sound at certain times. The reason for this sound production is not known, but it probably scares away small predators or parasites, from the virtually immobile and defenseless pupa.

Several nymphalid butterflies, the most famous of which is the "calico" *(Ageronia feronia)* and its relatives, make clicking sounds in flight. In the New World tropics calicos commonly perch with head downward and wings outspread on tree trunks about ten feet above the ground. When another butterfly flutters into range, the perching calico darts out in quick pursuit, flying only a few inches behind the intruder. During the chase, the calico often emits a rapid series of loud, sharp clicks, audible to the human ear as much as 100 feet away. The butterfly makes this sound by snapping two body segments together while moving both pairs of wings in a peculiar alternating beat. The significance of these sounds is not known, but they are probably related to territorial defense or courtship.

Scent tufts

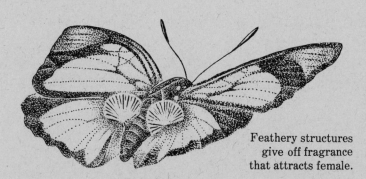

Feathery structures give off fragrance that attracts female.

Scents and Sensory Capacities

Caterpillars depend so much on taste to identify their food that they can even be deceived into eating gelatin if it is smeared with juices from the normal host plant. Their taste organs are mainly associated with the mouth parts, but adults also have many taste sensors on their feet: the long tongue reflexively uncoils to feed when the feet come in contact with a sweet solution. Biologists have found that monarchs respond when their feet are touched by sugar solutions of only 1/120,400 part per thousand. This is more than 2000 times the sensitivity of the human tongue.

In adult butterflies the sense of smell is chiefly associated with the antennae, although the bristly palpi also serve this function. Females use smell to locate the correct kind of plant on which to lay their eggs, and nymphalids may increase the sensitivity of their taste receptors by "drumming" on the chosen leaf with their short forefeet.

The sense of smell is also used extensively in courtship. In moths, it is usually the female that produces a powerful sex pheromone (a chemical that attracts other members of the same species) capable of luring males from as far as five miles away. Among butterflies, the male frequently has the scent-producing organs. These are usually special scales, called androconia, or pouches on the forewings or hindwings, but scent structures may also be present on the abdomen. Androconia are found on the wings of many satyrs, nymphs, skippers, hairstreaks, sulphurs, and some swallowtails. On kite, birdwing, and *Parides* swallowtails, conspicuous, long white hairs occur in folds of the inner margin of the male's hindwings and are used to waft scent during courtship.

Male monarchs and American queens have a noticeable black pocket of scent glands on the upper surface of each hindwing. During courtship they extend a pair of hair-pencils from the tip of their abdomens by contracting the abdominal muscles and increasing the hemolymph ("blood") pressure. They dip these cylindrical bundles of hairs into their wing glands and disperse the scent into the air or across the head and antennae of the female. Similar elaborate hair-pencils are found in danaids in other parts of the world, such as *Lycorea* in the American tropics and *Euploea* in the Indo-Australian region. Each species has its own characteristic scent, which it uses in courtship to insure that mating will occur with the proper virgin female.

Courtship and Mating

Entire butterfly courtships are rarely observed in nature, probably because they often last only a few minutes and occur in secluded places. The male initiates courtship with a long period of searching flight. On finding a female, he flies after her and tries to force her to land, or hovers over her if she has already alighted. A virgin female receptive to courtship will respond to the hovering male by holding her wings in a partially spread position. This allows the male to land beside her and push his way underneath her wings to line himself up next to her body. If the female has previously mated and is unreceptive, she will either fly off, tighten her wings around the abdomen, or flatten her wings and raise her abdomen high so that the male cannot approach her.

Once the male is accepted, he is allowed to curve the tip of his abdomen around 180° to link his genitalia with hers. Some stroking of the antennae may be necessary to reach this stage. As soon as a union occurs, the male straightens out in the common tail-to-tail position and the pair remains together as long as is necessary for the male to pass the "package" of sperm (called the spermatophore) to the female. Copulation may last from thirty minutes to several hours. The pair is inactive during this time, but if they do take flight, the immobile male is pulled backward through the air by his mate.

Scientists have recently discovered that males of many species, especially the sulphurs, are attracted to the proper females by ultraviolet wing colors. Our eyes cannot see these patterns, but butterflies are receptive to the ultraviolet wavelengths and can perceive totally different pigments from those we can see.

Visual signals in mating are extremely important,

as can be seen in many nymphs, pierids, and swallowtails, where the females mimic various distasteful butterflies but the males keep their ancestral color and pattern. Because females choose between males at mating, rather than vice versa, it is important for the male to be easily recognized as a mate of the correct species. This kind of selection means that the males must forgo the personal survival advantages of mimicry.

The immense migratory movements of birds, lemmings, and locusts have always attracted the attention of man. It is little wonder that migrations of huge numbers of butterflies, although they are not as commonly observed as bird migrations, prove equally fascinating. More than 200 species of butterflies, mostly tropical, have been known to migrate. The number of individuals involved often defies calculation. A northward flight of three species of sulphurs in Ceylon was estimated to involve the passage of 26,000 butterflies per minute along a mile-wide front. A three-day migration of painted ladies across a forty-mile-wide area in California was computed to have at least 3 billion butterflies passing through during thirty-six hours of daylight flying time.

There are various reasons for these mass movements. Some flights are caused by seasonal conditions, with species moving from a hot, drying area to a cooler moist area; or even moving up a mountain range or along a jungle river to seek a more satisfactory environment. Other migrations seem to be generated by temporary overpopulation, adults moving out en masse to seek new larval host plants. Different species move for different reasons and so may be traveling in opposite directions within the same region.

The best documented of all butterfly migrants are the painted ladies and the monarchs. In North America, the painted lady flies up from Mexico in the spring, arriving in Canada and Newfoundland by late summer. Waves of successive generations leap-frog north, living on a wide variety of food plants. In the Old World, painted lady migrations swing north out of North Africa and the Middle East to Europe in the spring, even scaling the seemingly insurmountable barrier of the Alps. On both Old and New World continents, a partial migration of their offspring returns southward in the fall.

Monarchs fly in regular seasonal migrations with fairly definite routes down the length of North America. How they orient themselves over such tremendous distances, often more then 2000 miles, and across countless mountains, rivers, lakes, and arid wastes is still one of the greatest mysteries of butterfly behavior.

67, 68. *All motion, a fritillary, the essence of a butterfly, flutters away from a buttercup (67). Alighting at an evening roost in Ecuador, a* Heliconius erato *(68) joins two sleeping companions. Communal resting is most common among such distasteful butterflies, which have little to fear from predators.*

Migration

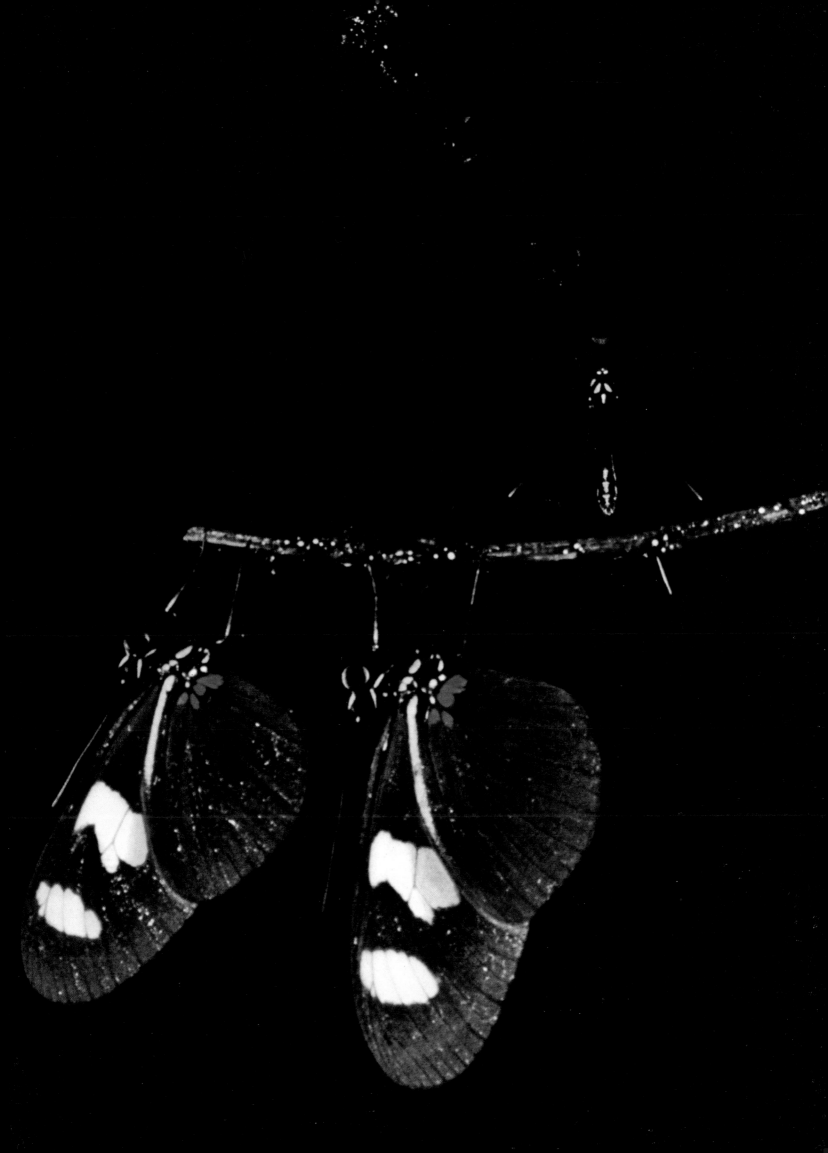

69. Heliconius species: Ecuador

69-77. Mimicry is common among many tropical butterflies. Although those illustrated here look amazingly alike, each is actually a different species. They are all poisonous and have evolved a similar bold "tiger stripe" coloration that warns predators, a form of protection called Müllerian mimicry. These butterflies all inhabit the same rain forest area at Limoncocha in eastern Ecuador.

70. Forbestra equicola equicoloides: *Ecuador*

74. Melinaea egesta rileyi: *Ecuador*

71. Melinaea menophilus menophilus: *Ecuador*

75. Hypothyris fluona berna: *Ecuador*

72. Hypothyris mamercus mamercus: *Ecuador*

76. Napeogenes apobsoleta: *Ecuador*

73. Tithorea harmonia hermias: *Ecuador*

77. Heliconius *species: Ecuador*

78, 79. Copying the protection from enemies used by distasteful species, harmless butterflies often mimic poisonous models in the same habitat, a type of behavior called Batesian mimicry. An edible pierid, Dismorphia orise *(79)*, mimics a bitter-tasting model, Thyridia confusa *(78)*. Mistaking it for the poisonous Thyridia *danaid, predators tend to avoid the harmless* Dismorphia.

78.

80. Adelpha bredowii: *California*

84. Anaea morvus: *Peru*

81. Caligo telucer: *Trinidad*

85. Polygonia zephyrus: *California*

82. Strymon melinus: *Florida*

86. Anaea itys: *Peru*

83. Hamadryas feronia: *Brazil*

87. Precis tugela: *Africa*

80-88. *Protective coloration takes many forms among butterflies. Bold stripes that break up the outline of the wings, as in this California sister* (Adelpha bredowii) *(80), is called disruptive coloration. Large eyespots frighten predators of the owl butterflies (81). Hairstreaks frequently have tails that look like antennae and eyespots that seem like eyes, confusing enemies into attacking the expendable edges of the hindwings (82). Resembling inedible objects such as the bark pattern of a tree (83) or a leaf (84-88) are other means of protection. Such devices camouflage a butterfly even when it is in open view on a tree trunk or mud flat. The southern dogface* (Zerene cesonia) *resembles a greenish yellow leaf as it hangs from a weed along a Mexican roadside (88).*

89-105. *Butterflies eat an extraordinary variety of foods. Flower nectar provides a rich source of sugar and water for many, especially in the northern temperate zones. On the following spread, a fiery skipper* (Hylephilia phyleus) *delicately probes a California* Grindelia *bloom with its long tongue (89). No flower is too small, too large or too complex for a determined butterfly (90-93). Other species prefer the juices of ripe fruits (94-96). Some nymphs and satyrs drink fermenting tree sap (97). A great many species, especially in the tropics, sip the putrid juices of animal dung and bird droppings (98-101). Soil moisture attracts great congregations of butterflies in many parts of the world (102-105). Some remain in these "mud puddle clubs" for hours, absorbing essential sodium salts as well as water.*

106. *A mating pair of* Dismorphia leuconoe melanoides *hangs from a vine tendril in the rain forest of eastern Ecuador. Most copulating butterflies rest quietly while the sperm is being transferred from the male to the female, a process that can take several hours, but if they become alarmed the female usually flies off, carrying the passive male attached to the tip of her abdomen.*

107. *Gathering by the millions each fall, southward-migrating monarch butterflies mass together in pine grove roosts on California's Monterey Peninsula, and points as far south as Mexico. After passing the winter, surviving butterflies begin the northward migration, laying eggs as they go; their offspring continue the journey as far north as Canada. Similar monarch migrations occur along the Gulf and east coasts of North America.*

88.

90. Eumaeus minyas costaricensis: *Costa Rica*

94. Polygonia c-album: *England*

91. Euphydryas chalcedona: *California*

95. Eurybia nicaeus: *Ecuador*

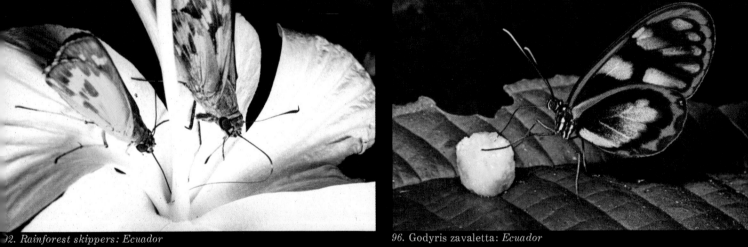

92. *Rainforest skippers: Ecuador*

96. Godyris zavaletta: *Ecuador*

93. *Itaballia demophile: Ecuador*

97. *Anteros sp.: Ecuador*

98. Charaxes *and other butterflies: Congo*

102. Papilio *species: Peru*

99. *Thecline hairstreak: Zambia*

103. Papilio troilus: *eastern United States*

100. *Butterfly congregation: Congo*

104. Eurema hecabe oeta: *New Guinea*

101. Salamis aethiops: *Tanzania*

105. Papilio glaucus: *New York*

The Families of Butterflies

At first glance, many butterflies appear to be rather similar. But a closer look reveals a surprising diversity of color, size, and structure among them. Some 20,000 species are known, ranging from the pygmy blue of North America, less than half an inch wide, to the goliath birdwing of the South Pacific, with a wingspan of ten or more inches. Some butterflies have chunky bodies so densely clothed with furry scales that they look like moths. Others are slender and delicate, with so few scales on their wings that they seem transparent. Many groups are dusted in dull browns and blacks and often pass unnoticed. Others, splashed with bold stripes and spots, flaunt a dazzling array of colors: pearly white, bright yellow, orange and crimson, brilliant iridescent blue, violet, green, and glittering gold.

Butterflies and Moths

Along with the moths, butterflies compose the insect order Lepidoptera, a term derived from the Greek words meaning scale-winged. No other group of insects possess these fragile, overlapping shingles in such abundance on their wings and bodies, which rub off as colored powder when the insects are handled. Technically, they are separated by the shape of their antennae, moths usually having feathery, tapering or hairlike structures, while the antennae of butterflies end in small knobs. Most moths alight with their wings stretched out flat, while butterflies generally rest with their wings held upright over their bodies. Moths usually have stout bodies covered with long, furry scales, whereas butterflies have relatively slender bodies with fewer, smoother and shorter scales. The difference in the scales is explained by the fact that nearly all butterflies love the sun, flying about in the warm daylight hours and remaining inactive even on cloudy days. Moths, on the other hand, are mostly nocturnal and need a thicker layer of scales to insulate their bodies against cooler nighttime temperatures.

There are some exceptions to these generalizations, of course. A few butterflies, especially tropical satyrs and the giant skippers, as well as many moths, prefer to move about only at dawn and dusk. In addition, some moths fly during the daylight hours and are so brightly colored that they may be mistaken for butterflies.

How Butterflies are Classified

Butterfly species are defined according to differences in the network of veins in the wings, leg peculiarities, mouth parts, position and shape of the eyes, genital organs and the earlier life stages. Related butterflies are grouped in a genus, the scientific name of each species consisting of both generic and specific names, as for example, *Papilio rutulus,* in which *Papilio* is the genus and *rutulus* is the species. The name of the scientist who described the species may follow the scientific name, e.g., *Papilio rutulus* Lucas. The scientific name makes it possible to identify a species no matter what the local people call it. Thus a butterfly known in the United States as the mourning cloak, as the Camberwell beauty in England, le morio in France, sorgmantel in Sweden, trauermantel in Germany, and so forth, is internationally recognized as *Nymphalis antiopa*.

Today butterflies are separated into two super-families: Hesperoidea, the primitive skippers, and Papilionoidea or true butterflies.

HESPEROIDEA
The Skippers (Family Hesperiidae)

Named for their rapid, darting flight, skippers are only one-quarter of an inch to two inches wide and are actually intermediates between the true butterflies and the moths. These robust-bodied little creatures are usually rather drab, their plain brown or blackish wings sprinkled with only occasional spots of yellow or white. This somber appearance has invoked such common names as cloudy wing, dusky wing and sooty wing among the North American species. In the New World tropics, however, where more skippers are found than anywhere else, many are brightly colored, some having wings crossed with white, black and iridescent blue or orange stripes, others with brilliant golden undersides.

Because of the similarity in wing pattern and their dodging, erratic flight patterns, this family of butterflies has been largely ignored by collectors. Actually, the skippers have many interesting habits. Some lay their eggs on lichens, others fly about for only one hour a day, still others have long tails that they bounce about during elaborate courtship flights. The skippers (some 3000 species) are found world-wide, from the deepest rain forest to the highest alpine meadow. They always seem to be in a rush, buzzing about like hummingbirds as they zip in short bursts from flower to flower, often stopping to sun themselves on a rock or leafy perch. Many of the males maintain territories around these sites from which they dart out to court passing females. Unlike most caterpillars, a skipper larva has a prominent head that seems to be separated from the body by a neck. The caterpillars rest during the day in tubes made of leaves pulled together loosely by silk strands, or in webs of grass. The pupae are formed in similar cocoon-like shelters, usually on the ground.

The Giant Skippers (Family Megathymidae)

These stout-bodied butterflies are the largest of the skippers, with wingspans often more than three inches wide. Found only in the deserts and drier plains of the southern United States and northern Mexico (one species reaches Costa Rica and Panama), the giant skippers are swift and elusive fliers, moving about in the dim hours of twilight. The larvae bore a silk-lined tunnel in the fleshy leaf bases and underground roots of yucca and agave plants. Later on, the pupae of one genus display a remarkable ability to move up and down inside this tube. Armed with a flashlight, an observer can find the adults sleeping on desert shrubs. To study these rarely seen butterflies more closely, however, collectors often seek out larval holes in the base of the plants and take the plant away to watch the caterpillar pupate and finally emerge as an adult.

PAPILIONOIDEA
The Swallowtails (Family Papilionidae)

Perhaps best known and most popular of all the butterflies, the swallowtails form an incredibly diverse and worldwide family. Many have brilliant colors, including dazzling metallic sheens, which makes this group a favorite. Their popular name came into use more than a century ago in Europe, where these butterflies frequently have slender "tails" projecting from their hindwings. But many tropical as well as arctic swallowtails are, in fact, tailless.

Some of the world's largest and most spectacular butterflies are found in this family. The magnificent male birdwings, found in the Indo-Australian region, are velvety black with bands, spots or patches of brilliant iridescent blue, green or red. Crimson heads and golden bodies make some even more striking. Their beauty and inaccessibility (many live in remote regions or fly at great heights in the forest canopy) make the birdwings among the most prized by collectors.

Among the more than twenty species in North America, the tiger swallowtail *(Papilio glaucus)* is the most beautiful. Its bright yellow wings are striped with broad black bands, and the outer blue margins of the hindwings are scalloped with yellow and orange crescents and terminate in slender black tails. These swallowtails have a strong but leisurely flight, often sailing across open fields with outstretched wings.

The parnassians, or Apollo butterflies, are more primitive swallowtails, pale white with black and red eyespots on the hindwings. They are found only in high mountain habitats, a few extremely rare species being known only from a handful of specimens from the inaccessible ranges of central Asia.

When feeding at flowers, most swallowtails hold their wings nearly erect above the body with their long legs outstretched and the wings fluttering quickly to maintain balance. Most are forest or woodland butterflies. Males are attracted to damp muddy spots along roads or trails but, for reasons not yet understood, females rarely join these mud puddle clubs. The males of some species commonly dart about on hilltops. This "hill-topping" behavior is apparently a way of establishing a point where males and females can meet and mate, for when a female flies into view near such a summit, she is immediately pursued.

The Whites and Yellows (Family Pieridae)

Among the first butterflies to be seen fluttering across open fields and congregating at mud puddles in spring are the whites and yellows. The brimstone *(Gonepteryx rhamni)*, found from Europe to Japan, is a striking butterfly with deep orange-colored wings; it passes the winter in the adult stage and flies in the first warm days of early spring. The pierids, only two to four inches wide, are unique in that their white, yellow, and orange colors are the result of uric acid pigments circulated through their systems. An extraordinary exception is the blue "clouded yellow" *(Colias sagartia)* of central Asia.

The orange-tip *(Anthocharis cardamines)* is one of the most delicate of the European whites. The male flaunts bright orange patches on the tips of his forewings; the female is completely white. When at rest, the pattern of black and yellow scales on the underside of the hindwings gives a mottled green effect, enabling the butterfly to blend with the foliage.

Among the many species in North America are the dog-face butterflies, named for the pink "poodle face" markings on their forewings. Other North American species have such charming names as dainty dwarf, fairy yellow, and sleepy sulphur, so called because its flight is slower and lazier than that of the other sulphurs.

Several serious argicultural pests are included in this butterfly family. The pine white *(Neophasia menapia)*, is the only pierid butterfly to feed on conifers, and can do extensive damage. The cabbage butterfly *(Pieris rapae)* and the alfalfa butterfly *(Colias eurytheme)* damage several commercial crops, particularly those in the mustard family. In 1910 a Dutch scientist named Verschaefft discovered that caterpillars of these butterflies would eat flour, starch, and even filter paper that was smeared with juice from plants containing mustard oils.

Because of the short caterpillar life of almost all species, most whites and yellows are able to produce two, three, four, or even more broods a year. In some cases, the broods match the predominant color of the vegetation at the particular season in which they fly. Because pierid males often differ from the females in color and pattern, freak butterflies in which half the body is male and the other half female are easily noticed. Like incorrectly printed postage stamps, these rare specimens bring high prices from collectors.

In tropical regions, mass migrations of some whites and yellows are spectacular. Charles Darwin recorded a vast seaward migration from his ship, the *Beagle*, when it was off the coast of South America. In the central highlands of Ceylon, millions migrate yearly toward Adams Peak, where, according to legend, they pay tribute to the gods before they die.

Restricted almost entirely to the tropical rain forests of Central and South America, these medium-sized butterflies appear to be a primitive offshoot of the stock that gave rise to the great family Nymphalidae. Most are poisonous as a result of the chemicals accumulated in the tissues of the caterpillars from eating plants in the deadly nightshade family.

Along with their distastefulness, many of these butterflies have evolved bright colors and bold patterns that make them easily recognizable to predators such as monkeys, lizards, and birds. They participate in a bewildering array of mimicry relationships, copying each other as well as being copied by other butterflies. On the wing, many of these species are impossible to tell apart. In fact there are so many almost identically marked butterflies within this family that one wonders how the males of one species can recognize the females of their own kind, except by a distinctive scent.

A very common color pattern adopted by great numbers of these butterflies is a bold orange and black "tiger stripe" design. By sharing this same form of warning coloration, they advertise their inedibility and gain a mutual protection from enemies, which soon learn to leave them alone. In addition, some edible butterflies in different families, such as pierids and nymphalids, copy the bad-tasting ithomiids and are also protected from predators.

The bright-colored ithomiids are bold fliers, seeming to flaunt themselves fearlessly as they slowly glide across open clearings in the jungle.

Deep in the forest interior, another group of ithomiids moves secretively through the undergrowth with wings as transparent as glass. Almost undetectable in the dim light, these butterflies have lost their colorful wing scales and rely on virtual invisibility to insure their survival. Even these clear-winged ithomiids are mimicked by a considerable number of moths and butterflies in other families, including some sulphurs, metalmarks, and a swallowtail.

Strangely, the single ithomiid living outside tropical America, *Tellervo zoilus*, is found several continents away—from northeastern Australia through New Guinea and east to the Solomon Islands. It, too, is a poisonous butterfly and is mimicked by a variety of other insects.

The ithomiids feed on bird droppings, tree sap and many types of tropical flowers. Individuals in Costa Rica and Ecuador that have been marked and later recaptured have been found to live up to six months in the wild, a relatively long lifespan for a butterfly.

The Ithomiids (Family Ithomiidae)

The Danaids (Family Danaidae)

This small family includes one of the best known butterflies in North America, the monarch *(Danaus plexippus)*. Most species occur in the Indo-Australian region, with only a few living in tropical America and Africa. Because their caterpillars feed on poisonous plants such as milkweeds, oleanders, dogbanes, and figs, the butterflies in this family are distasteful and rarely pursued by predators. In addition, they have rubbery bodies and very tough, leathery wings that enable them to survive an attack that would kill most butterflies.

Compared to other families, the danaids are rather dull colored, ranging from the autumnal amber of the monarch, queen, and lesser wanderer to the Australian crow butterflies, whose blackish wings often have iridescent purple or blue surfaces. All of these medium-to-large butterflies, some with wing-spreads of over five inches, have a slow, labored, gliding flight. Most male danaids have thin pencils of hair extending from the tip of their abdomens that they can twist and dip into scent pouches on their hindwings, dispensing an odor that attracts the females. In the monarch, the two scent glands are visible as black patches in the center of the male's hindwings.

The caterpillars are striped or spotted in bright warning colors and often have several pairs of fleshy filaments which they lash about in the air when disturbed. The hanging pupae are marked with metallic silver, gold, green or yellow dots.

The monarch is probably the most celebrated of migratory butterflies and is the only one in the world with a regular round-trip migration route. Every fall, millions work their way down both coasts of North America, often roosting for the night in huge concentrations at the same location year after year. They spend the winter in the subtropics and tropics and then begin drifting back in smaller groups in the early spring. The females lay their eggs along the way and their offspring continue the journey northward as far as Canada. Many have been sighted far out to sea, and it is believed that these incredibly powerful fliers have been able to reach Europe and the other continents by crossing the oceans.

The Browns and Satyrs (Family Satyridae)

These shy butterflies are usually somber brown, gray, or black, often with eyespots on both the upper and lower sides of their wings. Most are shade-loving woodland species and have an erratic dancing flight that has prompted such common names as wood nymph and little wood satyr. When alarmed, they may drop down into tall grass or other shelters to hide. The fork-tailed caterpillars are seldom seen as they feed on grasses under the cover of night. Unlike most butterflies, which spend the cold winter months sealed in a protective pupal casing, the larvae of

browns and satyrs often live through the winter as
caterpillars. In some groups, the caterpillar
excavates a shallow hole in the ground to pupate,
wrapping itself up in leaf litter with many
strands of silk.

The adults have a noticeable hollow swelling at the
base of their main wing veins. It is believed that
these swollen "drums" act as resonators to aid in
hearing sounds (butterflies do not have true ears).
The males frequently have patches of scent glands
on their forewings.

The browns and satyrs are found worldwide, but
reach their greatest diversity and development in
the tropics. Among the seven groups, ghost satyrs
are considered to be the most primitive. Their wings
are almost transparent, with lovely pink and bluish
tints on the outer margins, and they are almost
impossible to see as they float in the gloom near the
forest floor. A Chilean species which flies about in
open fields on the highest mountains has pure
silvery white wings.

Another group of interesting tropical satyrids
includes the large owl butterflies, with wingspans
often over six inches. These butterflies fly at dusk
and have a pair of very large eye-like spots on the
underside of each hindwing. The spots, with yellow
irises and black pupils, strikingly resemble the eyes
of an owl, and may startle predators when suddenly
displayed. The fraction of a second gained by
momentarily surprising the enemy gives the owl
butterfly time to escape.

Other primitive types of satyrs, found in both the
Old and New World tropics, are brightly colored
above and camouflaged on the underside with a few
poorly developed eyespots on the wings. Some have
short, tail-like projections. One group, in the
Indo-Australian region is brown with a broad central
white band or with alternating stripes of brown
and white.

Many satyrs are familiar butterflies in Europe and
North America. The ringlets, demurely colored
denizens of grassy plains, steppes, and mountain
meadows, are named for the light rings encircling
their hindwing eyespots. They are among the most
common butterflies of early spring, but few people
notice them as they slip in bobbing flight through
the tall grasses.

In the early summer months, the alpines and arctics
are abundant above timberline near mountain peaks
and in the tundra of the far north. They blend
superbly with the gravelly slopes and rocks on which
they frequently land. The alpines, *Erebia*, chiefly
dark brown with deep red spots, are perhaps the
most interesting of all the satyrs. Distinct, isolated
species have evolved on various mountain ranges.
One species, *Erebia christi*, occurs only in the
southern Alps of Switzerland, others are restricted
to the Pyrenees. The arctics, *Oeneis*, also include

several isolated subspecies, one of which is found only on the summits of New Hampshire's White Mountains and another is restricted to the alpine zone of Mount Katahdin in Maine.

The Nymphalids (Family Nymphalidae)

Fritillaries, crescents, anglewings, and tortoiseshells are included in this familiar group of butterflies, which contains over 4000 species. Many of the North American and European nymphs are checkered orange-brown and black with white spangles, perhaps serving to conceal them as they rest among the fallen leaves. Some northern species hibernate as adults, managing to withstand subzero temperatures and appear again the following spring. All of the butterflies in this large family are swift, powerful fliers, and are often seen basking in the sun with their wings spread open wide. Adults feed on numerous kinds of flowers as well as fermenting sap, rotting fruit, animal dung, and urine. Their common name of brush-footed butterflies arises from the fact that their hairy front legs have been reduced to tiny, useless appendages so that they have only four walking legs instead of the usual six.

The painted lady *(Cynthia cardui)* is a migratory species; great swarms have been recorded from all over the world. Unlike the monarch, painted lady migrations seem to have no seasonal pattern, but rather are the result of overpopulation of an area. The Virginia lady *(Cynthia virginiensis)* does not seem to have the migratory habit. Some of the other temperate zone nymphs, such as the admirals, emperors, and peacocks are as brightly colored as most of the tropical species.

Among the most famous of all the butterflies are the morphos, a small group of less than 100 species confined to the tropical American rain forests. Their dazzling iridescent wings twinkle and flash in the sun like brilliant blue semaphores as they soar high above the jungle canopy. The undersides of these large and spectacular butterflies are mottled brown, camouflaging them perfectly when they come down to rest near the forest floor. In Brazil, large numbers of the showier species are bred and reared commercially, their wings used to make jewelry and other decorative items.

Another group of tropical nymphs are famous as dead-leaf imitators. The edges of their wings are ragged and uneven, the forewings slightly pointed and the hindwings tailed. The upper sides are brightly colored but as soon as the butterflies alight on a twig they press their wings together and immediately blend with the surroundings. Even their wing veins simulate the veins of a leaf, and many species have irregular spots that imitate the damaged areas often found on foliage.

The beautifully colored and highly variable *Heliconius* butterflies of the American tropics are involved in extensive mimicry complexes. Their larvae feed on the poisonous passionflower vines and pass on the poisons to the adults, which are avoided by predators. Many butterflies from other families copy the various color patterns of the heliconians for protection.

The soft-winged bright orange and red acraeines, another distasteful group of nymphs, are found in the tropical and subtropical regions of both hemispheres, the vast majority living in Central and South America and tropical Africa. Four species are recorded from the Asian and Australian regions. These are very slow-flying butterflies. In colonies of one species, *Acraea encedon*, found in Uganda, as many as 99 out 100 butterflies were found to be females. The reason for such "biased" sex ratios is still unknown.

The Snout Butterflies (Family Libytheidae)

The most unusual feature of these butterflies is the length of their hairy mouth parts, called palpi, that form the long "snout" in both sexes. These structures are flattened and are four times as long as the head, protruding forward from it like a beak. This small and in many ways peculiar family has an ancient history, being first recorded in the fossil shales of Florissant, Colorado by a species that lived 35 million years ago. Although the snout butterflies are found on every continent, there are only ten living species, and usually only one species is found in any one region. They are medium-sized mottled brown butterflies with a rapid and jerky flight, alighting to rest frequently..Males of the African species are highly gregarious, often settling in considerable numbers on damp mud to drink. The females are more retiring and less frequently encountered. Several migrations of the North American snout butterfly *(Libytheana bachmanii)* have been observed in Arizona, Texas and in Mexico.

The Blues, Coppers, and Hairstreaks (Family Lycaenidae)

With perhaps 6000 species, the lycaenids are the largest of the butterfly families. In Africa alone there are over 1050 species. More than one-third of all the butterflies in the Australian region and close to a third of all North American butterflies are lycaenids. The percentage increases considerably in the tropics. These frail butterflies are small to medium in size, with wingspans from half an inch to three inches wide. They are swift fliers, their often metallic blue, violet, or orange wings winking in the sun as they dart from flower to flower.

Unlike most butterfly caterpillars, lycaenid larvae are usually flattened and sluglike. Many are associated with ants, which they attract with sweet secretions from glands in their skin. In turn, the ants often defend the caterpillars against enemies. Some caterpillars in this family are noted for their carnivorous habits. Lycaenid eggs generally resemble pincushions or turbans, with highly sculptured surfaces.

The hairstreaks received their name from the tiny hairlike "tails" on the hindwings of most species, and the finely streaked lines on the undersides of their wings. These small butterflies zip about so quickly and erratically that it is difficult to follow their flight. When they land, hairstreaks have the curious habit of rubbing their hindwings alternately back and forth, while keeping their front wings pressed tightly together over their backs. The short "tails" move like antennae and eyespots just behind the tails further enhance the impression of a false head. In some cases the camouflage is so realistic that it is virtually impossible to tell which end is the head and which the tail. The subtle wing movements probably provoke a predator into attacking the wrong end, allowing the tattered butterfly to make good its escape in the opposite direction.

Most of the North American hairstreaks are clothed in muted grays and browns. An exception is the great purple hairstreak *(Atlides halesus)*, a spectacularly iridescent species with two tails on each hindwing that is found locally in the southern United States from Florida to California. The common gray hairstreak *(Strymon melinus)*, which lives near urban environments from coast to coast, is sometimes called the hops hairstreak or bean lycaenid because of the damage it does to some cultivated crops.

In the American and Old World tropics, hairstreaks reach their greatest abundance and diversity of colors and sizes. Some are brilliant iridescent blue above and below, with bright black and white lines as well as orange and scarlet spots. Others are white with bold black zebra patterns; still others may be velvety green or black with broad metallic green-gold and blue bars splashed across their wings. One large Australian hairstreak is bright orange and black. Its thickly furred caterpillar lives in the nests of viciously stinging ants. When the fragile, unprotected adult emerges, it is attacked by the ants and must make a fast exit.

The coppers are an ancient worldwide group of butterflies with relatively few species. They often have brilliant metallic coppery orange uppersides, and are stout-bodied, fast-flying butterflies. Unlike the other members of this family, coppers are found only in the temperate zone, living on the forest rim of the Ngorongoro Crater in East Africa, the Alps of New Zealand, the forests of North America, and the rugged mountains of northern Europe. One of the most famous locally restricted butterflies in the world is the Hermes copper *(Lycaena hermes)*, found only in the San Diego area, where urban expansion is rapidly crowding out what remains of the butterfly's range and forcing it into extinction. Another western American species, the bright blue copper is extraordinary in that the males have brilliant sapphire wings instead of the usually coppery tone. These butterflies frequently perch on sagebrush stems and stake out "territories," driving away all intruders that come within four feet of the vantage point.

The blues reach their greatest diversity north of the equator in both the Old and New World. The males generally have bright blue uppersides, while the females are brownish. Perhaps the most beautifully colored blue is the Sonora blue *(Philotes sonorensis)*. It flies in early spring through the foothills of southern California, where its cobalt iridescence and prominent red splotches make a gaudy display among the canyon wildflowers. It was first discovered by Pierre Lorquin, a French naturalist who came to California for the 1849 Gold Rush and stayed on to collect many butterflies. The world's smallest butterfly is the pygmy blue *(Brephidium exilis)*, some males measuring less than three-eighths of an inch in wingspan. It feeds on pigweed and saltbush and is found from 178 feet below sea level in California's Death Valley to elevations of over 6000 feet in desert mountain ranges.

Many of the loveliest butterflies in Europe are found among the blues, such as the chalk-hill blue *(Lysandra coridon)* and the Adonis blue *(Lysandra bellargus)*. The large blue *(Maculinea arion)* is remarkable in that its caterpillar is totally dependent on the aid of certain ants for its survival. During the third molt, the larva wanders about until it encounters one of the ants which, after stroking the larva for a drop of honeydew, carries it to its nest. There the caterpillar spends the winter, feeding on ant larvae and being milked of its sweet secretions by the ants. Finally it emerges from the nest in late spring as an adult butterfly. If the caterpillar fails to meet with the correct type of ant it dies.

The Metalmarks (Family Riodinidae)

The common name for this worldwide but largely American family of butterflies arises from the presence of metallic flecks on their wings. When alighting to rest, often upside down on the underside of a leaf, metalmarks have the almost unique habit among the butterflies of holding their wings stretched out flat. The fifteen or so species in North America are dressed in rather drab browns, but several have a delicate metallic silver thread stitched along the outer margin of their wings. The little metalmark *(Lephelisca virginiensis)* is found in the South, where it flies in open, grassy fields and wet meadows. The weak-flying swamp metalmark *(Lephelisca muticum)* occurs from Pennsylvania and Ohio west to Michigan and Wisconsin. The somewhat rare northern metalmark *(Lephelisca borealis)* prefers open woods and dry, hilly countryside.

In the American tropics, however, the metalmarks run riot with an incredible range of shapes, sizes, colors, and patterns that closely resemble the butterflies of every other family. Dark, demure "satyrs," bright yellow "pierids," broad-winged orange "acraeines" and even "swallowtails" turn out, on closer inspection, to be metalmarks. Some species mimic the tiger-striped ithomiids, others copy the clear-winged butterflies. Some have long tails of brilliant iridescent blue ending in scarlet patches. Others are dusted with glittering green and gold scales. One tiny metalmark with a wing expanse of only half an inch is solid crimson with narrow, dark wing margins. Although there are hundreds of species of tropical metalmarks, most of them are uncommon and only a few specimens of each species are likely to be collected in any one area. The classification of this confusing family is still incomplete. Hundreds of new species may be expected to be discovered in the American tropics, and probably quite a few in the Asian and Pacific regions.

108-115. The family Hesperiidae, known as skippers because of their irregular, darting flight, are usually small and rather drab, although some tropical species have brilliant splashes of color across their wings. Found from the Arctic tundra to the tropical rain forests, skippers visit flowers and moist river banks or muddy trail sides. A few of the African species feed at flowers during twilight, remaining on the wing until well after nightfall. In Costa Rica, a large rain forest skipper visits morning-glory blossoms more than an hour before sunrise.

108. Elbella azeta: *Peru*

109. Pyrgus syrichtus: *Texas*

110. Carterocephalus palaemon: *Canada*

111. Pyrropyge cometes: *Peru*

112. Polites peckius: *Ontario*

113. Ochlodes sylvanoides: *California*

114. Paratrytone melane: *California*

115. Atrytone dukesi: *Alabama*

116.

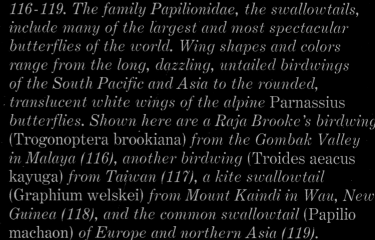

116-119. *The family Papilionidae, the swallowtails,
include many of the largest and most spectacular
butterflies of the world. Wing shapes and colors
range from the long, dazzling, untailed birdwings
of the South Pacific and Asia to the rounded,
translucent white wings of the alpine* Parnassius
butterflies. Shown here are a Raja Brooke's birdwing
(Trogonoptera brookiana) *from the Gombak Valley
in Malaya (116), another birdwing* (Troides aeacus
kayuga) *from Taiwan (117), a kite swallowtail*
(Graphium welskei) *from Mount Kaindi in Wau, New
Guinea (118), and the common swallowtail* (Papilio
machaon) *of Europe and northern Asia (119).*

117.

118.

120-122. The Pieridae are usually plain white or yellow with black markings. A number of tropical varieties, however, such as the large Phoebis and Catopsilia *sulphurs are more brightly colored.* The pierids shown here are a Delias eucharis *from India (120), a migratory great southern white* Ascia monuste *(121), and the white* Belenois aurota, *shown refueling at a flower during a migration in South Africa (122).*

121.

122.

123.

124.

123-124. *The family Danaidae numbers less than 200 species but they are well distributed in most areas of the world. Distasteful insects with tough bodies and rubbery wings, they are generally avoided by predators. Most are large and glide in a leisurely fashion, displaying their orange or purplish warning coloration to good advantage. The monarch* (Danaus plexippus) *(123) is a familiar danaid across North America and Asia. In subtropical and tropical America it flies in company with the queen butterflies, such as* Danaus gilippus *from the Everglades in Florida (124).*

125. *The family Ithomiidae contains some 400 species of colored and glassy-winged butterflies found throughout the lowlands of Central and South America, with one species occurring in Australia and across some of the South Pacific islands. Ithomiids form great mimicry complexes in the tropical rain forests.* Oleria *species (125) are common in the Amazon areas of Ecuador.*

126. Euptychia drymo: *Costa Rica*

130. Pararge megera: *England*

127. Lethe portlandia: *Virginia*

131. Tisiphone abeona: *Australia*

128. Coenonympha tullia: *England*

132. Bia actorion: *Ecuador*

129. Euptychia *species: Ecuador*

133. Taygetis *species: Ecuador*

flight, barely clearing the grasses. Many select surfaces such as lichen-covered rocks or exposed leaves and orient their wings to receive maximum benefit of the sun's rays, as shown by the hedge brown (Maniola tithonus) in England (134).

135-150. The family Nymphalidae is a huge group of butterflies including the well-known fritillaries, anglewings, crescentspots, buckeyes, "88" butterflies and a host of others amounting to some 3000 species. The majority are robust-bodied butterflies with a strong rapid flight. The acraeines are distasteful bright orange nymphs with long abdomens and rounded, often partially transparent wings. The heliconians are narrow-winged poisonous butterflies and are a familiar sight in the American tropics.

151. The family Libytheidae, containing ten species of snout butterflies, is recognized by the length of their mouth parts which project like a beak from the head. Each continent has one or two species. Pictured here is the North American snout butterfly (Libytheana bachmanii).

152-167. The Lycaenidae, a huge group composed of the blues, coppers, and hairstreaks, are often called the "living jewels" of the insect world because of their brilliant colors and small size. Several metal-marks in the family Riodinidae, such as the Charis species from Ecuador (167), so closely resemble hair-streaks that some authorities combine the two families.

134.

135. Heliconius wallacei flavescens: *Ecuador*

139. Mesoacidalia aglaja: *Austria*

136. Heliconius *species: Peru*

140. Limenitis archippus: *New Jersey*

137. Acraea quirina: *Kenya*

141. Argynnis paphia: *Germany*

138. Acraea cerasa: *Kenya*

142. Polygonia progne: *United States*

143. Phyciodes phaon: *Louisiana*

144. Issoria lathonia: *Spain*

145. Aglais urticae: *England*

146. Precis orithya: *Nigeria*

147. Catagramma eunomia: *Peru*

148. Catagramma *species: Peru*

149. Apatura ilia: *Europe*

150. Precis oenone: *Kenya*

152. Polyommatus icarus: *England*

156. Lycaena dispar batava: *England*

153. Cyaniris semiargus: *England*

157. Heodes virgaureae: *Austria*

154. Lycaena helloides, *female: California*

158. Lycaena thoe: *United States*

155. Lycaena helloides, *male: California*

159. Lycaena phlaeas americanus: *United States*

60. Strymon melinus: *Louisiana*

164. Callophrys rubi: *Austria*

61. Strymon liparops: *eastern United States*

165. Thecla betulae: *Austria*

62. Atlides halesus: *California*

166. Axiocerses harpax: *Zambia*

63. Thecla betulae, *female: Switzerland*

167. Charis *metalmark: Ecuador*

168-170. *The family Riodinidae, the metalmarks, forms a group of a thousand species reaching its maximum development in the American tropics. The metalmarks are a conspicuous part of the butterfly population across South America, frequently encountered along sunlit forest paths, moist river banks or mud flats, spreading their wings to expose brilliant metallic colors. Shown here are three metalmarks from Tingo Maria in Peru,* Ancyluris melipoeus *(168),* Amarynthis micalia *(169), and a* Caria *species (170).*

168.

169.

170.

Part Two

Where Butterflies Are Found

Butterflies have invaded every region of the world except those that are perpetually cold or wet. They fly up to nearly 20,000 feet in the Himalaya, exist more than 100 feet below sea level in desert valleys of the American southwest and the Middle East, and even survive on the wind-blown tundra north of the Arctic Circle. However, they reach their greatest diversity in the lush tropical jungles, where all butterflies probably originated.

The pierids, or whites and yellows, have the widest distribution of the butterfly families. In the western hemisphere they are found from northern Greenland and Alaska to the tip of South America, inhabiting every elevation where their food plants exist. The nymphalids have a similar range, but are not usually found as high in the equatorial mountains. The lycaenids, or blues, coppers and hairstreaks, extend as far north as the preceding two families, but are not found farther south than Argentina and Chile in the western hemisphere, or New Zealand in the eastern hemisphere. The satyrids and the papilionids, or swallowtails, range as far north as southern Greenland and Alaska and south to the tip of South America. The riodinids, or metalmarks, are largely tropical but several groups can be found as far north as southern Canada and south to central Argentina and Chile, flying up to 11,000 feet in the equatorial mountains. Most of the danaids and the hesperiids, or skippers, live in the central tropics and subtropical regions, while the ithomiids are almost exclusively a tropical American group, with only one species inhabiting some of the South Pacific islands and the rain forests of northern Australia. The megathymids, or giant skippers, occur only in the southern and southwestern portions of the United States, and extend south through Mexico to Central America. The smallest of the butterfly families, the libytheids, or snout butterflies, includes only ten species but is found worldwide in both the tropical and temperate zones.

In the New World, the Nearctic region includes the temperate areas of northern Mexico, the United States and Canada, while the Neotropical region includes the rest of Mexico and all of Central and South America. In the Old World, the Palearctic region is composed of the temperate northern parts of Europe, the Near East, Middle East, Mediterranean Africa and Asia, as well as offshore islands such as much of Japan and the British Isles. (The term Holarctic refers to the combined Nearctic and Palearctic regions, which share many butterfly genera and even some species). The Ethiopian region includes all of Africa except for its northern fringe, while the Oriental and Australian regions (often combined as the Indo-Australian realm) comprise the tropical Asian lands from China, India, and Malaysia south through the Australian area.

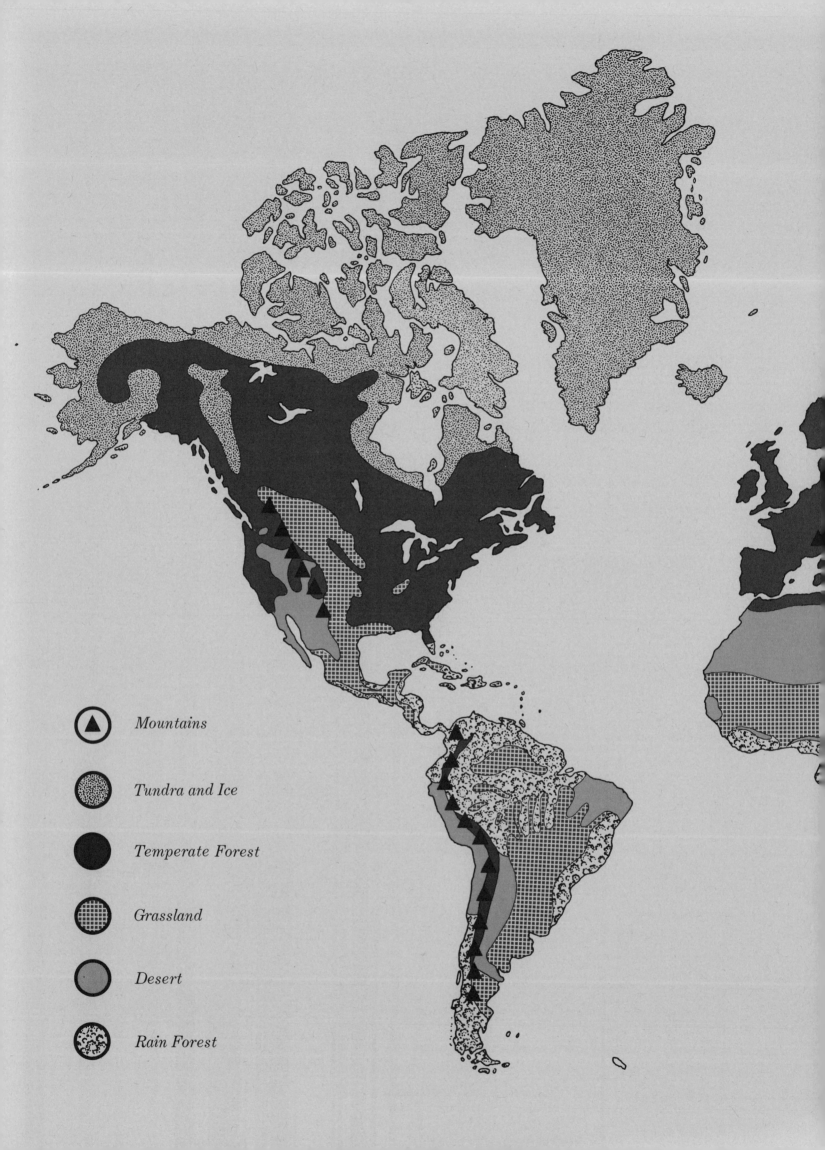

Mountains

Tundra and Ice

Temperate Forest

Grassland

Desert

Rain Forest

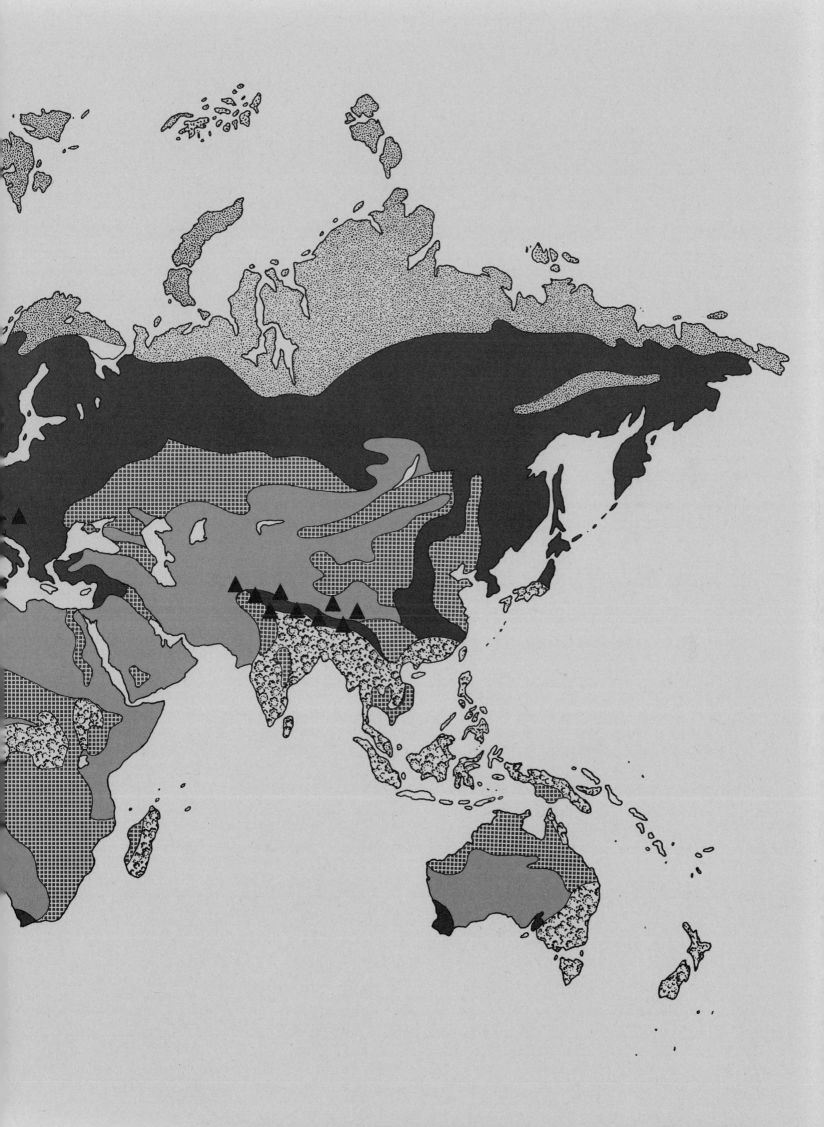

Butterflies of the Rain Forest

A naturalist's first day in a tropical rain forest is an unforgettable experience. My first such adventure came in Vera Cruz, a southern state in Mexico caressed by moisture-laden winds from the Gulf of Mexico. Walking among the green welter of giant, vine-festooned trees with their far-flung buttresses, I was more concerned with spotting snakes than butterflies. But soon all other thoughts were swept from my mind as I began to see the great number of gorgeous butterflies fluttering and gliding along the trail. The brilliant blue flashes of giant morphos and tiny iridescent green hairstreaks, the gaudily patterned undersides of the "88" and *Catagramma* butterflies, and the strange, loud, clicking sounds broadcast by the *Hamadryas* nymphs as they flew from trunk to trunk, combined to create a very exciting moment for an impressionable student. Since that day I have visited many rain forests and the even more productive jungles of second-growth forest throughout the American tropics, and every trip reinforces my belief that here is the true paradise on earth for the biologist. No other life zone has butterflies so diverse in structure and behavior, so numerous and visible, or so important a part of the community of plant and animal life.

Tropical rain forests straddle the equator in central Africa, the continental and island areas of southeast Asia, and the South Pacific islands, as well as northeastern Australia. But the most extensive rain forests of all spread a dense green carpet across Central and South America. These steaming jungles fascinated European naturalists during the nineteenth century. Such men as Charles Darwin, Henry Walter Bates, and Alfred Russel Wallace came to South America as young naturalists and left as seasoned biologists with a store of insights that would enrich the world. Darwin and Wallace published their theories on the origin of species by natural selection in 1859 and became famous biologists. Not so familiar is Henry Walter Bates's contribution. At twenty-three he set off with Wallace up the Amazon River to explore the natural history of Brazil. After traveling for two years together, they separated, Bates staying on in Brazil for eleven years. He collected and sent back to England 14,712 species of animals, of which over 8,000 proved to be new to science. It is a record that will probably never be equaled. Bates's book, *The Naturalist on the River Amazons*, published in 1863, four years after his return to England, contained many of his observations on Neotropical butterflies. It proved an instant commercial success and stimulated a great interest in the natural history of the American tropics.

Aside from the large number of new species that Bates discovered, his most significant contribution was his observations on insect mimicry. While collecting on the lower reaches of the Amazon, Bates had noted uncanny resemblances in shapes, colors, and behavior between butterflies of very distinct families. He encountered many transparent-winged species of *Ithomia* butterflies floating in abundance in the shady ravines of the tropical forest. Now and then, flying among the *Ithomia* was a *Dismorphia*, also a clear-winged butterfly but belonging to a totally different family, the Pieridae. Unlike the *Ithomia*, these pierids were unprotected by distasteful chemical secretions. Bates was quite unable to distinguish the two butterflies on the wing, and on every occasion when he captured an *"Ithomia"* only to find it was a mimicking pierid, he could scarcely restrain an exclamation of surprise, because the mimicry in behavior, color pattern, and size was so perfect.

Bates made many observations on mimicry in Brazil, and in 1859, after reading Darwin's *Origin of Species*, he saw that the most logical explanation was that a harmless insect like *Dismorphia* improved its chances of survival by looking like a common distasteful species. Bates concluded that the case offered a most beautiful proof of the theory of natural selection. After reading Bates's detailed account, Darwin felt moved to comment, "We feel to be as near witnesses, as we can ever hope to be, of the creation of a new species on this earth." As discussed in an earlier chapter, this form of imitation has come to be known as Batesian mimicry.

Fritz Müller, a German zoologist, came to the Brazilian Amazon a few years after Bates and discovered another important kind of mimicry among butterflies. While collecting ithomiids, Müller observed that a great many of these butterflies shared the same general color pattern, yet all of them were presumably distasteful as their larvae fed on poisonous plants in the deadly nightshade family. In his 1878 theory, which has become known as Müllerian mimicry, he suggested that sharing a common warning color pattern and behavior was a survival advantage to each of the distasteful species because the predators learned to associate a bitter taste with that pattern and had only to try one species of ithomiid to learn that it would suffer a severely upset stomach. Thereafter it would avoid all butterflies of a similar appearance.

What has made tropical butterflies so interesting to biologist and collector alike? Part of the reason is the tremendous variety of species in tropical regions. Some indication of this abundance is revealed in Bates's data. In all of South America (only partially collected even today), Bates became acquainted with 4560 species of butterflies at a time when only 716 species were known to inhabit the entire Palearctic Region, from Europe to Manchuria, the best-studied area in the world. All of Europe contains only about 400 butterfly species, whereas within the radius of an hour's walk at Pará (now Belém, Brazil) Bates easily collected 700 species.

The conditions that have produced such sharply contrasting figures are not yet completely understood. Biologists have observed the strikingly brief period of development for tropical insects. The danaid butterfly *Danaus chrysippus* usually goes through only one generation a year in the northern parts of its range in Asia; but in the southern Philippines it has a steady progression of generations throughout the year, each one taking only twenty-three days to develop from egg to adult. So many additional generations a year in the tropics result in more mutation, variation and recombination of inherited traits, thus producing a greater variety of butterflies.

The butterflies can accomplish this rapid growth rate because most tropical rain forests do not have well-defined seasons. They inhabit a world without winter and so do not need to hibernate through cold seasons or estivate through hot dry seasons. Rainfall is a more or less constant quantity every month of the year, and the temperature range and length of day barely change. With high temperatures and humidity, much light, and a great quantity of rapidly growing food, cold-blooded butterflies find an ideal environment.

The great variety of plants available as food for the caterpillars results in a wide diversity of insects and allows a much greater range of specialization than in temperate zones. Many plants live only at certain heights in the forest layers, from the topmost canopy, more than 200 feet high, to ground level. Most butterflies are limited to one particular layer, and this stratification increases the opportunities for additional butterflies.

The vast number of predators in the tropics also greatly influences butterfly variety. In their struggle for survival, many have adopted devices such as extensive mimicry of each other or imitation of inedible objects like leaves or bird droppings, particularly in their larval and pupal stages.

Central and South America

The spectacular butterflies characteristic of the dense rain forests in the New World tropics are nowhere more impressive than on the Osa Peninsula of Costa Rica, in Central America, or in the Amazon Basin of South America. A collector can wander for weeks along the trails and rivers in these forests constantly collecting species new to him. Some of these butterflies make their permanent homes in the canopy several hundred feet above the ground, darting down into clearings or over streams for only a few moments before zooming up into the treetops again. Others flutter along the rain forest floor, settling in the leaf litter only a few yards from where they took off. Gossamer ghosts of transparent ithomiid butterflies float on delicate wings among the hanging vines and palms. Suddenly, a brilliant iridescent flash of blue

scatters all thoughts of other butterflies and the collector is racing along after a saucer-sized morpho. But it zigzags off the trail into the undergrowth and disappears, perhaps to reappear at another clearing later on.

The eighty or so morpho species of the American tropics are interesting in many ways. The upper surfaces of their wings are usually brightly colored, ranging from white to light blue to dazzling deep blue and purple, although several species lack iridescence and flit about in somber yellow-spotted brown. The undersurfaces of all the species are brown, camouflaging them perfectly when they suddenly alight. The females are often less brilliant then their mates, are slightly larger in size, and have more retiring habits, which is probably why females of many species are seldom found in collections. Some, such as *Morpho cypris* and *Morpho theseus*, spend their lives in the treetops, while others, such as *Morpho peleides,* normally fly near the ground along paths and trails. Adults have been found to live close to nine months, and they apparently learn quite a bit about their environment. Many morphos follow regular flight routes during their daily movements through the rain forest, and in Central America these flight paths apparently function as territories for male butterflies of *Morpho amathonte.*

The small male populations of this species form sleeping roosts, each consisting of a few individuals that pass the night on top of large leaves within a few feet of each other. In the early morning hours, the males fly off to nearby feeding sites, which are accumulations of fermenting fruit on the forest floor. They usually feed between 7:30 and 9:30 A.M., without notably aggressive behavior. Females always feed after the males have left the fruits; thus no courtship occurs at the feeding sites. Between 9:30 and noon the butterflies move along somewhat circular flight paths. At this time, the males, each flying its own daily patrol route, attract, court, and mate with the females. This territorial behavior spaces out the males and draws them into a regular flight schedule through the forest understory, while the iridescence of their wings helps to attract females from afar. Courtship is aided and successful mating results despite the low-density adult population of the species. Early in the afternoon, before the usual daily rains begin, the morphos, especially the males, return to the general area of the feeding sites and roost there for the night. This complex daily activity pattern probably prevents aggressive behavior among the males when they are crowded together at feeding sites and nocturnal roosts. Their large but fragile wings would soon be battered by fighting if courtship and mating took place when several males were on hand.

One question may come to mind. If a morpho passes

the same point on a trail at about the same time each day, and if the morpho is flaunting conspicuous wing coloration to attract females, why don't predators watch these flight paths and catch all the morphos that come along? The answer is that they are not easy to catch. A number of long-beaked birds such as jacamars, flycatchers, and motmots feed on butterflies, especially the brownish winged morphos. But the brilliant blue species do not seem to be attacked very often. They rarely have "beak marks" on their wings, where a bird tried to seize them, and blue morpho wings are rarely found in the piles of insect remains on the forest floor under the perches of these birds. Predators may learn to ignore these bright and showy butterflies, since a flying male morpho can quickly alter its pattern and speed of flight by increasing its characteristic vertical bobbing. As its mirror-like iridescent wings flash in the sun the morpho's flight is further confused and almost inevitably insures its escape. A bird quickly learns that it is unprofitable to chase after this flashing, bobbing beauty.

Another curious Neotropical rain forest group is the ithomiid butterflies—the 400 or so species are characterized by a host of Batesian and Müllerian mimicry associations. The caterpillars feed on plants of the deadly nightshade family, absorbing the poisonous alkaloids in the leaves. When passed along to the pupal and adult stages, these poisons continue to protect the butterfly against being eaten by a bird, lizard, or other predator. These butterflies, among other insects, have discovered ways to detoxify the compounds they absorb, rendering them harmless to their own body tissues.

The life histories of the ithomiids have not been well studied, but those that have been traced reveal fascinating differences from the developmental stages of other butterfly groups. The larvae are often yellowish to green, with deeply crevassed body segments; some resemble our flattened species of common garden millipede, while others are cylindrical and are encircled by black and white bands. In the species that lay clusters of eggs, the hatching larvae feed together as a group and move around communally for at least several instars. Some pupae are brilliant silver over the wing areas, while one species has dazzling reflective gold rings around its pupa. To the human observer, ithomiid pupae hanging from plants in the forest look like large drops of dew or rainwater reflecting the sunlight. For those species whose life histories have been studied, it is known to take only twenty-five to forty-five days to develop from freshly laid egg to the emerging adult.

All of the ithomiids exhibit a slow, fluttering flight, the slowest and weakest being the transparent-winged species. Because most of their wing scales have been reduced to hairs, leaving the membrane exposed, these ithomiids achieve a kind of transparency. Deep in the forest interior, moving over dark leaf litter in heavy shade, they are almost impossible to see or follow in flight. Many retain white marginal spots on their wings, however, which may deflect a predator's attention from vital body parts, and probably also aid as courtship signals. Most of the sex recognition is the result of complex scent-scale brushes and glands that the males use to disseminate attractant chemicals and thus seduce the females.

Many of the ithomiids take an alternate course and assume bright warning colors that advertise their bitter taste to predators. *Mechanitis* and other "tiger striped" ithomiids resemble each other so closely in pattern and behavior that sex scents must play an essential role in courtship and successful mating. These boldly patterned species are commonly found along open trails and in clearings along the edge of the forest.

The ithomiids visit flowers and also descend on fermenting sap, fresh animal dung, bird droppings, and rotting fruit. In full flight the legs of these butterflies are slung back along the sides of the body but when they alight, their long, fragile-looking legs are stretched out in front like landing gear on a plane. The front pair of legs is quite small and is not used in walking or perching. The long proboscis can be flexed at several points, and the butterfly often probes about with it like a delicate young lady with a straw in a nearly empty soda glass, and then settles down to feed for many minutes on end.

Rather similar to the ithomiids in appearance are the long-winged heliconians, found only in the New World. These butterflies have specialized in eating the 500 or so types of passionflowers in the tropical jungles. Wherever these colorful plants blossom in the forest canopy, in clearings or at roadside, one or more of the eighty-odd species of heliconians are sure to be found. They are long-lived butterflies, some with life-spans up to six months, and like the ithomiids and morphos they need to supplement their usual sugary nectar diet with nutritionally richer sources of nitrogen and vitamins. The most advanced species in the genus *Heliconius* do not depend on accidental opportunities like bird droppings but take advantage of a second nutritious component of the flowers they visit: the pollen. The *Heliconius* butterfly has a specially constructed tongue for collecting it. Nectar and enzymes regurgitated onto the pollen, release free amino acids that can then be sucked up from the "pollen lollipop" and absorbed by the butterfly. These amino acids, the building blocks of proteins, are passed into the butterfly's tissues, and if it is a female, into her eggs. Lawrence E. Gilbert, a lepidopterist at the University of Texas who has done considerable research with *Heliconius*, has found that adults of some species actually patrol a regular route each day between nectar and pollen sources over miles of forest, and that males of at

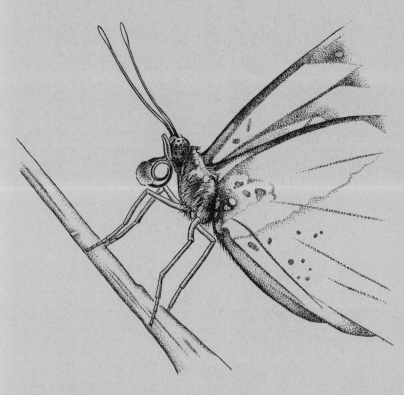

"Pollen lollipop." The specialized tongue of a heliconian butterfly can extract protein parts from flower pollen.

least one species actively fight off other butterflies from the flowers selected for their daily early morning feeding.

Heliconians usually deposit their eggs on the very tips of the vine tendrils of passionflowers. Yellowish orange in color and emitting a slight odor, these prominently placed eggs warn other females that this plant is already "taken." Thus a single vine does not become overloaded with caterpillars. At least one species of passion vine has orange tips on its tendrils, which could deceive a *Heliconius* female into thinking that the plant has already had an egg laid on it. That passion vine then escapes being fed on by *Heliconius* caterpillars.

These poisonous butterflies are mimicked extensively by other species, and part of our knowledge of how such mimicry systems are established comes from work done with South American heliconians. Biologists from England have successfully bred several species and crossed the various color forms to determine the inheritance of genetic differences, Lincoln P. Brower of Amherst College in Massachusetts has worked for many years testing the effectiveness of mimicry in these and other butterflies with predators on the island of Trinidad.

In the twilight between sunset and the tropical night, the giant owl butterflies, or *Caligo* species, bat their way through the forest in a brief flurry of activity. At rest on tree trunks during the daytime and concealed by cryptically marked undersurfaces, the *Caligos* bear prominent, lifelike eyespots on the hindwings, and if they "threaten" a predator by nervously opening and closing their wings, the bird or other animal will often take off. The *Caligo* collector rarely gets a clear view of his quarry in the dusk and must swing his net more by intuition and the rush of the wind from their powerful wing beats than by vision. Fortunately, the owl butterflies and others of their kind come to rotting fruit bait such as bananas or mangoes in the early morning or late afternoon, where they may be more easily captured. The caterpillars of some of the tropical American *Caligos* feed on commercially imported palms and bananas and have become economic pests.

The hairstreaks and the metalmarks are represented by an extraordinary diversity of species in Central and South America. Their taxonomy is so complex that museum specialists have largely avoided these groups, and with the spectacular larger butterflies such as *Morpho* and *Agrias* species drawing the collectors, these small but interesting butterflies are in fact rarely collected in proportion to their numbers. Most of the hairstreaks and metalmarks dwell in the forest canopy layer and so are not as accessible as the ground-dwelling satyrs and nymphs.

Tropical hairstreaks have correctly been called the "living jewels" of the butterfly world. Many have brilliant iridescent blue or purple colors across their upper wing surfaces, which flash in the sunlight as brightly as those of any morpho. A favorite perch becomes a vantage point from which a male will challenge passing hairstreaks or even larger butterflies. With a darting flight, he zips across a dozen yards of the canopy and returns a few seconds later: a challenge has been met and another male banished from his territory. Then he sits in the sun again, rubbing his hindwings together, wiggling the antenna-like tails at the rear margins. Should an observant predator take in this sudden flight and return and swoop in on the perching hairstreak, the attacker will probably end up with only a mouthful of scales and perhaps a piece of hindwing or a fractured tail dangling from its mouth.

The metalmarks have been aptly named. Splashes of brilliant green and iridescent silver and gold dot the wings of many a tropical species. Like the ithomiids, they are almost exclusively a Neotropical group, with only a few representatives scattered in the Old World. But more than any other family, the metalmarks dazzle the lepidopterist with a truly astonishing array of shapes and sizes. Some look like miniature swallowtails, pierids, satyrids, or nymphalids; others imitate ithomiids, acraeines, hairstreaks, blues, coppers, danaids, and even snout butterflies. Many species are inhabitants of the deep forest, flying furtively from the underside of one leaf to another during an hour or two each morning or afternoon when the sun angles down through the foliage to create sun spots here and there. Others flaunt their gorgeous, iridescent coat of scales on the forest paths or along clearings and water courses. The populations are small and localized, and often groups of adults emerge almost simultaneously, fly for a few weeks, and then disappear again for several months as the new brood of eggs and larvae develop. Thus it is often possible for a diligent collector to take a small series of adults of a rarely encountered metalmark if he has the time to return again and again to the same spot in the rain forest. Collectors may also take advantage of the fact that animal dung or urine-soaked ground will draw many metalmarks.

Africa

Unlike the richly populated rain forests of South America, those of Africa contain fewer butterfly species. The African continent south of the Sahara (including Madagascar) has just over 2600 described species (compared with over 6000 for South America), and a leading African lepidopterist, Robert Carcasson, estimates that this figure represents about 85 percent of the true total. A majority of Africa's species are found in the rain forests and mountains of West and Central Africa. In the temperate part of Southern Africa, there are roughly 550 species—still a considerable number when one realizes that this approaches the total number of

butterflies found in temperate North America. Although many coppers and other lycaenids occur in the grasslands of South Africa, and other specialized groups reside in the rugged mountain ranges, the rain forest forms are most characteristic of tropical Africa. The remarkable variety of trees, climbing vines, and other vegetation provides a rich source of food for caterpillars, and, as in the American tropics, the small seasonal change in the wettest rain forests allows continuous reproduction. A collector can sample the canopy fauna when high-flying butterflies dip down toward bright sunlit patches on the ground or along the water's edge. To secure the more secretive species that keep to the deep shade of the forest interior, one must leave the trails and wander about in the undisturbed primary forest.

The most sought-after butterflies of the African forests are the robust species of *Charaxes*. Large and colorful, the nymphalids have been favorites of collectors for more than a century. Because they are powerful fliers and very alert and wary, they are not easily netted. To get perfect specimens, collectors use trap nets set on top of fermenting fruit, rotting meat, or even monkey or hyena dung. Sometimes the intently feeding butterflies can simply be picked up with tweezers. Some species favor the drier thorn scrub, and they are easily captured on top of ridges as they engage in whirling "hill-topping" flight. Like most nymphs in normal flight, they usually flap their wings a few times, sail forward, and then resume a leisurely flapping after a few yards. But as soon as another butterfly comes into view, the pugnacious *Charaxes* takes off in pursuit with swift wing beat. Some species are known only from male specimens, others from only the female; this rarity adds to the excitement of hunting *Charaxes*.

The current drier climate along with the influence of human cultivation and the extensive burning of the plains has reduced the rain forests and separated the remaining stands by long stretches of grassland and sparse thorn scrub. As their habitat has been broken up over the past several thousand years, the *Charaxes* species of the wet forests have formed different geographic races. Apparently the butterflies are unable to move from one forest area to another because of differences in humidity and other conditions in the intervening territory.

Among the tropical nymphalids one attractive butterfly that is remarkable for its seasonal changes in color is *Precis*, a relative of the North American buckeye, whose many species are common throughout the woodlands and forests of Africa. The wet-season form is small and bright orange with black markings. In the moist forests, this form flies all year. In the dry season, the adults of *Precis octavia* are heavily marked with black areas and blue spots that perhaps blend with the deep shadows of the sere vegetation.

In *Precis pelarga* populations, two dry-season forms appear. One is orange-banded like the wet-season form, while the other has an intense blue band instead of orange. The wing margins of the dry-season forms are deeply scalloped and extended at the forewing tip and at the trailing edge of the hindwing. When the butterfly sits with folded wings among dead leaves, the false "stems" and the mottled browns and oranges on the underside make its resemblance to a leaf truly striking. Many of the satyrs also have seasonal forms, with more variable coloration and smaller eye spots appearing in the dry-season adults. These changes presumably aid in concealing the adult at a time when many plants in seasonal forest areas have lost their foliage and predators are avidly searching for food among the greatly reduced insect populations.

The largest butterfly on the African continent, *Papilio antimachus*, is a rain forest inhabitant and resembles a giant *Acraea* in its orange and reddish brown coat trimmed with black markings. Males will occasionally visit mud at the edge of a forest stream, but the huge wingspan (more than nine inches) swiftly carries these swallowtails away from danger if a predator intrudes. Many of the Papilionidae have tails, which may aid in deflecting a bird's attack to this nonvital part of the hindwing. All are strong fliers, keeping to the forest or woodlands and often sailing high overhead among the canopy blossoms with only an infrequent dip to a wet bank or understory flower. One species has the common name of mocker swallowtail *(Papilio dardanus)* because many of the females imitate a wide variety of distasteful butterflies. More than a dozen color forms are known, ranging from black and white, black and yellow, black and orange, white and orange, to nearly all black. In fact, the females of this mimetic species have even lost their tails except in the races found in Ethiopia and Madagascar, where they are tailed like the creamy yellow male. This extensive mimicry in the females probably has become established because it allows larger numbers of the swallowtails to live in the same area. In Batesian mimicry assemblages, where edible butterflies imitate poisonous species, the mimic must never be more abundant than the bad tasting model, or else the predators will often try a mimic and associate its appearance with a good taste experience. Mocker swallowtail females solve this dilemma by looking like several different poisonous butterflies in a given region and thus parceling out the mimetic advantage over a number of color forms. A host of kite swallowtails brighten the forest scene with delicate translucent green, yellow, and blue on dusky backgrounds. In typical swallowtail fashion, they flutter their wings gently while clinging to a flower, ready for an instant takeoff. Usually it is only when they are at mud or bait, and totally occupied in feasting, that one has a reasonable chance to net or photograph these extremely agile and fast-flying swallowtails.

The remarkable family Acraeidae reaches its fullest diversity in the forests of central Africa. Only a handful of species are found elsewhere in the world: about four dozen in tropical America, and four species in the Asian and Australian regions. *Acraea encedon* in East and West Africa occurs in almost exclusively female communities in certain cultivated areas, an extraordinary situation that appears to be part of the way this species regulates its population. This is also one of the most varied butterfly species in Africa with as many as ten or more color forms. Four match the four African forms of the golden danaid *Danaus chrysippus*, a butterfly that has proved distasteful to birds in feeding experiments. Other *Acraea* species resemble each other, and many nymphalids seem to mimic acraeines. The complexities of these mimetic associations are great, and it is often quite unclear which species are the models and which are mimics, or even perhaps just coincidentally similar in color pattern. Certain acraeine caterpillars feed on passionflowers, some of which are known to contain toxic compounds. Others, like the *Acraea encedon*, apparently feed on nontoxic plants; or perhaps these butterflies do not derive the toxic compounds from plants but produce them metabolically. These acraeines and their many mimics, along with *Papilio dardanus* and its diverse mimetic female forms, are providing key material to geneticists and students of ecology in unlocking the secrets of complex evolutionary histories.

The Indo-Australian Region

In southwestern India and Ceylon, and from northeastern India and Burma down through the Malayan Peninsula and neighboring islands to the Philippines and south to northeastern Australia, the wetter lowlands and mountain foothills are covered with tropical rain forest. Many areas that were formerly extensive jungles have been lumbered and cleared for agriculture, which has also been the fate of rain forests in other parts of the world as well. But one can still find fabulously lush jungles rich in spectacular birdwings and other unique butterflies, and experience the thrill that the great biologist and explorer Alfred Russel Wallace had while collecting on the island of Bachan west of New Guinea in late 1858 and 1859. His account of the first capture of the golden *Ornithoptera croesus* is now famous in butterfly lore.

Wallace landed at Bachan on October 21, 1858, and set up housekeeping near the coastal village of Batchian. During his very first walk into the virgin forest he came upon an immense, dark-colored butterfly marked with white and yellow spots. He saw at once that it was a female of a new species of *Ornithoptera*, or "bird-winged butterfly." Wallace

was very anxious to get a male, which he guessed
would be extraordinarily beautiful. During the next
two months he saw the butterfly only once again. He
had begun to despair of ever collecting a specimen
until one day early in January he saw one hovering
over an unusual shrub with large white leafy bracts
and yellow flowers. It got away from him, but the
next day he returned and succeeded in catching a
female, and the day after that a fine male, with black
and orange wings more than seven inches wide.
He wrote:

"I found it to be as I had expected, a perfectly new . . .
species, and one of the most gorgeously coloured
butterflies in the world. Fine specimens of the male
are more than seven inches across the wings, which
are velvety black and fiery orange. . . . On taking
it out of my net and opening the glorious wings,
my heart began to beat violently . . . and I felt much
more like fainting than I have done when in
apprehension of immediate death. I had a headache
the rest of the day, so great was the excitement
produced by what will appear to most people a very
inadequate cause."

The Indo-Australian butterfly population is extraordinarily rich. The Malayan Peninsula alone has
over 1000 species; even Singapore, the small island
at the tip of Malaya, has had no less than 368 species
of butterflies taken on it, although fifty-six of these
have disappeared since the 1920s. Burma boasts 1014
species, while the Indian subcontinent contains some
1443 species distributed from the tropical rain forests
of the Western Ghats to the high Himalayan meadows.
Australia, on the other hand, has only 364 butterfly
species of which 85 percent are recorded from
Queensland alone, where most of Australia's tropical
forest is located.

The low mountain range that runs like a spine down
the center of the Malayan Peninsula supports a
tremendously diverse butterfly fauna. More than
half of the total number of butterfly species are found
in the lowlands, where the rainfall reaches ninety
inches a year and the change in season is barely
perceptible. About one-seventh of the butterfly
population is restricted to habitats about 2500 feet
in the mountains, where the rainfall increases to as
much as 250 inches, and the remaining butterflies,
less restricted by altitude, are found in great
abundance wherever there is second-growth forest
and weedy areas.

Some of these cosmopolitan butterflies include the
beautiful *Catopsilia* sulphurs (closely related to the
American sulphurs), the Old World buckeyes in the
genus *Precis*, the widely distributed golden danaid,
and the swallowtail butterflies *Papilio memnon* and
Papilio polytes. The mimic forms in both these latter
species resemble various distasteful butterflies that
live in the same area.

The vast majority of Malayan species may be found

121

from the lowlands up to about 2500 feet in primary forest. They are usually represented by comparatively few individuals, as with butterflies in other rain forests of the world, but the diversity of form and color is a never-failing fascination to the naturalist. Almost all of the swallowtails are forest dwellers. The giant ghostly *Idea* danaids, their pale gray wings dusted with jet-black spots, float among the treetops seemingly at the mercy of the winds. But once alarmed they are quite capable of rapid flight. The deep shining blue and purple of the many *Euploea* danaids is a common sight throughout the peninsula. Typical denizens of the lower forest areas are the large, retiring amathusiids, a group unique to the Asian region. Skulking about like the owl butterflies of the New World tropics, these butterflies with their typical lustrous blue or purple uppersides quickly become invisible when they settle onto ground litter, camouflaged by the resemblance of their undersides to a dead, decaying leaf.

The most spectacular butterflies of the Malayan rain forests are the five resident species of "birdwing" swallowtails, particularly the famous Raja Brooke's birdwing. This magnificent creature was discovered in Borneo by Wallace in 1855 and named by him after Sir James Brooke, the dashing young British adventurer who, after helping the rulers of Borneo subdue a rebellion of native chiefs, was proclaimed "white Raja" of Sarawak. With emerald-green stripes on velvety black forewings and a crimson head, this birdwing is truly a regal monarch of the forest. The males sail along the banks of streams, sometimes settling by the dozens at patches of moist urine on paths. Females are much less common, sometimes only one per 1000 males. They prefer higher elevations on ridges above rivers, and are found hovering around flowering trees some twenty to forty feet or more above the ground. The females also fly later in the day than the males, and may feed at flowers until sunset. The female's white wingtips are quite conspicuous during flight, and in the jungle shade they look not unlike the landing lights on a moving airplane.

Almost all the gorgeously colored *Delias* pierids are found in the montane rain forest of Malaya. Their vivid patches of red, orange, and yellow on blackish wings seem almost incongruous in the dark, misty forests. Still another group almost totally restricted to the highland forests are the large *Celastrina* "blues" that are also found in temperate areas of Mexico, the United States, North Africa, Europe, and Japan.

Despite its remoteness, the continent of Australia was explored very early by expeditions, and the first Australian insects were brought back to Europe for classification and description in the early 1600s. It was not until 1770, however, that the first butterflies were collected—by naturalists accompanying Captain Cook—in Australia. Since Cook's vessel, the *Endeavour*, first landed at Botany Bay in New South Wales in the dry season, few butterflies were visible. During the *Endeavour's* more extensive stay at the Endeavour River (now Cooktown)in the north of Queensland, the butterfly collecting was more successful; Cook's naturalist, Sir Joseph Banks, took thirty-six species during this visit. Banks was a wealthy botanist who accompanied Cook's first expedition to the South Pacific and made a remarkable collection of plant and animal specimens. It was he who commissioned Captain Bligh to transport bread-fruit trees from their native Tahiti to the West Indies. While anchored at Thirsty Sound, between Quail and Long islands and the Queensland mainland, Banks noted in his journal the abundance of some of the Australian butterflies and described the pupa of an *Euploea* danaid species:

"Insects in general were plentifull, Butterflies especialy: . . . the air was for the space of 3 or 4 acres crowded with them to a wonderfull degree: the eye could not be turned in any direction without seeing millions and yet every branch and twig was almost covered with those that sat still: of these we took as many as we chose, knocking them down with our caps or any thing that came to hand. On the leaves of the gum tree we found a Pupa or Chrysalis which shone almost all over as bright as if it has been silverd . . . it was brought on board and the next day came out into a butterfly of a velvet black changeable to blue, his wings both upper and under markd near the edges with many light brimstone colourd spots, those of his under wings being indented deeply at each end."

The specimen Banks described may have been *Euploea core*, a butterfly that in Australia now goes by the name of the common Australian crow.

The great majority of Australian butterflies are adapted to living only in the tropical and subtropical parts of that continent. Although the rain forests are located along the northeastern coast adjacent to the strings of islands coming south from the Malaysian regions, only about 20 percent of the Australian butterflies are the same as those of the Asian area. The rest (266 species out of 364 recorded from Australia) are found only in the general Australian region, and 175 (48 percent) are limited to the continent itself. Although fifty-eight butterfly species do occur in the extremely arid deserts of central Australia, just one species, *Jalmenus clementi*, a rare blue from northwestern Australia, is native. In the rain forests of Queensland, the kite swallow-tails and some of the gorgeous true swallowtails are among the most impressive butterflies. The Ulysses swallowtail flaunts its brilliant metallic blue wings like a Neotropical morpho high in the Cape York and northern Queensland forests. A collector can attract the male adults down to ground level by pinning out a dead specimen or even using bright blue cloth or paper fixed to a bush. The females are reputedly attracted by bright red. Both sexes feed on lantana flowers at the edge of the rain forest.

Isolated like an orphan waif from the ancestral home of its New World family by the world's largest ocean expanses, the single ithomiid species *Tellervo zoilus* is found in the forests of eastern Australia and in the islands north of the continent. Its slow, floating flight and the demure black and white pattern of its fragile wings suit it perfectly to the protecting dense shade of the forest undergrowth. The glasswing *(Acraea andromacha)* is another isolated representative of its family, the Acraeidae, which reaches its greatest evolutionary development of species in Africa and tropical America. The Australian variety occurs commonly in the rain forests and most other habitats in northern Australia and Queensland, where its caterpillars feed on a number of varieties of passionflower.

One of the lycaenids of special interest in these Australian rain forests is *Liphyra brassolis*, a very large, stout-bodied butterfly with orange and black wings. The adults are most active at dawn and dusk, but the astonishing feature of this butterfly is the special association it has throughout its life cycle with certain green tree ants. The female lays her eggs in groups of up to three beneath branches or on the trunk of a tree infested with the ants. Fairly soon after the caterpillars hatch, they find the ant nest and busily feed by sucking fluids from the bodies of the ant larvae. The oval and flattened caterpillar is protected against ant attack by its hard leathery skin, under which is concealed its soft body. At molting times the old skin splits around the side margins and downward under the front edge, so that it provides protection until the last possible moment. Even when the mature caterpillars pupate, the thin-walled pupa is formed and kept inside the tough larval skin. Three weeks later, the adult emerges by first shedding the pupal skin and then breaking open the outer larval shell. The butterfly's short, stout wings and antennae are initially covered with long woolly scales. These are easily shed when the jaws of any attacking ant attempt to grasp the butterfly as it scrambles toward the exit hole of the ant nest. Once outside, the adult climbs a twig and the wings are quickly expanded by fluid pumped from its body.

Just north of Australia, the Aru Islands were the scene of some spectacular butterfly collecting by Alfred Russel Wallace. His descriptions catch the mood of any lepidopterist who has been fortunate enough to visit a tropical rain forest. Wallace and a guide set off early in the morning, and after walking about half a mile along the beach, turned into the forest along a narrow path. The path was very little used and often swampy, so that they soon lost it

123

altogether. Wallace had already taken about thirty species including many rare and beautiful butterflies, hitherto known by only a few specimens from New Guinea. Among them were the large and handsome specter butterfly, the pale-winged peacock butterfly, and a brilliant clear-winged moth, as well as several little jewel-like blues.

The next two days were too wet and windy for going out but on the succeeding day the sun shone brightly. Wallace reports:

"I had the good fortune to capture one of the most magnificent insects the world contains, the great bird-winged butterfly *Ornithoptera poseidon*. I trembled with excitement as I saw it coming majestically toward me, and could hardly believe I had really succeeded in my stroke till I had taken it out of the net and was gazing, lost in admiration, at the velvet black and brilliant green of its wings, seven inches across, its golden body, and crimson breast. . . . I had seen similar insects in cabinets at home, but it is quite another thing to capture such one's self . . . to gaze upon its fresh and living beauty, a bright gem shining out amid the silent gloom of a dark and tangled forest. The village of Dobbo held that evening at least one contented man."

171. In the lush rain forest of Ecuador, hundreds of species of butterflies inhabit a single square mile, from the flowering vines at the tops of the tree canopy to the mosses on the forest floor. Brilliant blue morpho butterflies float through luxuriant tangles of lianas while clusters of transparent ithomiids jostle each other on the occasional flowers.

172.

173.

172-174. In the African rain forest certain edible nymphs of the genus Pseudacraea imitate highly distasteful butterflies of the genera Acraea and Bematistes so successfully that it is difficult to distinguish between them. Here are shown a Pseudacraea species from the Cameroun (172) and a false acraea (Pseudacraea boisduvali) from Rhodesia (173). On the opposite page, the noxious fiery acraea (Acraea acrita) (174) is found from Rhodesia north to Kenya and west to Angola.

175-190. The diversity of colors and patterns among rain forest butterflies is extraordinary. From the brilliant blues of swallowtails, the metallic greens of hairstreaks, and the yellows, oranges and reds of pierids and heliconians, to the mottled browns of the satyrs, every conceivable combination serves to advertise or conceal a butterfly's presence.

191. Deep in the shadows of the tropical rain forest, clear-winged satyrs float like ghostly spirits over the decaying leaf litter of the forest understory. The eyespots on the hindwings are often the only visible clue to the butterfly's progress until it alights in a sunbeam. Here a female satyr, Haetera piera, pauses for a moment on the forest floor in the Amazon Basin of eastern Ecuador.

75. Papilio ulysses: *New Guinea*

179. Heliconius erato cyrbia: *Ecuador*

76. Papilio demoleus: *Ceylon*

180. Heliconius erato amalfreda: *Guiana*

77. Ornithoptera priamus poseidon: *New Guinea*

181. Heliconius ethilla: *Ecuador*

83. Arcas ducalis, *female: Brazil*

187. Callitaera pireta: *Ecuador*

84. Helicopis acis: *Ecuador*

188. Haetera piera piera, *male: Ecuador*

85. Thecline hairstreak: *South America*

189. Haetera piera piera, *female: Ecuador*

192.

193.

192-194. *Many rain forest butterflies combine dazzling colors on their uppersides with camouflaged undersides. When* Cymanthoe coccinata *(192) of the Congo's tropical forests rests with wings upright, its brilliant orange upper wings are hidden and it looks like a dead leaf, complete with false midvein. The royal purple of* Chlorippe kallina *(193) from Santa Catarina, Brazil, is displayed only when it halts to spread its wings in the sun. The bold eyespots of a huge* Caligo *owl butterfly (194) from eastern Ecuador startles predators and often allows the butterfly to escape.*

195-210. *A kaleidoscope of nymphalids live in the rain forests of tropical America and Africa. Even the morphos, famous for their iridescent blue species from Brazil to Ecuador, flaunt pearly whites and yellows, reds, deep purples and blacks. The swirls of color on a* Catagramma *(196) are replaced by vivid stripes in* Anartia *(206) or checkerspot patterns in* Chlosyne *(207) and* Byblia *(210).*

195. Precis sophia: *Tanzania*

199. Morpho laertes: *Brazil*

196. Catagramma eunomia: *Peru*

200. Morpho cisseis: *Brazil*

197. Precis terea elgiva: *Tanzânia*

201. Morpho achillaena: *South America*

198. Precis oenone: *Kenya*

202. Najas normalis themis: *Congo*

203. Charaxes candiope: *Tanzania*

207. Chlosyne narva: *Costa Rica*

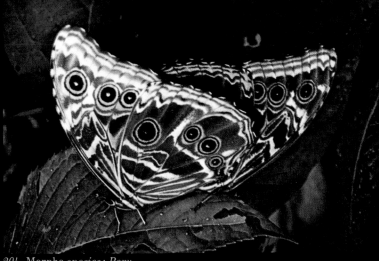

204. Morpho *species: Peru*

208. Agrias amydon ferdinandi: *Brazil*

205. Morpho *species: Peru*

209. Najas eleus: *Cameroun*

206. Anartia fatima: *Mexico*

210. Byblia acheloia: *Kenya*

211-214. *Many small metalmarks perch on sunlit
leaves along jungle paths and dart forth to challenge
any butterfly entering their "territory." Large*
Mesosemias *are frequently seen in open glades along
the Rio Napo in eastern Ecuador (211). Animal dung
attracts several species of* Symmachia *metalmarks
(212, 213). Alighting on a fern, a shy* Calydna
species (214) spreads its polka-dot wings.
215. *A transparent-winged ithomiid* (Prillwitzia
hymenaea) *from Brazil sucks juices from a decomposing grasshopper leg.*

212.

213.

Butterflies of the Desert

Deserts have an undeserved reputation as desolate wastelands of arid sand and abrasive winds. Actually, many are surprisingly beautiful, particularly after the brief spring rains when acres of brilliant wildflowers seem to spring up overnight, carpeting the desert floor with masses of white, rose, and yellow blooms. Desert butterflies take advantage of this temporarily rich supply of food and water. Having passed the harsh, dry season in a state of dormancy, they now come to life with a rush—eggs hatch out by the millions, caterpillars gorge on petals and leaves in their haste to exploit the brief growth, adult butterflies stir within pupal casings, pushing against their prisons in an urgency to escape.

If a region receives less than ten inches of rainfall during the course of a year, it is classified as a desert (some parts of the Arctic tundra, and certain arid oceanic islands also meet this requirement). Deserts spread across nearly one-fifth of the earth's surface, all sharing the common conditions of low rainfall, high temperatures, frequent winds, and rapid evaporation. There are several different types of deserts throughout the world. In North America, the Great Basin states of Nevada and Utah contain high-elevation "cool deserts" with arid sagebrush-covered valleys lying between great mountain ranges. The low deserts of Arizona and California, some even below sea level, are dotted with cacti, Joshua trees, palms, and shrubs such as the creosote bush. North Africa's Sahara has vast areas of blowing sand unrelieved by a single shrub. Although the soils may be quite fertile and rich in minerals, the small amount of moisture available in all of these deserts restricts plant and animal diversity. When rain does come, it is usually a cloudburst which sweeps over the surface in roiling floods leaving little moisture for the plant roots to absorb. Some deserts, such as the Atacama in Chile, may only receive rain at intervals of fifty years or more.

Deserts are often caused by mountains that capture the moisture-laden clouds before they reach the inland areas. When the rising clouds collide with the cooler air of the upper mountain slopes they become chilled themselves, and drop their load of moisture on the summits. Occasionally, as in coastal Peruvian deserts and in the Namib Desert of South West Africa, a cold ocean current off the coast has the same cooling effect on potential rain clouds.

Deserts are found on every continental land mass. The Eurasian Palearctic desert includes the Sahara of temperate northern Africa and the deserts of Asia Minor, as well as those of Russia, Pakistan, India, Tibet, China, and Mongolia. In southern Africa lie the Kalahari, Namib, and Great Karoo deserts. The Gibson, Great Sandy, and Great Victoria deserts cover most of the interior of Australia. In South America the strange Peruvian and Atacama deserts, as well as high, isolated inland valleys, lie in the rain shadow of the Andes. The North American deserts cover most of the southwest of the United States and much of northern Mexico as well as Baja California.

How do seemingly fragile butterflies adapt to the hostile environment of the desert? Local species avoid the dry season by going into a dormant state called diapause. The caterpillars, whose thin skins would dry out quickly in the heat, are active in the cooler and moister spring and fall months. Their appearance coincides with the period of maximum plant growth, when young and more succulent portions of the host plant are available. Virtually all desert caterpillars grow very rapidly, and some pierids such as orange-tips (*Anthocharis*) and marbles (*Euchloe*) take less than two weeks to reach pupation size from the time the tiny creature first crawls out of its egg. The pupa of the typical desert butterfly is protected against drying out by an almost impermeable outer cuticle. Most butterflies go into the resting stage as pupae and remain that way until the next rainy season. A few butterflies that have spring caterpillars, such as the checker-spots, can become dormant as shrunken larvae when they are partially grown. A whitish "plug" at both their oral and anal ends minimizes loss of water from the inside of the digestive tract, and the caterpillar's practice of hiding beneath boulders or in the ground when it is preparing to rest helps avoid exposure to heat and radiation during the long, hot summer in the desert.

With the onset of the rains the pupa develops rapidly, and the newly formed adult hatches within two weeks. Soon butterflies are streaking across the desert. They mate, and the females lay eggs on the rapidly leafing vegetation. A few desert butterflies, particularly the skippers, become dormant in the egg stage and await another year's growing season before hatching. The eggs of most species, however, develop quickly, hatching out within seven to ten days after they have been laid. The young caterpillars begin their hasty consumption of the leaves, flowers, or seed pods of their hosts. Some feed at night to minimize their exposure to the drying effects of daytime winds and sun.

The adult butterflies have also developed various means of adapting to the harsh conditions of deserts. The giant skippers fly at twilight when the air is cooler. Others, such as the tiny *Philotes* blues, choose the calm early morning hours to make their way over the desert sands. All the desert butterflies feed frequently on flowers, probing among the blossoms with their long tongues. Only a few satyrs, such as the little satyr (*Cercyonis sthenele paulus*) and Nabokov's wood nymph (*Euptychia dorothea*), have been able to establish a foothold in desert country since few other satyrs visit flowers regularly. Most of these butterflies have short tongues that restrict them to sipping surface water and nutrients from mud, excrement, or rotting fruits; they are not able to reach the nectar in flowers of even modest depth.

Usually, desert butterflies have only one flight season a year, although a fall brood sometimes emerges as well as the spring flight. With a dormant stage that often lasts several years or more, desert species can persist through droughts that may last for many growing seasons. The synchronization of butterfly hatchings with the occurrence of heavy rains guarantees that their food plants will be putting out new leaves at the same time that the adults are searching for egg-laying sites and the newly hatched caterpillars begin to feed.

The evolution of characteristics to overcome harsh conditions has led to interesting and quite distinctive types of desert butterflies around the world, particularly in the rich southwestern desert country of North America and the vast arid areas of North Africa and central Australia.

North America

There is something magical about the American southwest with its vast sweep of golden deserts, starkly eroded buttes and mesas casting long purple shadows across the flatlands, and distant snow-capped mountains looming deceptively near in the brilliant atmosphere. Some of the most interesting butterflies in the United States are found in the Colorado and Mojave deserts of southern California. Races of the black-and-yellow-banded short-tailed swallowtail *(Papilio indra)*, an uncommon butterfly yet found throughout thousands of miles in the higher and cooler elevations of the Sierra Nevada, Pacific Northwest, and Rocky Mountain ranges, live in the low, arid mountain ranges strewn across the southern California deserts. Each has developed in its own set of "ecological islands," probably isolated from the higher ranges to the north for thousands of years. The existence of this swallowtail in these deserts was not even suspected until the early 1950s despite the presence there of the greatest number of butterfly collectors in the United States. The first local race, *Papilio indra fordi*, was discovered in 1951 within one hundred miles of Los Angeles by a Californian, Robert J. Ford. In April of that year, Ford wandered into the Granite Mountains, a few miles northeast of Apple Valley, San Bernardino County. This is an extremely arid region strewn with giant boulders that looks something like a deserted battleground. Not even a plant, much less a fragile butterfly, would seem to be able to live there. But though the rainfall is exceedingly spare, whatever does fall drops on barren rock and is gathered in drainage basins, each flowing into a pocket of hidden soil, where it is shielded from evaporation and absorbed by the few plants that have managed to

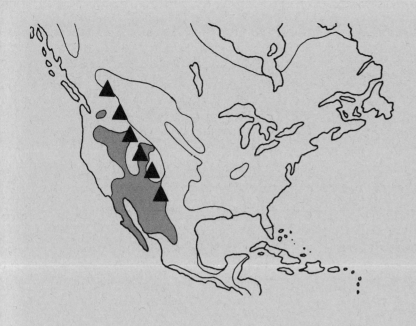

become established. On one of these plants, Ford found strange caterpillars surrounded by hovering swallowtails he had never seen before.

Once considered among the rarest of all swallowtails, Ford's swallowtail has since been found in many of the mountain ranges of the western half of the Mojave Desert. To the east, it is replaced by a still more recently discovered (1963) race in the Providence Mountains, Martin's swallowtail *(Papilio indra martini)*, a very unusual butterfly with a triangular yellow patch on its hindwing instead of the more typical wide yellow bands. These swallowtails sail majestically across the tumbled boulders of the desert mountain canyons each spring, while their bright pink-and-black-banded caterpillars feed into early summer on the serrated leaves of their food plants.

On the open desert another swallowtail, *Papilio rudkini*, dips and glides over the springtime flower-beds and appears again in abundance during the fall if heavy summer thundershowers have soaked its favored habitats. Unlike its closest relatives, which eat plants of the carrot family, Rudkin's swallowtail prefers the pungent turpentine broom *(Thamnosma montana)*, a member of the citrus family. There is a remarkable abundance of different color forms among three of the four life stages. The adults may be largely yellow, black, or an intermediate mixture of yellow and black with extensive blue areas; the pupae may be brown or green, and the caterpillars green, black, or banded with wide green and black stripes. The pupae of these swallowtails can remain dormant for as long as six years while waiting for favorable rains. This remarkable adaptation requires that all systems remain in a state of suspended animation for some sixty months beyond the normal time of emergence.

These large and glamorous swallowtails catch the eye first but a host of other interesting butterflies fly over the deserts during the spring peak. Starting in late February, as the desert annuals begin to poke their flower-laden stalks above the shifting sands, one finds orange-tips, marbles, checkerspots, and blues taking wing on warm mornings. In March and early April of years with good rainfall, the butterflies appear in masses among the yellow daisies, purple Mojave asters and other desert blooms. In the saltbush areas, small sooty-wing skippers scoot along from flower to flower, drinking deeply of nectar. The delicate yellow and orange forewings of the rare Felders' and Pima orange-tips decorate the landscape. Mottled greens conceal a southern marble, its head buried in a mustard flower.

Occasional monarchs and striated queens *(Danaus gilippus strigosus)* float on strong, white-spangled, amber wings above the desert gullies. In some years the painted ladies *(Cynthia cardui)* appear in huge numbers on the deserts, even as early as January.

This spring brood seems to originate in northern Mexico, flying north by the millions in tremendous migratory movements that last a month or more. They lay their eggs on a great many desert plants such as mallows, thistles, and lupines and the caterpillars develop rapidly, becoming a second brood of adults before the plants finish blooming and set seed. As the season progresses, they head north, as did their parents earlier in the spring. This movement is usually a minor annual affair, but it becomes a major "migration" in years of good rainfall when there is a spectacular overproduction of adults, and at such times draws wide public attention.

When the spring sun warms the sands on windless days, the tiny *Philotes* blues delicately fly here and there among the thousands of wildflowers. Bold black squares and dots are scattered on their soft gray undersides, while a bright orange band trails along the edge of the hindwing. Their favorite haunts are the glistening white and pinkish blooms of the fragrant buckwheats nestled between the sharp-spined cacti and rugged boulders of the desert canyons. During April, the small blue *(Philotes speciosa)*, less than half an inch wide, flutters weakly a few inches above the ground, pausing occasionally to rest and take a sip of nectar. To net it, the collector often has to swing at the moving shadow of this tiny desert wraith rather than at the butterfly itself since it is almost invisible against the light colored sands. Most of the other desert blues also fly in the springtime, but several species have switched to a fall flight period following the summer rains. Dammer's blue *(Philotes enoptes dammersi)* and the Rita blue *(Philotes rita elvirae)* are autumn visitors to the southern California deserts, apparently having adapted to different food plants to avoid competition with their spring-flying relatives.

Checkerspots are common wherever there are well-watered canyons. One of the most conspicuous and variable is the Chalcedon checkerspot *(Euphydryas chalcedona)*, which seems to have a different wing color and pattern in every desert mountain range. The familiar blackish race is found throughout the coastal mountains of southern California, but among the desert populations the colors are browns, reds, or whites. Neumoegen's checkerspot *(Chlosyne neumoegeni)* is a true creature of the desert, favoring rocky places, especially canyons and washes that are home to its colorful food plant, the purple Mohave aster. The lustrous, pearly white spots on its undersides are a prominent feature of this lovely spring butterfly. The leanira checkerspot *(Chlosyne leanira)* is much less common and is highly variable in color, ranging from a dark red and white patched form *(wrightii)* to a brick red form *(cerrita)* to an orange-washed subspecies *(alma)* that is found in Death Valley as well as in the Great Basin deserts.

Giant skipper Agathymus alliae *and its agave food plant*

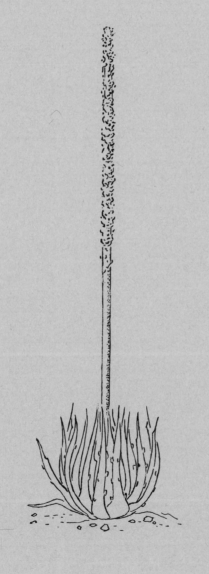

These beautiful checkerspots choose the equally colorful Indian paintbrushes as their food plants. The favored haunts of the bordered patch *(Chlosyne lacinia crocale)* are the sunflower-filled edges of agricultural fields in the desert country throughout the southwest and Mexico. It flies in great numbers from March to October in a series of broods. The adult butterflies display numerous color forms, including bands and patches of yellow, white, orange, and other bright colors on a glistening field of black pigment. The last three larval instars can be almost entirely black, black with a prominent yellow or orange-red stripe down the middle of the back, solid orange, or orange-red. The pupa itself may vary from almost pure white or black to white with rich black streaks.

A close relative, the California patch *(Chlosyne californica)*, flutters across the Colorado and Mojave deserts, usually in canyons and washes. As with most desert butterflies, its abundance is correlated with rainfall. If thunderstorms have been plentiful, small summer and fall populations may emerge in addition to the large spring brood of March and April. The tiniest one of all, the imperial checkerspot *(Microtia dymas)*, flaunts its half-inch wide, tan-and-black-checkered wings across the deserts from California to Texas and south into Sonora, Mexico.

Often desert butterflies share the same flowers. Blues hover around blooming buckwheat bushes and may be joined by a colony of the jaunty and attractive desert metalmark *(Apodemia mormo deserti)*. The white-spangled black and red Mormon metalmark *(Apodemia mormo mormo)* ranges from Salt Lake City, Utah, to southern California and Arizona. Both the caterpillar and the adult also feed on buckwheat. The miniature forests of junipers and piñon pines that dot the canyon country are home to the juniper and Skinner hairstreaks *(Mitoura siva)* and *(Mitoura loki)*. These two delightful sprites of the butterfly world are rather rare, and their delicately patterned undersides make them highly prized by the collector. The thick, greenish caterpillars have an incredibly detailed resemblance to the needles of the junipers on which they feed. They are sometimes common in juniper forests in early spring but are rarely seen unless the branches are shaken to scare up perched adults, or they are found gathered on a patch of blooming yellow flowers.

Another North American desert butterfly that is rare in collections and not often seen by the average lepidopterist is the giant skipper, which flies only at dusk or in the early morning hours. Almost unique to the American southwest and northern Mexico, these butterflies, with wings more than three inches long, zip about so rapidly that they are called the "jets" of the butterfly world. The caterpillars bore into the base of century plants and yuccas.

The average person thinks of a butterfly collector as someone who dashes blithely across flower-strewn meadows, net in hand, in eager pursuit of his specimen. But those of us who have collected in the West, especially in southern California, know that there are often considerable discomforts involved in butterfly collecting, as well as such hazards as rattlesnakes, sheer rocky cliffs, scorching sun, and flash floods that sweep across the desert without warning. The problems involved in trying to trace the life history of the giant skipper were described in 1956 by the noted lepidopterist John Adams Comstock, who did much of his investigations on butterflies in southern California.

It had long been thought by local collectors that some association must exist between century plants and giant skippers, since the two were always found in the same territory. In October, 1932, Comstock and his wife decided to solve the mystery of this strange butterfly. They left for the desert in a Model T Ford, heading toward La Puerta in the lower end of Mason Valley, San Diego County. The route led down an old stage road toward Box Canyon. Shortly after starting out they ran into rain, which increased so quickly that the wagon tracks turned into mud. Somewhat discouraged, they pushed on because they had been assured that "it never *really* rains in Mason Valley." After struggling to the top of the ridge at the southeastern end of San Felipe Valley, they came to a dry lake bed surrounded by hills that were covered with century plants.

Despite the downpour, Comstock dissected several of the plants from crown to root. It was an unpleasant task, with water trickling down his back and serrated century-plant leaves sawing at his knees. The job took time, the fleshy leaves being tough, and hard to remove. Then he noticed a peculiar dark stain at the base of one of them. Further probing revealed a cavity containing a plump grub within a chamber. The long-sought caterpillar of the giant skipper had at last been found. Soaked to the skin, they retreated to their car. That night, seven inches of rain poured down on one of the most arid spots in California. The morning light found them surrounded by an inland sea, with water lapping at the running boards. Impatiently they waded ashore and trudged several miles to the nearest ranch house, eager to announce that they had at last solved the mystery of the giant skipper.

Anyone anxious to seek out the still undiscovered lepidopteran treasures of the remote deserts of northern Mexico and the American southwest, Australia, Africa, or Eurasia, is likely to face much the same problems today that confronted the Comstocks in 1932. But even in such a populated area as California there is still much to be learned about butterfly distribution and the special adaptations required to exist in an arid climate.

Giant Skipper Megathymus coloradensis martini *and its yucca food plant*

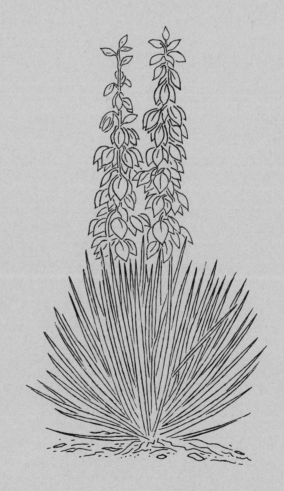

147

North Africa and the Palearctic Desert

When one thinks of northern Africa, an image of the vast Sahara comes to mind. Yet a map of the Old World shows that the Sahara is only a small part of the great band of the Palearctic desert ranging westward from the Gobi in Central Asia through Afghanistan, Iran, Arabia, and North Africa to the Atlantic Ocean. Included in this tremendous expanse are many separate deserts, each with its own mountain ranges. Chief among them is the Sahara, its 3 million square miles covering almost half the continent of Africa. Little is known of the butterflies in this inhospitable land.

The famous Gobi Desert of Mongolia is also poorly explored for butterflies. Although part of its 500,000 square miles has been traversed by major museum expeditions, including the famous Central Asiatic Expedition of 1928 led by Roy Chapman Andrews of the American Museum of Natural History, most biologists have come to search for its rich fossil beds rather than its living butterflies. Here, in the remotest part of central Asia, lies a land of immense undrained basins surrounded by high mountains that shut out moisture from all the seas. The Central Gobi basin includes areas like the Turfan Depression, which is 890 feet below sea level, yet only 100 miles away towers the 18,000-foot peak of Topotar Auliya. One of the Gobi's neighboring desert basins holds a shallow lake, Lop Nor, which is so flat that sediments carried in by wind and occasional streams sometimes fill the lake and move its body of water to other parts of the basin. For this reason the Swedish explorer of Central Asian deserts, Sven Hedin, called Lop Nor the "Wandering Lake." Today the basin is the site of China's main nuclear facilities.

Afghanistan is a fascinating land of deserts and majestic mountain ranges. The latter rise to 17,000 feet in the isolated central range of the Koh-i-Baba Mountains. Most of the desert and semidesert butterflies found in Afghanistan come in from neighboring Iran.

Between Iran and the Sahara, the Arabian Desert covers nearly half a million square miles of the Arabian peninsula, including much of Syria, Iraq, Israel, Jordan, and Saudi Arabia. Iraqi butterflies have been well studied and represent the desert species found in most of the arid Middle East. Of the 133 butterfly species recorded from Iraq, eleven are found only in the desert plains, ninety-four appear only in the mountains and some twenty-eight species occur in both habitats. These figures clearly show the difficulty of adaptation to the harsh, barren desert. Scattered here and there on the low plains are oases, ranging from cultivated gardens and fields irrigated by wells and seeps to marshes and riverbanks. These areas are often inhabited by butterflies that have been introduced by man. But such oases are only slightly richer in butterfly species than the desert and far less rich than the mountains, which climb to 13,000 feet above sea level and have substantially more rainfall.

The Iraq desert contains two groups of butterflies: local species, which tend to breed near their place of origin, and migrants, which fly long distances from their hatching grounds, breeding in new locations each year depending on the vagaries of winds and rains and the availability of desert vegetation. The residents live in the desert year-round, coping with the driest periods of the year by going into a dormant phase. Both caterpillars and butterflies are active for only several months at most.

Of the six members of the swallowtail family found in Iraq, most are confined to the high mountains, usually above treeline at 5000 feet. One swallowtail *(Papilio machaon centralis)*, however, dips down from its favored mountains to the northern and central deserts where it feeds on the cultivated rue, dill, and orange trees of the oases. The adults and their orange-spotted, green-and-black-banded caterpillars are familiar to European naturalists, for this butterfly also occurs throughout the Old World temperate zones. The pupae attached to tree trunks are brown or gray, while those hung from foliage are usually green, a camouflage adaptation that insures their survival. The spring swallowtail *(zerynthia cerisyi deyrollei)* thrives as low as 2000-3000 feet in the mountains and is occasionally encountered in the northern deserts.

The small white *(Pieris rapae iranica)* is a local race of the cabbage white found in the temperate parts of the northern hemisphere. It is one of the most common butterflies in the mountains and oases of Iraq's deserts. The bath white *(Pieris daplidice)* and the desert white *(Pontia glauconome iranica)* are found on the open desert in the spring and early summer, and also inhabit the oases all year. Several beautiful *Euchloe* marbles and the delicately tinted desert orange-tips inhabit foothills and the stony desert floor. In April, green-dappled whites *(Euchloe ausonia)* and several brilliant orange-tips flutter about hilltops and the lower mountains bordering the deserts. The more sedately colored greenish black-tip *(Anthocharis charlonia)* is a collector's prize in the desert foothills.

The thirty-eight species of lycaenids in Iraq are almost entirely restricted to the oak zone and higher areas in the mountains. However, the small copper *(Lycaena phlaeas)* comes down out of the mountains to oases where it feeds on dock, its favored food throughout the temperate areas of Eurasia and in isolated areas of North America. The desert small blue *(Chilades galba)* may be encountered anywhere on the desert from April to late summer. Its caterpillar is closely attended by a small ant which milks a sweet secretion from it and defends the

caterpillar against parasites and small predatory insects. The minute butterfly called the grass jewel *(Freyeria trochylus)* hatches out in several broods in the desert foothills, and two species of tiger blues occur in oases near nebek trees, the food plant used by its larvae. The common blue, found throughout Europe and Asia to Siberia, flies along watercourses in the desert foothills and the northern plains of the Arabian peninsula, where the caterpillars feed on vetches and trefoils.

A collector in the deserts in Arabia inevitably comes away with migrant nymphs since most of the native species are only found in mountain retreats. The painted lady is common in the spring, large migrations coming into Iraq from the south. As in North America, these migrant butterflies visit mallows, thistles, and nettle. The red admiral is also a migrant but is found only as single individuals in the desert oases. A prized little butterfly, the mullein fritillary *(Melitaea trivia robertsi)* is found in the desert foothills, where three generations hatch each year. The males are fond of flying around and settling to sun themselves on the tops of hills or mountains. They are often found at great heights, while the females stay closer to the breeding grounds. Several satyrs, such as the pelopea grayling *(Pseudochazara pelopea)* and the wall butterfly *(Pararge megera iranica)* inhabit the desert foothills but are more common in the mountains along with the rest of the twenty-four species of satyrs found in Iraq.

The jaunty little skippers are common in the desert oases, in part because most of them require green growing grasses as food plants. Garden flowers in the cultivated oases also provide a rich source of nectar for adult skippers and the other desert butterflies.

Australia The great interior expanses of Australia are largely desert; one section alone, the Great Sandy Desert, covers some 160,000 square miles. These vast stretches are constantly swept by the desert wind, or as the Australians call it, the brick-fielder. Hot, dry, and dusty, it blows from the interior of the continent and dehydrates butterflies and humans alike. Extraordinarily few butterfly species—some fifty-nine in all—have managed to adapt to these arid regions of the continent, and only one exceedingly rare "blue" species, *Jalmenus clementi*, is known to be a native there.

During the Australian springtime, from September to November, carpets of brightly colored wildflowers spring up everywhere after the winter rains. As a naturalist from southern California I feel especially at home in western Australia among the chaparral-covered hills and sandy deserts. Zipping here and there among composite flowers around Geraldton on the west coast are silver-spotted skippers *(Anisyn-*

toides argenteoornatus). On the islands off the coast of western Australia the caterpillar of one race spins a shelter of whitish silk nestled in the foliage near the top of its food plant.Unlike the desert butterflies of California, however, only one swallowtail inhabits these inland and western deserts of Australia. The bold, rapid flight of the checkered swallowtail *(Papilio demoleus sthenelus)* is a familiar sight in the Australian interior. It is an extraordinarily successful species elsewhere, too, for its range extends up through Malaya to southern China and west through India to Iran.

The amber-and-white orange migrants *(Catopsilia scylla etesia)* and the whitish common migrants *(Catopsilia pyranthe crokera)* are the only large pierids that penetrate the deserts of the interior. They often settle in large numbers to sip water at mud banks after a rain storm. The small grass yellow *(Eurema smilax)* also migrates in great numbers from time to time, and individuals may be spotted each spring on the deserts. The narrow-winged pearl white *(Elodina padusa)* whose black forewing tips in flight seem to float off from its delicate, nacreous wings, may be seen fluttering across the inland deserts. Sometimes great numbers of pupae of the red-spotted wood white *(Delias aganippe)* are gathered together near mistletoes that serve as food for their caterpillars.

The common caper white *(Anaphaeis java teutonia)* has a truly remarkable range of habitats in Australia, from lush rain forest to open desert. The colors of the females are quite variable, ranging from black checks on white to densely black wings, with a patch of white or orange near the body. Tremendous migratory movements of this butterfly frequently occur in certain parts of Australia, but the reasons for these flights are still unknown.

The golden danaid *(Danaus chrysippus petilia)* is found throughout Australia, where its slow, labored flight is a familiar sight. The monarch, which spread across the Pacific from North America in recent times, reached Australia about 1870. It is now well established along the entire east coast and will undoubtedly spread into the deserts, feeding on milkweeds. One of Australia's velvety blackish brown crow butterflies has become common near Alice Springs, in the center of the largest desert.

Two kinds of the elaborately patterned orange and black painted ladies are found in the Australian deserts. *Cynthia cardui* has a worldwide distribution, but it is known in Australia from only a few specimens—possibly migrants from Africa. Australia's native painted lady *(Cynthia kershawi)* has a less finely etched wing pattern with blue centers in its hindwing spots. Like all of its relatives, the caterpillar forms a shelter by curling a leaf of the food plant into a nest and fastening it together with silk. Great southward-moving migrations are common between September and early November, which are comparable to the northward spring movements of *Cynthia cardui* in the southwestern United States and northern Africa. In both hemispheres, the painted ladies move in the direction in which new spring plant growth will be available for egg-laying and for their caterpillars to eat as the season advances.

Another interesting nymphalid in the desert is the meadow argus *(Precis villida calybe)*, a beautiful purplish butterfly with two large eyespots on each wing. It frequently settles on the ground with wings outspread, apparently to soak up the warm radiation from the morning sun. Later in the day, the meadow argus keeps its wings closed above the body when it alights, minimizing the solar heat it receives. This adaptation for regulating body temperature appears in many butterflies all over the world.

The small blues of the genus *Jalmenus* are a diverse Australian group of nine species, some of which fly in the deserts. Like other lycaenids, the caterpillars are attended by ants. Some of these butterflies pupate in a communal web spun by the caterpillars. The rarest desert blue, *Jalmenus clementi*, is known only from a few adult specimens taken in north-western Australia. The amaryllis azure blue *(Ogyris amaryllis)* is found throughout the interior. Its caterpillars feed at night on mistletoe growing on trees that fringe the rivers. During the day the caterpillars hide under loose bark, in crevices on the trunks of the trees, or in tunnels created by insects boring into the branches.

The shining brilliant metallic blues and purples of the western jewel *(Hypochrysops halyaetus)* flash about the small yellow flowers of acacia trees along with the double-spotted lineblue *(Nacaduba biocellata)*, one of the smallest and most abundant of the Australian lycaenids. The caterpillars resemble the acacia buds and flowers upon which they feed. Another delightful blue associated with acacia is *Theclinesthes onycha*, whose males often fly around hilltops, which apparently serve as courtship sites. The male is blue or lilac in color, while the female is grayish brown.

Finally, the most common butterfly in Australia, found everywhere from the open deserts to rain forest clearings is the common grass-blue *(Zizina otis labradus)*. It usually is the first butterfly seen on a spring morning hike into the Australian desert wilderness, and with its ability to feed on a broad range of garden as well as wildflowers, it is undoubtedly the best adapted and most successful species among the Australian desert butterflies. The butterflies of the world's deserts are models of evolution. They have conquered environments that men have not entirely mastered and so exemplify the irresistible drive of life to find a place for itself anywhere on earth.

216. During the brief rains in California's Mojave Desert, white dune primrose and purple sand verbena carpet the ground all the way to the Little Chuckwalla Mountains. In some years masses of painted ladies shimmer in a never-ending flow across the deserts of North America and North Africa. Other desert butterflies include delicate blues and orange-tips, marbles, checkerspots, and swallowtails.

217-219. *Swallowtails successfully invaded the deserts of the American southwest. Even tropical and subtropical butterflies such as the giant swallowtail* (Papilio cresphontes) *(217) and the pipevine swallowtail* (Papilio philenor) *(218-219) have large populations in the Arizona deserts wherever their food plants grow. The giant swallowtail is also slowly invading California citrus groves in arid southern valleys and the pipevine swallowtail is frequently encountered in canyons and washes wherever* Aristolochia *pipevines are found.*

218.

219.

220-221. A butterfly of open desert country, Rudkin's swallowtail (Papilio rudkini) *has several adult color forms. The yellow one (220) is predominant east of San Diego, while the black version (221) is more common in the Death Valley region.*
222. Desert skippers are usually small and drab, blending with the light soils and strong shadows of their harshly sunlit environment. This tropical checkered skipper (Pyrgus syrichtus) *has paused at a desert flower near Trinity River, Texas.*
223. A surprising number of blues and hairstreaks are abundant in the hot, wind-blown deserts. The green siva hairstreak (Mitoura siva) *lives in the juniper belt of the desert ranges of the American southwest.*

220.

Butterflies of the Temperate Forest and Grassland

The first book to mention British butterflies was *Theatrum Insectorum*, a work in Latin published in 1634 by a physician to Charles I. After it came many other publications on butterflies by the English, and the books became more numerous over the next three centuries. This was a reflection not only of the developing curiosity of the English about nature, but of the fact that butterflies in the northern temperate zones are so visible and so common in the densely settled farmlands of Europe.

The rich soils and the productivity of temperate forest and grasslands country led to their development for agriculture and as hunting territory for aristocrats. The native butterflies aroused the wonder of ordinary men, the curiosity of the more intelligent.

Renaissance scholars rediscovered classical Greek works on natural history at a time when centers of learning were being established throughout Europe. The science of the Greeks was revived. Moreover, the voyages of exploration that began toward the end of the fifteenth century brought many new specimens of the world's flora and fauna back to Europe. Study and classification began. At the same time, the invention of printing spread textbooks on natural history throughout the European world. With the expansion of knowledge the interest of laymen in such subjects grew and the study of butterflies became an avocation. Thus, the butterflies of the European temperate zones are the best known in the world.

England has a butterfly fauna of only sixty-eight species, including local residents and migrants, and by the end of the eighteenth century, all but five of them had been catalogued. This work was paralleled in France, Germany, and Japan. Not until the middle of the nineteenth century did equivalent work begin in North America, primarily by Samuel Scudder and William Henry Edwards. The lateness of this research, which was matched in South Africa by resident Europeans, suggests that serious scientific research on butterflies cannot start before a certain level of national development has been reached. There must be an educated and leisured class to pursue it.

Whatever the reason, the deciduous and coniferous forests of North America—and also Eurasia—are a rich hunting ground for the lepidopterist. The early butterfly collectors ventured into the vast grasslands and steppes of the midcontinent regions in search of lepidopteran rarities. In the nineteenth century, throughout the mountain ranges of Arizona, Colorado, Nevada, and other western territories of North America, adventurous naturalists accompanied exploring expeditions sent out by the United States Army. The butterflies they found were not as large and gaudy as many tropical species, but this temperate fauna proved to have unique attributes.

Satyrs and nymphalids, in particular, have adopted the temperate forests and grasslands as their homeland, diversifying into a great many closely related species. The wood nymphs, satyrs, and ringlets of the *Euptychia*, *Lethe*, *Cercyonis*, and *Coenonympha* genera found plants in temperate North America, as have their counterparts among the Eurasian species of graylings *(Hipparchia)*, browns and ringlets *(Erebia)*, and heaths *(Coenonympha)*. These satyrs occur on open meadows, mountain slopes or open woodland, wherever their food plants can grow.

The spread of species has not been evenly distributed despite the diversity of suitable environments. The temperate satyrs are best represented in the warmer parts of Europe where they make up almost one-third of the butterfly population there. But some of the nymphalid groups, such as the fritillaries *(Speyeria* and *Argynnis)*, the checkerspots *(Euphydryas* and *Chlosyne)*, and the anglewings *(Polygonia)* have fanned out widely through the temperate woodlands of both Holarctic continents and have diversified in an abundance of species and local races.

To be successful in temperate zone habitats, a butterfly species must not only find a useful host plant but it must be able to hibernate in the winter. The tropical rain forest butterflies may breed in continuous generations all year. On the deserts, they must estivate in a resting stage through the long periods of drought until rains bring new growth to their food plants. Temperate forests and grasslands have freezing temperatures during at least part of the winter season, and besides the directly detrimental effect weather has on a cold-blooded insect, the host plants are leafless or buried under snow. Thus temperate zone butterflies hibernate either in sheltered hollow logs as adults or, more commonly, as eggs, caterpillars, or pupae.

This quiescent period, while the tissues are fortified against frost damage with "anti-freeze" chemicals, carries the species into the next annual cycle.

The natural history of these temperate zone butterflies has been so well studied that butterfly books 100 years old can still be used today as identification manuals. Because the English led the way in this early study, Britain is a good place to begin any observation trip through all the environments of these fascinating creatures.

The European Region

When the spring or early summer is warm and clear in Great Britain, which is rare enough, the butterfly hunter will see hosts of the insects. He may be disappointed that there are so few species, but he will immediately observe how precisely the butterflies are restricted to their special worlds. The most localized butterflies are those which fly only in the chalk downs or limestone hills in southern and central England: the brightly marked chalk-hill blue (*Lysandra coridon*), the Adonis blue (*Lysandra bellargus*), and the silver-spotted skipper (*Hesperia comma*). These are difficult to detect or to net. Often there is considerable variation in underside markings on the two blues, and specimens with exceptional markings are highly valued by collectors.

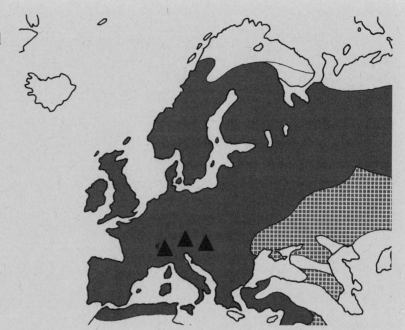

The rapid-flying dark green fritillary (*Argynnis aglaia*) sails here and there across the downs, but it is rather rare in the woods where its relative, the high brown fritillary (*Argynnis cydippe*), lurks. The small blue (*Cupido minimus*) and the brown argus (*Aricia agestis*) dart about on the downs and rough grassy slopes in late spring and summer, and even the casual observer soon notes that, while in other blue species the male is blue and the female is chiefly brown, the brown argus is brown in both sexes. The undersides of the wings of the brown argus are punctuated with dots and eyelike spots which caused it to be named after the many-eyed giant of mythology. Most of the downland butterflies fly along the seashore as well, and are especially attracted to sand hills covered with marram grass and shrubs. The glanville fritillary (*Melitaea cinxia*) is even confined to just the southern shore of the Isle of Wight.

In the first book wholly devoted to British butterflies, *Papilionum Britanniae*, published in 1717, James Petiver used the name "half-mourner" to describe a species of boldly marked black and white satyrid butterfly, *Melanargia galathea*. Petiver wandered widely through the open meadows and fields so characteristic of the settled English countryside. In many places, this country begins inland from the downs of the coasts. Today called the marbled white, *Melanargia galathea* is commonly found in these grassy areas, flaunting its checkerboard wings along the roadsides of southern and central England and looking very much like the ordinary white pierid. It is perhaps the most unusual of all the satyrids commonly flushed from the grass by the trudging butterfly hunter.

The caterpillars of the marbled whites, like those of the common satyrs, feed on grass. The adults are quite variable in coloring, some even being yellow instead of white. The meadow brown (*Maniola jurtina*) is abundant everywhere in the grassy meadows and displays its eyespots in bouncing flight over swales. They may be driven up almost in swarms from the grass. They fly unhurriedly, stopping often to feed on the colorful June flowers. The yellow rings on the brownish wings of the ringlet (*Aphantopus hyperanthus*) are concealed in the grassy tangles which also hide a satyrid larva or two that might be feeding in the day. If the tall grasses are hunted at night with a lantern light and sweep-net, meadow brown and ringlet caterpillars might be found.

The English countryside is a charming mixture of fields and woods, copses and spinneys, streams and forests, and these give shelter to many butterflies. At the edge of the forest, the wall butterfly (Parage megera) scuttles along hedgerow and stone wall. Its tan and brown wings are outspread in the afternoon sun before it takes off again and flies away. Occasionally, a hedge brown (Maniola tithonus) or a bright green hairstreak (Callophrys rubi) zips out from its perch on a bramble blossom to challenge intruders. The green hairstreak is the only all-green butterfly in Europe, and is superbly concealed when it perches on a bramble bush with its wings closed. Hunting it may lead the collector to the edge of the New Forest.

There, in the oak woods, the purple emperor shows itself sparingly. One of the most sought-after species in Britain, this resplendent butterfly, Apatura iris, ignores flowers and seems to delight in spending hours flying around and settling on the topmost branches of forest giants. It gives only glimpses of the open wings of a male flashing a beautiful purple sheen from its unreachable perch.

The oak forests of England are famous, protected for hundreds of years by royal edict after disastrous overcutting during the Middle Ages. They are a home for other butterflies. High brown fritillaries float down from oaks after brief rests during cloudy periods at midday. Commas (Polygonia c-album—its scientific name refers to the C-shaped silver mark on its hindwing), and the famous white admirals (Limenitis camilla) of the New Forest are likewise about in numbers, and a few spiny black caterpillars of the comma feed on a nearby nettle patch. The female white admirals lay eggs on the leaves of honeysuckle vines, a reproductive investment that will not yield fruit until the following spring. After the admiral caterpillars hatch, they will feed slowly until October, and then settle down for the winter. As a protective "quilt," the larva constructs a hibernation shelter by fastening a dead honeysuckle leaf to the vine stem with a silken binding, drawing the edges of the leaf together around it with more silk. The following April the surviving caterpillars come out and again feed on honeysuckle leaves until fully mature, when they pupate and become jewel-like butterflies of green, purple, and orange, with a golden sheen and several glistening metallic spots on their vertical sides.

The English countryside, with its varied habitats, offers the butterfly collector the chance of seeing or catching twenty or more species within a limited area in one day's work. But what is delightful are the number of surprises offered by the English butterflies. At any moment, a prize may appear, such as the heath fritillary (Melitaea athalia). Unlike the high-flying purple emperors, this butterfly stays near the ground and, if followed, often leads the collector to a colony concentrated around a patch of cowwheat. Many of the known colonies of this extremely localized insect have disappeared, perhaps because of overcollecting, so the wise butterfly enthusiast may only take a perfect matched pair of the beautifully checkered adults.

The limited number of species of British butterflies is a result of the barrier of the English Channel. Many species that could thrive in Britain were unable to cross the channel after the retreat of the last Pleistocene ice sheet. On the mainland of Europe, however, the butterfly picture changes. There, although some still tend to be rather limited in any given area, the entire Palearctic region, from the Atlantic to the Pacific oceans, contains about 1450 species of butterflies.

They are spread wide across the land, however. The entire Iberian Peninsula, for instance, with all its diversity of mountainous topography, has only 229 recorded butterfly species, a fauna actually smaller than that of California or Colorado. It is still quite impressive when compared with the 364 Australian species, and the approximately 713 species in all of temperate North America. But it cannot compare with the richness of species in tropical America, Asia, and Africa.

Nevertheless, the temperate species are interesting for other reasons. It is easier to see the individuals and focus on special adaptations and features. The environments with their distinctive species often lie close together.

The Atlas Mountains of Morocco are not often visited by lepidopterists, but they offer rich rewards. In this group of mountains is the Middle Atlas Range, with peaks averaging 5500 feet and rising to a height of 7500 feet. The ancient range is marked by the cones of old volcanic craters, crowned here and there with groves of cedars, and it is good country for butterflies. Colin Wyatt, a leading English lepidopterist, who has collected some of the rarities of this temperate region, has described it: "On the northern slopes lie great forests of Cedars and Ilex, together with areas of Pines and Oaks, forming a wonderful parkland whose flower-spangled glades are alive with insects. In the spring Paeonies and Saxifrages flower everywhere, the lush valleys by the creeks are fringed with Poplars and Ash and Hawthorne, and only the occasional Macacus monkey and the howling of the jackals at night remind one that he is in Africa after all."

The most interesting butterflies of the middle Atlas are the blues. The native Vogel's blue (Plebejus vogellii) is one of the most restricted species in the world, known in only three localities at 7000 feet elevation within a twenty-mile radius of the Taghzeft Pass. Even here, it is limited to areas of only about five acres, where its equally rare geranium-like food plant grows in the rough stony soil. Small black ants tend the caterpillars of the Vogel's blue and obtain sweet secretions from their honeydew glands. During the daytime, the caterpillars move down the stems and hide near the roots. The adults are on the wing by mid-August. A much more plentiful but also very local and lovely lycaenid is the bavius blue *(Philotes bavius fatma)* found only in wet grassy meadows near the edge of the cedar forests where its food plant, a giant woolly-leaved Salvia grows. If a collector is lucky, he may find a fine hesperiid, Mohammed's skipper *(Sloperia mohammed)*, in the forest clearings. Wyatt noted that he "never saw it on the wing but bred a fine series from larvae taken in mid-June. These spin a sort of light cocoon in a fold of a leaf in which they aestivate through the hot month of July, taking no food until early August when they feed up rapidly and pupate, emerging in late August and September."

Another unusual species is the giant, batlike satyr *(Satyrus abdelkader)* which lives on steep, dry mountain slopes where the esparto grass grows. The males sail up and down over the tall tussocks in persistent search for the more secretive females. "It is a very hard species to catch," Wyatt observed, "for while it appears to be gliding slowly it is extremely wary, and the 'blast' of wind at the stroke of the net seems to catch its wide wings and waft it suddenly away at the last moment." Coming to feed on sage and thyme are handsome specimens of the Moroccan ringlet *(Coenonympha vaucheri)*. The very scarce and local orange-tip, *Anthocharis tagis mauretanica*, lives here along with the exceptionally rare white, *Pieris mani haroldi*. The finest of all Middle Atlas butterflies, the magnificent fritillary *(Argynnis lyauteyi)*, is the ultimate spectacle for the lepidopterist.

Japan

William J. Holland, author of *The Butterfly Book* and a noted director of the Carnegie Museum, worked in Japan almost a century ago. He gave lepidopterists a first picture of the pleasures of butterfly-watching there. Japan's rich subtropical and temperate zones are a mixture of climates and environments ideal for butterflies. The islands lie at about the same latitudes north of the equator as southern Europe and the Pacific Coast of the United States, but they are made specially interesting for butterfly lovers because of their climate.

The powerful interaction of cool air coming off the Siberian land mass and colliding with the warm Japan Current, produces immense rainfalls along the western sides of the Japanese mountains. Extremes of wet and dry, coupled with the height of the mountains and the scope of the foothills, create many habitats in one area.

Holland was particularly impressed by this. In that age, he could afford to travel with a group of native workers and so he was able to mount an ideal butterfly-collecting expedition. Very early, he experienced the sharply changeable weather which characterizes Japan. As he headed toward the Usui-toge, a pass through the mountains, he noted: "What a sunset when we reached an elevation of three thousand feet above the paddy-fields, which stretch across the Kwanto of the Gulf of Yeddo! What a furious thunderstorm came on just as the night closed in! Then at half-past nine the moon struggled out from behind the clouds, and we pushed on up over the muddy roads, until at last a cold breath of night air sweeping from the west began to fan our faces, and we realized that we were at the top of the pass, and before us in the dim moonlight loomed the huge form of Asama-Yama which more than once has laid the land waste for leagues around, and compared with which Vesuvius is a pygmy."

He had felt the Siberian air on his face, and he had experienced the rains, but the following morning he saw immediately that he was in real butterfly country. Seven species of lilies flourished in the hedges and fields around him, growing so thickly that their blossoms scented the air. Everywhere, butter-flies and bees mingled with the flowers. To this paradise was added the magnificent backdrop of the volcano which sent up a continuous plume of smoke that had gathered in a cloud overhead. Holland wrote: "Five species of Fritillaries flashed their silvery wings by copse and stream; great black Papilios soared across the meadows; blue Lycaenas, bright Chrysophani [coppers], and a dozen species of Wood-nymphs gamboled over the low herbage and among the grass. . . . And so we wandered down the mountain-slope, taking species new alike to American and Japanese."

It was an extraordinary expedition. With such a large number of collectors, Holland accomplished one of the major collecting feats of entomology in this area. He brought back a thousand butterflies and moths as well as two thousand beetles.

The Japanese, with their long history of affinity for nature, are today among the most enthusiastic of all butterfly lovers. They have amassed life-history details on practically all of Japan's 215 species. The fauna is a curious mixture of tropical Asian and Palearctic species, from the Asian map butterfly (*Cyrestis thyodamas mabella*) and the tropical green *Graphium* swallowtails to the Palearctic copper and the high mountain satyrs in the *Oeneis* and *Erebia* groups. In the bogs in the northern islands and in the higher mountains thrive five species of bog fritillaries, and over the meadows fly nine larger fritillaries with ruddy topcoats, greenish underclothing, and boldly silvered spots. The two small temperate zone orange-tips. *Anthocharis*

solymus and *Anthocharis cardamines isshikii*, are dwarfed by the giant pierid invader from further south, *Hebomoia glaucippe shirozui*, whose broad white forewings end in flaring points of bright orange nearly four inches apart. Surely the most spectacular in coloration are the large swallowtails, especially *Papilio maackii* and *Papilio bianor* with their vivid mixture of rich iridescent green or purple against a jet-black background. One of the most interesting groups to the collector are the large and very colorful hairstreaks for which Japan is renowned. Many have shimmering greens and blues covering the entire surface of the wings.

Another great lepidopterist, George B. Longstaff, arrived in Japan around the turn of the century, and reported his experiences in *Butterfly-Hunting in Many Lands* in 1912. He set out from a small fishing village, Mogi, on a peninsula. Unlike Holland, he did not head for the high country immediately; at sea level, he was already in butterfly country, a region swarming with flowers. He wrote: "The country was pretty and all arrayed in bright spring colours. The wild flowers most of English type, e.g., two sorts of scentless Violet, a Potentilla, and the good old Dandelion. A prominent plant new to me was like Lucerne [American alfalfa], but smaller, and with flowers the colour of Thrift. On the way to and fro (all too short) I got some delight-ful collecting. The Fauna even more than the Flora afforded illustrations of the strange mixture of the Oriental with the Palearctic which is so characteristic of the Japanese archipelago, and which is, presumably, most marked in the southern island Kiusiu. . . ."

The mixture of Palearctic and Oriental species puzzled Longstaff, as it did many early collectors in Japan. But when the weather of Japan was analyzed more closely, and the influence of the Siberian air mass on the islands was understood, it became reasonable to assume that many Palearctic species had been swept across the Sea of Japan by the Siberian winds.

Longstaff collected blues and swallowtails, such as the fine *Papilio xanthus*, which reminded him of European species. Mixed among these Palearctic forms were magnificent oriental species—blue-green swallowtails and exotic satyrids—that landed on the road to drink at mud puddles.

After his delightful introduction to Japanese butterfly life, Longstaff set out along the Tokaido, the old high road from Kyoto, at the head of the Inland Sea, traveling toward Tokyo through the narrow plains of the eastern shores of Honshu. But he had read Holland, and he knew the real delights still lay ahead of him. He prepared to go inland immediately.

On the first day of his journey into the mountains, along the lower part of a road below 2000 feet, he caught a satyr *(Blanaida goschkevitschii)*, two

Argynnis anadyomene and a fritillary in mud on the
road, a *Cynthia cardui*, a snout butterfly *(Libythea
lepita)* and three swallowtails *(Papilio macilentus,
Papilio demetrius,* and *Papilio bianor).* At about 3500
feet he took a gorgeous peacock blue swallowtail
(Papilio maackii). He then climbed Asama-Yama, at
8280 feet the highest of the active volcanoes of Japan.
He wrote:

"The ascent is quite easy, being for the most part
over small scoria, but we were unfortunate in our
weather. The strong smell of sulphur declared our
proximity to the crater, but the cloud was so dense
that we literally could not see more than five yards;
moreover, the wind was so strong that it drove the
rain horizontally . . . so we had to beat a rapid
retreat. The next morning it was tantalizing to see
from the train the summit of Asama-Yama far above
the clouds, with a wreath of steam slowly rising from
the crater—the very ideal of peaceful repose."

As Longstaff climbed, he passed through zone after
zone of different butterfly habitats, so that his view
of the insects was constantly changing with the
sighting of new species. This led him, finally, to a
puzzling occurrence of several species concentrated
in the area of a man-made ruin. He reported:

"Together with the now familiar *Blanaida
goschkevitschii* was the wet-season form of the
comparatively insignificant satyrid, *Yphthima zodia.*
In a wood at the foot of Toyama, at an altitude of some
2100 ft., the pretty *Araschnia burejana* was not un-
uncommon; *Neptis sangaica* was in larger numbers,
while but two *Grapta* [*Polygonia*] *c-album* were
taken. The Blues were represented by two *Everes
argiades* but at the summit of the small wooded hill
Cyaniris ladonides was in abundance though worn.
This pretty knoll culminates in a tiny ruined temple
of very remarkable construction. It is of wood to which
thin slabs of lava are cramped vertically, just as
weather-boarding is fixed on old riverside cottages
in England . . ."

Around that shrine he found innumerable swallowtails
of four species: *Papilio demetrius, Papilio bianor,
Papilio maackii,* and most abundant, *Papilio machaon.*
He ends with an unanswered question: "None of these
Papilios were common on the sides, or at the foot of
the hill. Why did they behave in this manner? I wish
I could tell whether both sexes were so occupied . . ."
Since the days of Holland and Longstaff, many of the
questions about Japanese butterflies have been
answered in the meticulous life studies done by the
Japanese themselves.

Butterfly collecting has been graced by a Russian
master of the English language, Vladimir Nabokov,
who, in his field work, has ranged widely about the
temperate zone of North America. This is one of the
most exciting and diverse regions for a butterfly

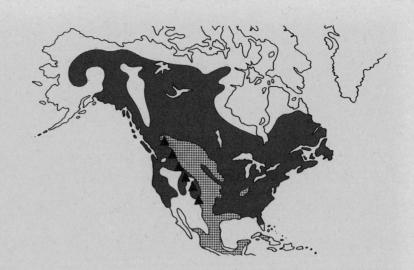

North America

167

hunt. Nabokov's talent for relating butterfly to man touches his work. Once, exploring a vast Russian marsh beyond the Oredezh, he crossed the river by a rickety footbridge near a hamlet and headed toward a green bank. He could see, he writes:

". . . the bright patches made on the turf by the scattered clothes of peasant girls, who, stark naked in shallow water, romped and yelled, heeding me as little as if I were the discarnate carrier of my present reminiscences.

"On the other side of the river, a dense crowd of small, bright blue male butterflies that had been tippling on the rich, trampled mud and cow dung through which I trudged rose all together into the spangled air and settled again as soon as I had passed."

Nabokov began collecting butterflies in his youth. His interest continued and was brought to fruition during his stay in America, while he was working at the Museum of Comparative Zoology at Harvard University. He experienced the pleasures of summer collecting on the Great Plains and in the Rocky Mountains, and he learned all about the joys of late spring hikes in the Sierra Nevada and the Cascades, and strolls in early autumn along the dunes on both the Atlantic and Pacific coasts.

His experience was wide, and his memory sharp. He recalled a collecting trip he once made in Colorado while exploring butterfly country in Russia:

"After making my way through some pine groves and alder scrub I came to the bog. No sooner had my ear caught the hum of diptera around me, the guttural cry of a snipe overhead, the gulping sound of the morass under my foot, than I knew I would find here quite special arctic butterflies, whose pictures, or, still better, nonillustrated descriptions I had worshiped for several seasons. And the next moment I was among them. Over the small shrubs of bog bilberry with fruit of a dim, dreamy blue, over the brown eye of stagnant water, over moss and mire, over the flower spikes of the fragrant bog orchid (the *nochnaya fialka* of Russian poets), a dusky little Fritillary bearing the name of a Norse goddess passed in low, skimming flight. Pretty Cordigera, a gemlike moth, buzzed all over its uliginose food plant. I pursued rose-margined Sulphurs, gray-marbled Satyrs. Unmindful of the mosquitoes that furred my forearms, I stooped with a grunt of delight to snuff out the life of some silver-studded lepidopteron throbbing in the folds of my net. Through the smells of the bog, I caught the subtle perfume of butterfly wings on my fingers, a perfume which varies with the species—vanilla, or lemon, or musk, or a musty, sweetish odor difficult to define. Still unsated, I pressed forward. At last I saw I had come to the end of the marsh. The rising ground beyond was a paradise of lupines, columbines, and pentstemons. Mariposa lilies bloomed under

Ponderosa pines. In the distance, fleeting cloud shadows dappled the dull green of slopes above timber line, and the gray and white of Longs Peak." The lush meadows and aspen-conifer forests of the Colorado Rockies never fail to make the skin of a confirmed naturalist tingle. Sweeping vistas of nodding sunflowers, pink pentstemons, and delicate blue harebells, framed by grand 14,000-foot peaks, provide an incomparable stage for the richest variety of butterfly species in North America—over 250. (Even Florida has only 144 species.) And a number of the species in Colorado are represented by different subspecies at various elevations and localities. Certainly one of the most striking butterfly groups of these Colorado forests and meadows are the fritillaries of the genus *Speyeria*. Their golden brown and tawny orange wings are decorated with checks and patches of jet-black, and beneath lies a darker brown or greenish disk with brilliant silver spots. The great spangled fritillary *(Speyeria cybele)* visits the yellow coneflowers nodding in a moist forest glen, while the Aphrodite fritillary *(Speyeria aphrodite)* haunts the grassy slopes and foothill canyons.

Donald Eff, the noted Colorado collector, worked in these localities. "The males," Eff has commented, "are especially common and easy to capture in the early morning hours as soon as the sun is up and has warmed them sufficiently for flight. The females are a different story and never found in the places where the males are most common. Instead they prefer the flowers of the hillsides and ridge tops of the foothills." There the Aphrodite females swarm about the deep-scented flowers of mint plants. Occasionally, they fly off into sheltered woodland patches to lay their eggs singly among the violets, which, as with all the *Speyeria* fritillaries, form their larval food plant.

There is no more prized butterfly in Colorado than the huge Nokomis fritillary *(Speyeria nokomis)*. It must be sought during August in the wet meadows of rather arid mountain canyons bordering the lower desert country of western Colorado. But the fritillaries are hard to find. Despite repeated visits to a host of these environments, the discovery of one of the Nokomis colonies is rare. The male has a bright tawny orange upperside, while the female has a beautiful whitish buff ground color sprinkled with bold black and blue-green on the inner half of the wings. Underneath, the orange colors are more intense and the large silver spots, edged with black, stand out dramatically. This dimorphic Colorado species has been found recently in numbers in Unaweep Canyon and Paradox Valley, both around the 5200-6000 feet elevation. At these willow-thicketed sites, a constant flow of water seeps from granite or shale canyon walls, and this maintains the violets necessary as larval food plants.

Most of the other eight fritillary species of Colorado

Neophasia menapia menapia (male)

Neophasia menapia menapia (female)

Philotes sonorensis (male)

Philotes sonorensis (female)

are common in the forested zone of the mountains, where they are found in grassy clearings along roads and streams. During hot days, the callippe fritillaries *(Speyeria callippe)* dash in and out of oak thickets in the foothills, making them difficult to catch until evening, when they congregate on flowers. The other species occupy more luxuriant surroundings higher in the mountains, wafting, gliding, and occasionally darting in strong confident flight on the summer afternoon breezes among the rustling pines and quaking aspens. Here and there in a sunlit clearing they will be briefly joined by a playing zephyrus anglewing *(Polygonia zephyrus)* whose hoary, mottled underside camouflages it beautifully against the ground when it alights.

In the Rockies, the peak of the flowering season is from June to August and then the golden yellows and oranges of the mountain pierids are seen on the wing. The common orange alfalfa sulphur *(Colias eurytheme)* is found everywhere in the mountain fields and meadows; the early spring brood is small in size and has reduced orange patches on yellow wings, while the summer brood has much larger wings and the orange coloring on the uppersides sweeps all the way to their broad black borders. In the lowlands its larvae feed on alfalfa and may occasionally become agricultural pests, but here in the mountains the soft green caterpillars feed on the vetches *(Astragulus)*. Sometimes, adult hybrid specimens are seen. They are crosses between this orange alfalfa sulphur and a common black-bordered yellow butterfly, the western sulphur *(Colias philodice eriphyle)*, which is also abundant in these mountain meadows. Still another larger sulphur is the gorgeous Queen Alexandra's sulphur *(Colias alexandra)*, which is a common roadside and dry meadow butterfly in late June and July. Soaring with strong effortless flight across the mountain valleys, it is easily recognized by the pale lemon yellow of the uppersides and the cool, pale, grayish green of the hindwing undersides. The females lack the strong black border of the males. Wherever a summer thundershower has left a mud puddle, the males of Queen Alexandra's sulphur cluster about the edges, drinking in the company of its smaller orange and yellow relatives.

Clouds of mosquitoes swarm out from high altitude Rocky Mountain bogs when the butterfly collector arrives, but he may give no heed. This unlikely environment provides the rich experience of seeing relict populations of butterflies, left behind in this mountain fastness by the last retreating Pleistocene glaciers about 10,000 years ago.

Dense clumps of willows make walking difficult; the ground is muddy or rough. Suddenly a Scudder's sulphur *(Colias scudderi scudderi)* bursts out of a blueberry patch and with a hasty and lucky swing of the net the collector finds he has captured an immaculate pink-fringed beauty from the Arctic—every scale in place! With the warming morning sunshine, other Pleistocene species, otherwise restricted to the Arctic and subarctic north, begin flying here among the willows and the neighboring spruce. The prim-looking little bog fritillaries of the genus *Boloria* dodge in and out of the grasses, searching for mates and violet food plants for their eggs. The checkerspots of the genus *Euphydryas* settle and sip nectar for long minutes on the yellow head of each composite and shrubby cinquefoil. The darting, jabbing flight of the brilliant male ruddy coppers *(Lycaena rubidus sirius)* trace fiery trails across the bog as they fly off their perches to challenge any intruding species. They are especially abundant around the tall curly-leaved dock, where the females come to lay their eggs. Aerial "dogfights" occasionally erupt between the red males of the ruddy copper and the beautiful iridescent males of the purplish copper *(Lycaena dorcas florus)* as they cruise among the stately dock plants searching for their mates. Patrolling low in the grasses are the abundant adults of the greenish blue *(Plebejus saepiolus)*. The males have lustrous light blue uppersides with a tint of green while the females bear a multicolored coat of warm browns and blues. Another Pleistocene relict in these bogs and other montane meadows is the mountain blue *(Agriades glandon rustica)*, a race of a blue species which also occurs in the mountain meadows of Europe. The uppersides of the male of this demurely colored butterfly are lustrous gray-blue, while its mate wears a covering of dark brown scales. The mountain blues are often encountered with the proboscis and even the entire head sunk deep in the throat of a clover blossom, seemingly drunk on the richness of the nectar.

Many highly desirable and beautiful species of butterflies make up the eastern fauna, but they do not equal the abundance of species and races in the west. Kansas, for instance, has 155 species (many of them nonresident strays from across the southern and eastern borders), and Nebraska has had 159 species collected within its borders. Virginia has about 143 species, Georgia 145, Pennsylvania about 122, and Minnesota only 118.

One of the most famous and spectacular of the eastern group is the Diana fritillary *(Speyeria diana)*. The males bear the typical bright orange and black fritillary pattern but the females are a lustrous blue, with black near the body. It is thought that the female's coloration makes her a successful mimic of the distasteful blue and black pipevine swallowtail *(Papilio philenor)*. Birds avoid the Diana, allowing the female to complete her egg-laying without the bird predation that such a succulent insect would normally suffer. Dianas are found gliding in a leisurely fashion along valleys and deep, wooded ravines near cold streams or seepages at moderate elevations in the mountains of Virginia and adjacent southern states. There they visit thistle blooms, and it is said that they can also be attracted with baits of manure or dung. The males are more frequently collected than the females, which are secretive and usually occupied in slowly searching the rhododendron and alder undergrowth for the violets that serve as their hosts.

Another eastern rarity is the West Virginia white *(Pieris virginiensis)*, which flies in scattered woodland localities from central New England south to West Virginia. It must be sought deep in the rich transition zone woods where its food plant, the toothwort, grows. Once a lepidopterist has collected or seen such a rarity as *virginiensis* in one of its known colony areas, he acquires a strong urge to seek it out in the unsearched territory of his own state.

An eastern lepidopterist, Walfried J. Reinthal, once spent an exciting day in such a search, hunting with a party in the Wahconah State Park northeast of Pittsfield, Massachusetts. There, he came on a wooded area where a stream fell into a gorge and formed a small waterfall. Reinthal's description indicates both the enthusiasm of the lepidopterist and also his attention to fine details:

"As soon as we stepped down to the waterfall, I got a butterfly in my net in a damp place along the path in the woods. To my surprise it was a male of *P. virginiensis*. Of course, a feverish and diligent search began immediately. Along a tiny stream running down a shady, woody slope, we found some patches of *Dentaria* in bloom, the food plant of the species. And here we soon obtained a few other specimens some of which, however, turned out to be *Pieris napi*. So both species flew here together in the same biotope. . . . We then turned our attention to the swampy forested area below the waterfall. . . . Here a few *P. napi* and *P. virginiensis* were caught. The other place, even better, was a shady, swampy, deciduous woods at the foot of that slope, along the banks of a small stream. We noticed some small open spaces along the water where the sun found ready access and white flowers of *Dentaria* were waiting for guests to feed upon. Both species were flying in those open spaces. . . ."

Reinthal, like most good butterfly men, was sensitive to both the biology of the creatures he was studying, and also to the atmospheres created by their colors, their movements, and their seeming "personalities." He was particularly impressed by the differences in the behavior of *P. virginiensis* and *P. napi*. He continued, referring to the *virginiensis*:

"Its normal flight is slow, zigzagging a foot or two above the ground, stopping for a while on flowers or resting on the ground enjoying the sun.

P. virginiensis is a rather 'nervous' and jerky species. If disturbed it gets panicky and goes into an erratic flight, and at times it really soars. I have seen it fly as high as the tree tops or hasten up a steep woody slope. There was some opportunity in this place to compare both species in their habits, and it probably would not be wrong to say that their habits are quite similar, except that perhaps *P. napi* is more temperamental, more sensitive, and is more easily disturbed. When this happens it flies away fast . . ."

By the time Reinthal and his party left the park they had seen about twenty *Pieris* and had collected one male and three females of *Pieris napi*, and one female of *Pieris virginiensis*.

Not only does the abundance of widely distributed species make every field trip worthwhile, but there is always the chance of making a unique observation on some facet of butterfly natural history. It may be a territorial dragonfly plucking an admiral butterfly out of the air, or a female laying her eggs on a previously unrecorded type of food plant. With luck, the entire courtship sequence culminating in successful mating may be seen. Even though the temperate zone butterflies have been studied for centuries, there is always the exciting possibility of being able to add something new to the fund of knowledge.

224. In late summer nodding heads of goldenrod and ripe pokeberries fill a field in the Great Smokies. Collecting in the southern mountains is best done around flowers, which nearly all hairstreaks, nymphs, skippers, pierids and the elusive swallowtails visit frequently.

225-249. *Temperate butterflies include many mountain and forest species as well as those of the lowland plains and grasslands. Butterflies of the East African savannas inhabit a relatively cool plateau region 5000 feet high. In Japan and America, invasions by northern and southern species have led to a merging of butterflies from both the tropics and the Arctic. In temperate Australia, the tropical influence enters from the north and contributes to the diversity of form and color of the grassland and coastal forest species. The spicebush swallowtail* (Papilio troilus) *is a particularly colorful American example of these temperate butterflies (225).*

225.

226. *Scarce swallowtail* (Iphiclides podalirius): *France.*

227. *Two-tailed swallowtail* (Papilio multicaudatus): *Idaho.*

228. *Apollo butterfly* (Parnassius apollo): *Europe.*

229. *Janson's swallowtail* (Papilio macilentus): *Japan*

230. *European skipper* (Adopaea lineola): *Michigan*

231. *Large skipper* (Ochlodes venatus): *England.*

232. *Whirlabout skipper* (Polites vibex): *eastern United States.*

233. *Clouded skipper* (Lerema accius): *Louisiana*

234. *Mourning cloak or Camberwell beauty* (Nymphalis antiopa): *Britain*

238. *Peacock butterfly* (Inachis io): *England*

235. *Silvery checkerspot* (Melitaea nycteis): *New York*

239. *Meadow fritillary* (Boloria toddi ammiralis): *United States*

236. *Zebra butterfly* (Heliconius charitonius): *Florida*

240. *Patch butterfly* (Chlosyne lacinia): *Texas*

237. *California sister* (Adelpha bredowii californica): *California*

241. *Viceroy* (Limenitis archippus): *eastern United States*

242. *Buckeye* (Junonia coenia): *Georgia*

246. *Map butterfly* (Araschnia levana): *Germany*

243. *Florida leafwing* (Anaea floridalis): *Florida*

247. *Virginia lady* (Cynthia virginiensis): *Ontario*

244. *Eyed pansy* (Precis orithya): *Tanzania*

248. *Poplar admiral* (Limenitis populi): *Germany*

245. *Pearl crescent* (Phyciodes tharos): *Indiana*

249. *Pearl-bordered fritillary* (Clossiana euphrosyne): *England*

250. *Lesser purple emperor* (Apatura ilia substituta): *Japan*

254. *Julia* (Dryas julia cillene): *Florida*

251. *Purple emperor* (Apatura iris): *England*

255. *Comma anglewing* (Polygonia c-album): *England*

252. *High brown fritillary* (Fabriciana adippe chlorodippe): *Spain*

256. *Pearl crescent* (Phyciodes tharos): *eastern United States*

253. *Red spotted purple* (Limenitis astyanax): *Georgia*

257. *Great spangled fritillary* (Speyeria cybele): *Ontario*

250-258. *Many temperate nymphalid butterflies are orange and brown, spotted with black, although an iridescent purple sheen decorates a few admirals. Some have beautifully checkered undersides such as the pearl-bordered fritillary* (Clossiana euphrosyne) *from Europe (258).*

259. The Gulf fritillary (Agraulis vanillae incarnata) *is common from southern California through the Gulf Coast states and south into the American tropics. Its brilliant orange wings are spangled underneath with silvery spots and streaks, and have a magenta flush at the base of the forewings.*

260-275. The colors of the temperate pierids are reflected in their common names—sulphurs, whites, orangetips, and yellows—just as names such as wood nymphs and browns suggest the somber tones of the satyrs. The small Colias *sulphurs are found throughout the temperate zones, and even range far south into the equatorial regions along the mountain ranges. Many satyrs such as the tiny* Coenonympha *ringlets are found in great abundance in the temperate grasslands and forests.*

276. A little satyr (Euptychia cymela) *spreads its wings an instant before it flies off in a Georgia woods.*

258.

260. *Topaz Arab* (Colotis calais): *Tanzania*

264. *Alfalfa butterfly* (Colias eurytheme): *California*

261. *Dappled white* (Euchloe ausonia crameri): *southern Europe*

265. *Moorland clouded yellow* (Colias palaeno): *northern Europe*

262. *Veined white* (Pieris napi venosa): *California*

266. *Clouded sulphur* (Colias philodice): *eastern United States*

263. *Green-striped white* (Euchloe belemia): *Spain*

267. *Sleepy yellow* (Eurema nicippe): *southern California*

268. *Gatekeeper* (Pyronia tithonus): *England*

269. *Grayling* (Eumenis semele): *England*

270. *Meadow brown butterfly* (Maniola jurtina): *England*

271. *Scotch Argus* (Erebia aethiops), *female: Scotland*

272. *Small heath* (Coenonympha pamphilus): *England*

273. *Marbled white* (Melanargia galathea): *England*

274. *Pearly eye* (Lethe portlandia), *male: Louisiana*

275. *Pearly eye* (Lethe portlandia), *female: eastern United States*

277, 278. *Hairstreaks are often found in shrubs or woods, and along the forested margins of fields, darting about from flower to flower. Shown here is a red-banded hairstreak* (Strymon cecrops), *common in the southeastern part of North America (277). Blues and coppers visit the flowers of marshes, meadows, and roadsides, but a few prefer woodlands. They frequently spread their wings to catch the sunlight, as in this view of a chalk-hill blue* (Lysandra coridon) *on a sedge (278).*
279. *The idas blue* (Lycaeides idas) *is widely distributed in western Europe. The size of this tiny butterfly varies with altitude, becoming smaller at higher elevations in the Alps.*

277.

Butterflies of the Mountains and Tundra

Each year the flower-spangled alpine meadows draw lepidopterists searching for elusive riders of the wind—mountain butterflies. Robert Michael Pyle, director of a butterfly society at Yale University, once summed up the experience: "As a young collector, hiking in Colorado, I passed into a high valley and saw dozens of butterfly nets. I thought I'd died and gone to heaven."

What Pyle had actually seen was the Rocky Mountain Biological Laboratory at the old ghost town of Gothic in the Gunnison River mining country. There, at nearly 10,000 feet, and surrounded by alpine peaks with rich meadows swarming with many kinds of butterflies, the laboratory is a perfect base for both professional and professing lepidopterists. Paul R. Ehrlich of Stanford University, author of *The Population Bomb*, often spends summer months at the lab studying the population biology and ecology of butterflies. He and others seek to apply the principles they have discovered to human population problems.

The high mountain environment is tough, and its peculiarities resemble those of the northern tundra. Life must survive freezing temperatures, strong winds, rugged terrain, and the risk that snow may smother all food, even in summer. In the alpine zones, the steep grassy slopes of the butterfly habitats often alternate with sheer cliffs, rock outcrops, and talus slopes where few butterflies can exist. Such varied geological features and the isolation of many mountain ranges keep alpine butterfly colonies widely separated. Different races of the same butterfly frequently live in adjacent mountains, or even on different peaks of the same range.

The cold temperatures of high altitudes bring early snows with deep drifts that linger through spring and create only two real seasons: a long winter and a short summer. In the Alps, the season of above-freezing temperatures lasts six months at 6500 feet, but only two months at 10,200 feet. In the Colorado Rockies, most alpine butterflies must compress their adult flight season into the first weeks of early July. In the Arctic, butterflies reach the peak of their flight period in the longest summer days of June.

The number of butterfly species adapted to survive drastically decreases as mountain height increases. Of ninety-six butterfly species living in the Swiss Alps, only twenty-seven range above timberline into the shrub and meadow zones, and only eight reach into the subsnow zone. Butterfly development slows down in low temperatures, as exemplified by the large white and the European and anise swallowtails, which produce multiple generations at low altitudes but can only breed once a year in the mountains. Species that need a year for development in the lowlands take two years in the alpine zone. The white *Pieris callidice* and a number of the *Oeneis* species, dull colored, medium-sized satyrs that usually fly among the granite boulders and rock slides of the highest peaks, emerge only in alternate years. Entire series of populations of the Jutta arctic *(Oeneis jutta)* which inhabit lodgepole pine and spruce forests in the Rockies and eastern North America, are synchronized to fly in either odd- or even-numbered years, depending on the year that the original founding individuals reached those areas and started the populations. Since the period of adult activity is short and all the individuals of a species emerge at once, alpine butterflies appear abruptly, flood an area, and disappear as quickly.

Many alpine and arctic butterflies are dark on both sides of their wings. Their somber hues better absorb radiant heat, helping them warm up faster and be more active in cold weather than their more brightly colored lowland relatives. The melanic pigment may also give protection against the increased amount of ultraviolet radiation that penetrates the thinner atmosphere at higher altitudes.

To conserve internal heat, the bodies of many arctic and alpine butterflies are also covered with a dense, hairy coat of long scales. They can absorb heat from warm surfaces. Ground temperatures in the arctic or alpine zones often rise to 70° F., while the air is seldom warmer than 50° F. To reach the temperature needed for flight, the butterflies press their wings against the sun-warmed ground and orient their bodies so that they get maximum heat from the sun. After flying for a few minutes in the brisk air, their body temperature falls. They must land in another sheltered hollow to bask in the sun again.

As soon as clouds cover the sun, and temperatures drop in the mountains or the tundra, most butterflies stop flying. Strong winds force them into shelter to avoid being blown into snow or ice fields or even into the foothills and valleys, away from their food plants. Almost constant winds sweep across alpine meadows and the tundra, and butterflies compensate by flying quite low, often in jerky, seemingly nervous flight. Some species, such as the parnassians, flatten themselves in sheltered nooks facing the wind. They fly only when the air is relatively calm; others, such as the *Oeneis* satyrs, dart rapidly from one shelter to another. Despite such adaptation, butterflies are sometimes caught by the wind and swept far above the snow line. The early nineteenth-century explorer, Alexander von Humboldt, saw butterflies at over 19,350 feet on Mount Chimborazo, a volcano in Ecuador, and other climbers have recorded butterflies at 20,670 feet in the Himalaya. The European satyr *Maniola glacialis* and a few others have evolved to cope with the highest of all habitats, the edge of the perpetual snow line.

The Himalayan massif surpasses all other mountain ranges in elevation, length and width. Himalaya (from Sanskrit *him* =snow, *alaya* =abode) was the name applied in ancient India to the Great Snowy Range, visible to the north from much of the vast plain between the Indus and Ganges rivers.
The Himalaya include the complex system of nearly parallel ranges of mountains stretching over 1800 miles from northern Burma in the east to Afghanistan in the west. Their width varies from less than 50 to more than 180 miles. The highest peaks on earth, such as Everest, are in the Nepal Himalaya, about 480 miles in length, and the three other basic subdivisions of the Himalaya are nearly as extensive.
The Himalaya of Pakistan's North-West Frontier Province differ markedly from the rest of the system, running southeast-northwest rather than east-west and are much wider. Few peaks reach above 22,000 feet, but many are 19,000 to 20,000 feet high. Until fairly recently, the northwest Himalaya were largely unexplored because of their enormous size, great heights, and inaccessibility. Mountaineers favor the Nepal and Kumaon sections because of the spectacular peaks in those ranges. Since 1951, however, entomologists under the direction of M. S. Mani have worked extensively in the little-known northwest Himalaya and have discovered fascinating new facts about alpine butterflies and other insects there.
The highest alpine butterfly is one of the Apollo species *(Parnassius acco)* which has made the adaptation to living at 19,030 feet. Nearly half of the other species are found between 9800 and 13,100 feet, and nearly one-fourth range between 13,100 and 16,400 feet. Oddly, most of the butterflies seem to favor environments at about 13,000 feet. The most common of the many families of Lepidoptera found in the snow (nival) zone are butterflies: swallowtails, whites and yellows, and the nymphs. About half a dozen species of lycaenids have been reported from the region, but practically nothing is known about their distribution and behavior.
All the alpine butterflies living in this zone of perpetual snow produce only one generation in the short summer; some, like the Nearctic *Oeneis* satyrs, probably need a two-year life cycle to complete development. Nearly all the butterflies deposit their eggs in rocky crevices or under stones instead of on leaves or flower buds. The caterpillars of these Himalayan species are mostly rock dwellers, as are many species in the European Alps. They usually remain at ground level or rest under stones where the temperature is much warmer.
At such exposed heights, butterflies find few plants for hosts. Many of the caterpillars are grass feeders. Forty (out of ninety) species of moths and butterflies in the northwest Himalayan system are Palearctic forms and are unrelated to the Indo-Malaysian species

Parnassius apollo

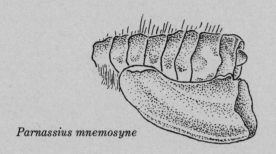

Parnassius mnemosyne

found at lower elevations and on the outer ranges of
the Himalaya. Nineteen species of butterflies belong
to the swallowtail family, three to the pierids, five
to the nymphalids, and three to the lycaenids. Both
the alpine butterflies of other high mountain ranges
and the nival species from the northwest Himalaya
have numerous separate races or subspecies, often
restricted to curiously localized patches or even
single peaks. Thus the diversity of appearance of
alpine butterflies is much greater than is indicated
by the number of species alone.

Although the swallowtails make up nearly one-third
of the snow zone Lepidoptera, most are the strange
orange-and-red-spotted, tailless white parnassians.
About three dozen true swallowtails live in the lower
elevations of India but only one species, the
European swallowtail, is found in the snow zone of
the northwest Himalaya. This yellow and black
butterfly is spread around the world in the Arctic as
well as in cool temperate areas of Europe. Subspecies have been named from North Africa, the
Pamirs, Siberia, Japan, Alaska, and eastern Canada,
and over forty subspecies have been claimed in
Europe. Two subspecies occupy the snow zone of the
northwest Himalaya. *Papilio machaon asiatica*,
common around 14,000 feet, ranges throughout the
Himalayan system and into the Tibetan plateau.
Papilio machaon ladakensis is darker, with shorter
tails and paler yellow on the uppersides. It flies
north of the main crest of the Great Himalaya and
in the Pamirs, and is common between 11,500 and
14,000 feet. The caterpillars of these races feed
on leaves of the carrot family.

Many of the other swallowtails belong to the
remarkable genus *Parnassius*, the dominant group
in the nival zone here, and of the alpine and arctic
areas around the northern hemisphere. The adults
of some species have been collected above 19,700
feet. Unlike most butterflies, which perch with
wings held vertically above their bodies, they rest
with wings outspread on flower heads or rocks. All
are clumsy fliers, but if given a head start and a
swing of a net to frighten them, the parnassians are
fast. Their wings are characteristically whitish and
translucent, with disk-shaped black spots and bands,
the hindwings often bearing red eyespots. Their
bodies are densely covered with long hairlike scales.
After mating, the females develop a conspicuous
horny white-colored pouch and carry this "chastity
belt," called a sphragus, for the rest of their lives.
It stops other males from copulating with them and
protects the reproductive investment of their first
mate. The dark-colored, hairy caterpillars move and
feed alone but are found resting in groups in sheltered places, usually under rocks.

Numerous local races of *Parnassius* have been
described. Most of the species from the northwest
Himalaya are found near 13,000 feet, but some like

Parnassius acco, delphius, and *simo* breed above 16,400 feet. *Parnassius delphius workmani* occurs up to 19,000 feet and is one of the few butterflies typically encountered around high mountain glaciers. Two widely distributed alpine white butterflies belong to the genus *Baltia*, which is found in the mountains of Tibet, Mongolia, Turkestan, and the Himalayan system. They fly rather poorly and close to the ground, ranging from 12,800 to 18,000 feet in the Himalaya. The tiny, brown-checked white *Baltia shawii* is common almost throughout the mountains north of the main crest of the Himalaya but is supplanted to the south by the somewhat larger and strongly brown-veined *Baltia butleri*. The caterpillars of another species of high-elevation, weak-flying white, *Aporia leucodice balucha*, are gregarious and hibernate under snow.

Several species and local races of *Pieris* whites occur in the Himalaya, but most of them fly only up to about 14,800 feet. This genus, which includes the well-known cabbage white *(Pieris rapae)* and other temperate zone species, is widely distributed in the Holarctic zone, including Alaska, and even occurs in the Indo-Malaysian region. The *Pontia* whites are another common group in the alpine zone. One species has been collected at 14,100 feet in the Lahaul area of extreme northern India, as well as in the high elevations of Tibet, Baluchistan, and Yünnan Province of southern China.

The most interesting alpine pierids are the *Colias* sulphurs, a group of butterflies also found in the lower temperate forests and grasslands. They range around the world in the arctic and temperate mountains of the northern hemisphere, the Andes of South America, and the Nilgiris of South India. The adults are yellow or orange, some with intense red-orange across their wings. The small, greenish colored *Colias cocandica* is only common north of the main crest of the Himalaya. *Colias electo fieldi* is found up to 14,800 feet and is the local but widespread representative of a butterfly known from China, Tibet, the Himalaya, and the whole of Africa. Some *Colias*, including the deep dusky orange *Colias eogene eogene*, are common up to 16,400 feet in the alpine zone of the northwest Himalaya. There are more species of nymphs than whites and yellows in this region. The fritillary genus *Argynnis*, found throughout the Holarctic and even the Indo-Malaysian and Australian realms, is represented by four tawny orange species. *Argynnis clara* is relatively common and occurs from the upper edges of the forest to 15,800 feet on the Pir Panjal Range. *Argynnis algaica vittata* has been collected as high as 16,400 feet. Four species of painted lady butterflies fly from the upper wooded slopes to perpetual snow in the Himalaya. One checkerspot, *Melitaea sindura*, is commonly found around 11,500 feet. *Maniola* satyrs are another common group in the

upper forest zone and the lower snow zone. The alpine forms have ochre-brown or orange-yellow wings and are typically poor fliers. *Maniola pulchella* is found frequently up to 14,100 feet. *Erebia* satyrs are common alpine butterflies here as they are elsewhere in the Holarctic region. In the Himalaya, the snow zone species are mostly brown on the upperside and tinged with red on the underside. The caterpillars feed on grasses in the mountain meadows.

Another exceptionally interesting satyrid group is the genus *Karanasa*. They prefer regions at and above the timberline on dry mountains or on high dry steppes, at 15,000 to 17,000 feet on the western border of Tibet; 12,000 to 13,000 feet in Kashmir; up to 13,000 feet in the northwest Himalaya, and at lower elevations in Afghanistan. To the north of the Himalaya and paralleling it lie the lofty Karakoram ranges where many species and races of *Karanasa* are found. The chronicler of a 1909 expedition to Karakoram and the western Himalaya gives a vivid impression of this *Karanasa* country:

"The whole land is one vast labyrinth of high, barren, desolate mountain chains, of cliffs split and shattered in every direction, usually precipitous; overhanging valleys full of rocks and stones, pebbles and sand; detritus of all shapes and sizes hurled down in avalanches and mingled with vast accumulations of alluvial deposits."

He reported that the disintegration was so continual and so vast that the valleys must change their shape at many points every few years.

Because of the tremendous geographical variety in the alpine portions of these arid ranges, more than seventy-five sets of local *Karanasa* populations are recognized, with possibly as many as twenty different species. This group of butterflies of the barren, rocky lands centering around the Pamir Mountains at the western end of the Himalayan Range is so incredibly complex, their homeland so high and hostile, that few specimens have been studied. Two investigators, André Avinoff and Walter Sweadner, have said that "the infinite variety nurtured by the isolated factors of high barren mountains and deep eroded valleys, has resulted in the impression that no two specimens are alike, that a chaotic condition exists . . . like the colors of pansies . . . among cultivated flowers."

Avinoff, who collected many *Karanasa* personally in Russian Turkestan northwest of India before World War I, writes that these rare alpine butterflies fly low with the irregular jerks and shifts of direction typical of many of the satyrs. They settle on the open ground with wings closed and press their bodies tightly against the surface, perhaps because of the prevailing winds and warmer ground in these open mountainous regions. At earth level, they are excellently disguised by their marbled underside, which blends with the pebbles and debris around them. Avinoff observed that these butterflies are very similar in their flight and habits to those of the small, pale Riding's satyr found in the rolling plains of Wyoming. He felt that Wyoming's Bad Lands were a natural setting comparable to that of the Pamirs.

Russet-colored *Karanasa leechi*, the smallest satyr, reaches the highest elevations. Avinoff found it hard to catch because of the strong winds in the passes. He saw these little satyrs only on warm days, fluttering around and chasing each other among the cliffs rising above the dry beds of temporary mountain streams. But they were quite numerous, and he collected 500 specimens during his party's summer season expedition in the Alai and Pamirs. These butterflies fly short distances within restricted zones, which Avinoff believes might account for the extreme localization of racial forms even in a region that does not have visible obstacles to their distribution.

While biologists write precisely of species, sub-species, and similar categories, such terms really have no fixed meanings. Within the *Karanasa*, hybridization occurs at all levels, and wing shape, colors and patterns vary apparently at random between one local population and the next. Avinoff and Sweadner proposed the local population as the basic biological unit many years before others interested in evolution began shifting their own emphasis from the importance of the species level to the population level.

South America

The great Andean ranges are second only to the Himalayan system in size and spectacle. They are strung along the western side of South America, and twist for nearly 4000 miles from Colombia through Ecuador, Peru, Bolivia, Chile, and parts of Argentina. The Andes are majestic barriers between the Pacific and the Amazonian rain forests in the north and the harsh coastal deserts and lush inland pampas in the south. The alpine wildlife of the Andes is hard to study and lepidopterists have concentrated on uncovering the butterfly treasures of the lowland rain forests. But the Andes do have rich butterfly populations, particularly satyrs, lycaenids, and the whites and yellows.

Curiously, some butterflies that might be expected in these high and extensive mountains are missing. The swallowtails drop out around 6500 feet, except for *Papilio asterius americus* which flies right up to the edge of the alpine zone at 11,000 feet. No parnassians occur here. Despite their dominance in the northern and central alpine parts of the eastern hemisphere, they do not range farther south than northern New Mexico. No similar group of swallowtails has evolved in South America.

This placement of species is precise and shows, with odd exceptions, how well evolution fits creatures into such specialized environments. The whites and yellows are quite common across the treeless alpine grasslands, which are called *páramo* in South America, and higher tundra-like areas on up to the perpetual snowline at around 17,000 feet.

The capacity of cold-blooded creatures to fly so high is surprising enough, although many species are active only when the days are warm, but the systematic colonizing of high places is one of the features of the insect world. A genus of whites, *Tatochila*, basically white butterflies with black wavy marks and lines on both wing surfaces, range wholly within the mountains of eastern South America and Central America where they fly to 13,500 feet all the way from Tierra del Fuego to Costa Rica. Thus, they are exact ecological replacements for the *Pieris* whites of North America and Asia.

Another genus, *Catasticta*, ranges from Mexico City to Bolivia where it flies to more than 10,000 feet. But only a few of these whites reach the alpine grasslands.

The truly showy pierids of the Andes are the sulphurs in the genus *Colias* which have developed bright colors and the capacity to live at really high altitudes. Some, particularly *Colias flaveola* which inhabits Chile and Bolivia, parade vivid orange wings with thin black borders. An Ecuadorian species, *Colias dinora*, is a small sulphur with dusky yellow-and-orange-patched wings. Most unusual is one butterfly from Ecuador, Peru, and Colombia, *Colias dimera*, the males of which have bright orange forewings and flashing yellow hindwings. At first, they look as though someone had glued the front half of an alfalfa sulphur to the back half of a common yellow sulphur. But once the collector has seen thousands of them coursing over an Andean meadow, he realizes that they actually emerge with those colors.

Among the many satyrs which penetrate the high mountain zones of South America is the spectacular *Argyrophorus argenteus*. Its broad wings are covered above and below with a shimmering metallic silver tarnished only by a single black forewing eyespot and a basal reddish patch on the underside. In flight, it looks like a silver dollar flashing its way through the montane grasses. A smaller version, *Punargentus lamna*, occurs in Bolivia. The many dark butterflies of the genus *Pedaliodes* move like their northern *Erebia* cousins, making short rapid flights across the *páramo* grasslands. Their mottled undersides conceal them admirably when they alight. In a number of species, the upper wing surfaces are crossed with bright bands of yellow, white, or orange.

The alpine lycaenids are numerous but little known. Most are dull-colored blues that settle in the tundra vegetation for long periods and rarely take flight

except during the calmest, most sunlit periods. The tiny brown "blue" (*Parachilades speciosa*) flies up to well over 14,000 feet around Cotopaxi volcano south of Quito in Ecuador; it is also found in the Andes of Peru and Bolivia. A very unusual lycaenid, which belongs to a subfamily (Styginae) all its own, is *Styx infernalis*. This large, dull, whitish butterfly superficially resembles a dusky Apollo in its elongated but stocky and rounded forewings and hindwings. Only a dusting of darker scales near the wing margins marks the translucent base coloration. Nothing is known of its life history. Judging from its Latin name, the lepidopterist who discovered it must have thought it resembled something straight from the region of hell.

North America The influence of wind on butterfly life at high altitudes is critical, particularly in the North American mountains which face the full force of Pacific gales. There, the fragile insects must take shelter from winds that often blow at more than 100 miles an hour. Their low and fast flight, their capacity to fly in the lee of rocks, or move not at all during persistent winds, are admirable adaptations to this world.

In the jumble of peaks in the northwest corner of the United States, the Olympic Range is typical of these conditions. It is accessible by car only at Hurricane Ridge where gale-force winds frequently sweep across the slopes. But in July, the alpine meadows, which tend to be sheltered, are alive with rich flower displays and hosts of butterflies. One of the rarest butterflies in the world is found only in the Olympics, a race of the chryxus arctic (*Oeneis chryxus valerata*). This satyr is on the wing as early as late June, flying among the gracefully nodding glacier and avalanche lilies that dot the patches of snow. It is supremely specialized and prefers alpine ridges and draws, alighting often on the rocks between the sparse wiry grasses that probably suit its caterpillars as food plants.

The North American alpine butterflies occupy a somewhat limited world. South of the Arctic Circle, the arctic-like alpine areas are found only at the tops of the highest mountain ranges. In Washington state, the upper limit of the timberline, and hence the start of alpine tundra and rocky areas, occurs at about 6000 feet on such mountains as Mount Rainier in the Cascades, and Mount Olympus in the Olympics. In central California, Colorado, and New Mexico, the timberline continues upward to almost 11,000 feet.

The butterflies, of course, can roam higher as the mountains move south, but most share common characteristics enabling them to cope with the altitude, at whatever longitude they are located. Vidler's alpine (*Erebia vidleri*) with a broad orange band splashed across its chocolate brown wings darts so rapidly across meadows and flower-strewn rock slides that it looks like a tiny, fast-moving bird. Occasionally it stops to sip nectar from yellow sunflowers and daisies. This haste of flight is matched by the many comma skippers (Hesperia comma) which zip about on Hurricane Ridge in the Olympics during the brief time that tundra plants are in bloom.

Farther to the south, in the Sierra Nevada range of eastern California, there are extensive areas of protected "high country" in Yosemite, Sequoia, and Kings Canyon National Parks as well as surrounding national forest areas. Here another rare satyr occurs: the ivallda arctic (Oeneis ivallda). Pale tan with whitish or yellowish areas around the forewing spots, this charming butterfly is found only on the pale granite pinnacles of the Sierra range, from Sequoia north through Yosemite to the Donner Pass near Truckee. The dark volcanic areas in the central Sierra are home to a somber, yellow-brown relative, the Stanislaus arctic (Oeneis chryxus stanislaus), which may overlap at the edges of its habitat with populations of the ivallda arctic. Of all the Sierra butterflies, however, the best known is a green pierid, Behr's sulphur (Colias behrii). In the late nineteenth century and the early part of the present century it was thought to be the rarest North American sulphur because of the isolation of its alpine habitat, restricted range, and short flight season. As roads penetrated the highest Sierra passes, and hiking and backpacking trails were established through the parks, the butterfly was found to be quite abundant. In the sunny days of late July, swarms of this black-bordered, deep green sulphur may be met in favored meadows above Yosemite Valley. Among the more lightly marked females are albino forms that have pink eyes and a richly developed rose fringe on their greenish white wings.

The alpine lycaenids of the Sierra Nevada are especially brilliant decorations along the flower-bordered trails. The lustrous copper (Lycaena cupreus) flashes its gaudy wings across the blossom-spangled, rock-strewn fields in mid-July. It visits the blooms of the yellow groundsel; and, as John Adams Comstock, the pioneer western lepidopterist, remarked, "delights the eye of the beholder with its rich metallic lustre." The nivalis copper (Lycaena nivalis) is one of the rarer species; the males are purplish copper while the females are yellowish tan with extensive dark brown checking. The brightly colored males of the greenish blue (Plebejus saepiolus) fill grassy meadows. A small butterfly with mouse-gray undersides, the shasta blue (Plebejus shasta) flies about the higher and more barren slopes.

Comstock, who wrote one of the earliest and best works on western natural history, Butterflies of California, and made many expeditions into the remote areas of the Sierra Nevada, recorded the earliest information on this rarely seen butterfly. He observed:

"The Shasta Blue strongly belies its appearance, which is that of a delicate insect with weak powers of flight. In reality it is at home in regions of rigorous climate. High on the alpine summits, where bleak exposures serve as a trysting ground for angry cloud and roaring blizzard, is the abode of this brave little species. In midsummer, when a few short days of sunshine encourage the stunted flowers of the alpine meadows to show their faces, shasta comes out to sport among them."

Extending north through New Mexico, Colorado, Wyoming, and Montana to Canada, the Rocky Mountains display an impressive progression of high peaks and extensive tundra regions. Almost every area above timberline has its own combination of alpine butterflies and each summer the more accessible mountain passes draw lepidopterists from across the continent. One group of butterflies especially sought after by collectors is the Oeneis arctic genus. Colorado has seven of these satyrs, four of which regularly fly above timberline. Bruce's arctic (Oeneis brucei brucei), the smallest of the true alpine species, has dull, smoky gray, transparent wings. It flies in July at 12,000 to 14,000 feet among lush patches of alpine grasses and flowers. The Colorado arctic (Oeneis melissa lucilla) is much more common, but like the Bruce's arctic, it rarely descends to timberline and flies only in July on the highest passes and peaks, preferring exposed ridges covered with alpine grasses.

The rarest species is Edwards's arctic (Oeneis taygete edwardsi), which has been caught in only a few localities. F. Martin Brown, dean of Colorado lepidopterists, was one of the first collectors to find this prize. His observations on it suggest that it has about the same habits as the Colorado arctic. He found it to be quite active in the late morning and early afternoon, but wary, tending to stay on the steep slopes at the top of the Continental Divide. "When disturbed," he wrote, "it moves uphill flying a foot or so above the ground, and if really frightened it dashes in a zigzag course that is impossible to follow uphill at 12,000 feet. None of the high altitude Oeneis are easy to catch. Steep slopes, treacherous footing and lack of oxygen handicap the collector."

The five alpine satyrs of the genus Erebia are abundant above timberline in Colorado. Davenport's alpine (Erebia theano demmia) flies in moist grassy areas well above 11,000 feet, while Edwards's alpine (Erebia theano ethela) occurs in bogs near timberline in the Front Range west of Boulder. Butler's alpine (Erebia epipsodea epipsodea) is the most abundant of these satyrs in Colorado. Its dark brown wings

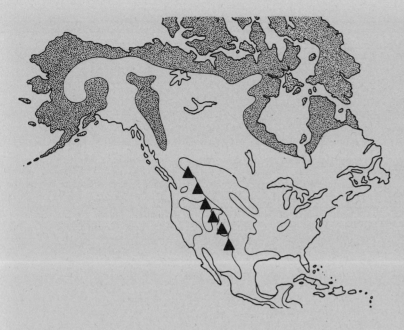

are decorated with eyespots set in distinctive patches of reddish brown. In midsummer, the adults cruise from flower to flower in boggy alpine meadows. Mead's alpine (*Erebia callias*) is a small butterfly with mottled soft gray coloring on the undersides of its dark brown wings. It flies in late summer high above the tree line.

The prize species for Colorado alpine collectors is the magnificent Magdalena alpine (*Erebia magdalena*), a large and uniformly black species. It haunts the rock slides on the steepest slopes at timberline during early July. Brown found it generally very difficult to catch because of the treacherous footing on the tumbled rocks and had to use a net with a six-foot-long handle.

Colorado's alpine summits abound with Apollo butterflies, which, as in the mountains of Europe and Asia, are found everywhere above timberline. Their flight across the meadows and rockslides is weak and fluttery. But the collector himself is handicapped by the altitude, and so these white and gray beauties are hard to catch. The females are much darker than the pale, translucent males, sometimes even colored grayish black. Like the European and Asian *Parnassius*, they develop a protective pouch on their abdomens after their first mating. The caterpillars of this Colorado swallowtail feed on stonecrop. They are flattened, sluglike creatures, velvety black and decorated with yellow spots and short black hairs at maturity. The pupa is surprisingly mothlike, which is considered one of the characteristics that mark these butterflies as an ancient genus of swallowtails. It forms in a loose cocoon built of debris in the shelter of a clump of grass or stones.

The alpine areas of Colorado are also the home of the state's most sought-after pierid butterfly: Mead's sulphur (*Colias meadi meadi*). It inhabits windswept alpine meadows, where the startling, fiery orange color of its uppersides seems incongruous until the butterfly settles and the deep green of its undersides blends into the environment. Perhaps such a sudden change from brilliant to cryptic coloration confuses the few predators such as horned larks or rosy finches that can survive at these high altitudes.

The earliest specimens of this sulphur were collected in 1871 by Theodore Mead, the first lepidopterist to penetrate the Colorado mountains. The butterflies were extremely difficult to chase even though in July the windy ridges above timberline swarmed with them. When these sulphurs alight they often allow the wind to blow them flat against the ground, and they blend into the lichen-covered gravel. Once disturbed, they dash off and let the wind blow them about. Mead found it almost impossible to chase specimens in the oxygen-thin air. He saw dozens for every one he trapped. Only on rare windless days when the females are just emerging can good catches be made. As the season develops, Mead's sulphurs seem to drift downslope, and by late August and early September they may be seen, somewhat tattered, at about 9500 feet.

Colorado has more than fifty peaks higher than 14,000 feet. The alpine zone begins at timberline, around 10,500 feet, so alpine butterflies have almost 4000 feet of useful habitat. In early July, Cottonwood Pass at 12,000 feet near Aspen, swarms with sulphurs, ringlets, *Erebia* alpines and *Oeneis* arctics, all flying across the blooming meadows and barren rocky slopes.

Another outstanding area for arctic butterflies is the famous Trailridge Road in Rocky Mountain National Park, which meanders for miles through alpine tundra, with breathtaking vistas of densely wooded valleys below.

The energetic naturalist may choose to climb one of the 14,000-foot alpine peaks outside the Park. In summer, on Mount Sherman for instance, a new race of alpine checkerspots was discovered in one sheltered valley. Left behind as the Pleistocene glaciers retreated, the ancestors of this isolated population could not enter the warming lowlands of Colorado. Thus, they diverged slowly in color and pattern from near relatives on other isolated peaks. The Mount Sherman checkerspots are small, dull and dusky, adapted to absorbing sunlight and withstanding winds.

The true tundra is found north of the tree line, where the weather is too severe to allow upright growth of woody vegetation. The brief summer allows only the top few inches of frozen soil to thaw. Below the surface is permafrost, a deep layer of permanently frozen ground thousands of feet thick in places. It prevents surface water from being absorbed and creates many shallow pools and marshy areas. The tundra is surprisingly rich in butterflies. But a collector must be willing to spend arduous weeks in the field fighting hordes of bloodthirsty mosquitoes, biting flies, cold winds, frustrating cloudy weather, and the uncertainties of arctic transportation.

Colin Wyatt, a noted English lepidopterist, explored the most remote alpine mountain and arctic regions for new butterflies. He once spent three months collecting in the Mackenzie River and in the western arctic of North America. When he arrived in May at Fort Smith, North West Territories, the ice still remained on the Slave River. But despite the chill, some butterflies were already out of hibernation, notably a few anglewings and a forlorn-looking mourning cloak.

By the middle of the month, other butterflies began appearing, when as Wyatt put it, "the season began with a rush." The little blue *Lycaenopsis pseudo-argielus* appeared, followed two days later by elfin hairstreaks *(Incisalia polios* and *augustinus)*, quickly swarming everywhere that bearberry was growing. The appearance of Arctic and subarctic life is timed precisely in the spring and summer. Because of the shortness of the growing season, each species of butterfly has to appear almost on the same day that its food starts to leaf out and flower. Wyatt saw bog fritillaries, whites, and an alpine *(Erebia discoidalis)* coming out just before the marbles; and by May 27, a third species of elfin hairstreak *(Incisalia eryphon)* emerged with orange-flushed wings among the females.

By June 6, another alpine specimen *(Erebia disa)* was caught, and soon they were common in the dry, fairly open forest. On the same day, the first arctic *(Oeneis chryxus caryi)* appeared, a genuine surprise, "a fine deep brown female . . . the first indication that I was a long way north of the normal west Canadian fauna."

Wyatt took a tugboat down the Mackenzie River toward the Arctic Ocean. The first stop was Norman Wells, from June 18 to 21. He went ashore with a net and headed towards the still snow-dotted Franklin Mountains east of the river. In the first large, open, heathy clearing he took several arctics and saw his first sulphurs among flowering Labrador tea.

Wyatt's descriptions were extremely valuable because he intensively covered a wide area. Each day brought surprises, but only at the cost of almost constant trudging amid clouds of biting insects. Once, walking into a steamy cloudberry bog, he saw:

". . . a huge brown thing the size of a big Saturniid moth fluttering around a spruce tree in amorous dalliance with a male *B. polaris;* out of curiosity I caught it, and to my amazement it proved to be a female, freshly emerged, of *P. glaucus,* the whole ground colour being a rich tawny colour instead of cream, and with all black markings heavily enlarged and suffused across the wings . . ."

Wyatt then went to the mountains of the Northwest Territory-Yukon border and camped in solitude, "apart from several quadrillion mosquitoes," at the foot of the mountains. Early in his climb, he took a small and dark male alpine *(Erebia rossii)*, and at about 1100 feet he netted another sulphur, *Colias nastes subarctica,* flying low over grassy slopes thickly covered with dwarf willows. There, with yellow arnica the most abundant flower, the sulphurs were feeding heavily.

At 1300 feet, he went through a belt of dwarf alders and above this came on damp slopes recently thawed, with moisture oozing out of large drifts of snow higher up the mountain slopes. He took a few alpines. At 2200 feet, Wyatt came to a large shelf shimmering with a silvery mass of cottongrass. Its countless tussocks made his walking difficult, but he sighted several European swallowtail males *(Papilio machaon aliaska)* chasing each other about and copulating with females. Wyatt then noted:

"Suddenly a *Boloria* skimmed past, sat for a second on a flat stone with outspread wings, and dashed off again. What the devil was this? It reminded me of *astarte*, but I had never heard of *astarte* up here. Back it came. I stalked it carefully and got it: a big *Boloria* of a pale ochre-yellow. I turned it over. Then I nearly fell over. *Distincta!* There was no doubt about it—I was holding a bug of which only three specimens were known, taken nearly forty years ago!"

Wyatt then went down the delta on a small schooner toward the Arctic Ocean, sailing through the ice pack to Coppermine. Here collecting was again good even though it was late July. By August 3, autumn was in the air. He went on to Victoria Island and the Boothia Peninsula, but the season was over. He did not find a single bug. He wrote:

"The flowers were all in seed, and the migratory birds already beginning to collect for their long flight south. At last an aircraft turned up and flew me out, but not until the first blizzard had come and the lakes begun to form ice. I had seen the short arctic summer come and go—it had been all too short for me. However, I had got pretty well everything I wanted, and a few things I had never expected to see in my life outside of a museum, so I was happy. Apart from that, there is a calmness and peace about the Arctic which is most soul-satisfying. I hung on in the North until the sea freeze-up started, and when I finally returned to the 'outside' at Halifax by way of Baffin Island and Labrador, I swore I would return to the Arctic at the first opportunity."

280. An alpine meadow at 11,000 feet in the Never Summer Range in Rocky Mountain National Park, Colorado, blazes with sunflowers. Parnassians, fritillaries and an occasional blue visit these flowers during the brief spring and summer months above timberline. Alpine butterflies are often descendants of arctic species left behind by retreating Pleistocene glaciers; their nearest relatives still live in the tundra north of the Arctic Circle.

281.

282.

281-283. The arctics are common butterflies of the tundra and high mountains. Macoun's arctic (Oeneis macounii) at Meadow Lake in Saskatchewan (281) ranges southward in jackpine or black spruce swamps and is sometimes found on dry prairie hilltops. Hoffman's checkerspot (Chlosyne hoffmanni), here photographed (282) in the Cascade Mountains, lives near timberline from northern California through Washington state. Gillett's checkerspot (Euphydryas gillettii) is found only in isolated colonies from Yellowstone National Park north to Glacier National Park. The rare form shown here (283) was recently discovered in the Sawtooth Mountains of Idaho.
284. European alpine fritillaries are often brightly colored and have hairy bodies. Shepherd's fritillary (Boloria pales) is found from timberline to the highest peaks, flying in July and August over grass slopes to elevations of 8000 feet or more.

285. *Baldur parnassian* (Parnassius clodius): *California*

289. *Northern cloudy wing* (Thorybes pylades): *Canada*

286. *Apollo butterfly* (Parnassius apollo rhodopensis): *Austria*

290. *Arctic skipper* (Carterocephalus palaemon): *Canada*

287. *Berger's clouded yellow* (Colias australia): *Austria*

291. *Bright blue copper* (Lycaena heteronea): *Colorado*

288. *Alpine white* (Hesperocharis *species*): *Ecuador*

292. *Small copper* (Lycaena phlaeas phlaeas): *England*

285-294. Alpine and arctic butterflies must cope with cold temperatures, thin air, and strong wind. Most species are small and have a rather weak flight, often stopping to rest and sun themselves with outstretched wings. On Ellesmere Island, just 600 miles from the North Pole, where the ground temperatures in July may rise to 70° F. while the air is only 42° F., the five resident butterfly species press themselves against the warm ground and orient their wings to the sun to increase their body temperature. The habitat preferred by arctic fritillaries is the sheltered side of dryas plant hummocks. The American copper (Lycaena phlaeas) is found across North America and arctic Europe and south to North Africa (293-294). An isolated alpine population is found on the heights above California's Yosemite Valley.

295. The purple-edge copper (Palaeochrysophanus hippothoe) flies in alpine meadows at 6000 feet during July and August in the French Pyrenees.

293.

294.

Butterflies of the Oceanic Islands

When a naturalist, John McGillivray, was exploring the Solomon Islands in the 1880s, he shot a butterfly. The Queen Victoria's birdwing *(Ornithoptera victoriae regis)*, found only on Bougainville, is such a large, powerful and high-flying species that McGillivray could not reach it with his net, and so was forced to use a shotgun loaded with small pellets to bring it down.

The incident is typical of the experiences of lepidopterists who first uncovered the remarkable world of oceanic island butterflies. Isolated, many of these butterflies have evolved into a multitude of spectacular forms. Brilliant colors are common. A few are giants, some flaunting wingspreads of nearly eleven inches.

With their bright colors, size, and majestic high-soaring flight some of these *Ornithoptera* butterflies look more like birds than insects. They exemplify the lure that islands have held for biologists and naturalists alike, particularly since the time of Darwin, who based part of his theories of evolutionary change on animals of the Galapagos Islands, which had been long isolated from their mainland relatives. Despite their isolation, island butterflies have not evolved any dramatic behavioral or flight adaptations. However, on several remote antarctic islands and other oceanic islands certain moths have lost their power of flight. The wings of the Hawaiian flightless moth have narrowed to stick-like projections. The males have slightly broader wings than the females, perhaps because they must move about to find mates. The totally flightless females need only walk around the site of their emergence to find food plants and places to lay their eggs. Although all butterflies have retained their wings, certain species on the Galapagos Islands have become dwarfed, perhaps to adapt to prevailing winds which might otherwise be more likely to blow them out to sea.

The Caribbean Islands

An extraordinary archipelago of lush green islands called the West Indies or the Antilles sweeps southeast from the tip of Florida in a wide curving arc, terminating in the relatively large island of Trinidad, just nine miles off the Venezuelan coast. Few of these thousands of islands are inhabited. Some are coral atolls built up from the ocean floor by the skeletons of billions of marine creatures. But most are the peaks of a large submarine volcanic mountain range. The Greater Antilles include the four large and mountainous islands of Cuba, Jamaica, Hispaniola (Haiti and the Dominican Republic), and Puerto Rico. The Lesser Antilles are all the smaller islands from the Virgin Islands south to Grenada, just north of Tobago and Trinidad. Each island in the chain is unique biologically, yet each shares with its neighbors an Eden-like beauty. The glorious blue waters of the Caribbean are a part of almost all the landscapes in this delightfully mild and tropical climate.

The butterflies of the West Indies have come almost equally from Central and South America. In the larger western islands there are more Central American species, whereas more of the species in the southern islands have come from South America. The butterflies apparently reached the islands from the mainland by overwater flights rather than by ancient land bridges.

The Antilles population of butterflies is not particularly rich, at least not in comparison with an area of equal size in Central and South America. Only 285 species are found in the entire region, with the greatest number, 175, on Hispaniola. The diversity is comparable to that of southern Florida, which has only 119 species of butterflies. Trinidad and Tobago, which are closer to the mainland, share the South American abundance of butterflies. Trinidad has 617 species, of which 99 percent are also found in northern Venezuela. Only six species are limited exclusively to the island: two metalmarks, two hairstreaks, and two skippers.

These Caribbean butterflies include spectacular species, often seen winging through almost idyllic glades and vales where forests still remain. The swallowtails, Coliadinae sulphurs and true nymphalids are more predominant in the Antilles and Florida than in Trinidad and South America. Several genera in the first two groups have radiated widely. The abundance of nymphalids seems to be due to repeated invasions from the United States and South America. Metalmarks, satyrs, and ithomiids are very rare here, probably because there are no known migratory species among them. Most are local, forest-inhabiting butterflies that would not cross water barriers and could not survive on the many low, drier islands in the Antilles chain even if they were blown there by the wind.

Three major types of butterflies inhabit the Antilles: 45 percent are local species found nowhere else, 40 percent are continental species restricted to a few islands, and 15 percent are continental species that are widespread on many islands. Biologists have concluded that the number of species, and especially the development of butterflies restricted to a particular island, depends on the size and variety of its habitats, such as grassy areas, wet forests and mountains. So, the Greater Antilles, which are larger and higher islands, have developed more local butterflies than the smaller islands.

Jamaica

When André Avinoff, at one time a director of the Carnegie Museum of Pittsburgh, was exploring the rugged Cockpit Country of central Jamaica in the early 1900s he collected a magnificent swallowtail, *Papilio homerus.* Its bold black and yellow pattern and broad spatula-like tails had made it a favorite of lepidopterists ever since its discovery in the eighteenth century.

This insect is probably the most famous native butterfly of the Caribbean Islands. It is the largest in its genus and is found most frequently between 1000 and 2000 feet in the forested central mountains. It deeply impressed Avinoff and he spent much time observing it.

The butterfly alighted on either high trees or bushes and was never seen on flowers. Avinoff found that it was quite common in the area and often saw it basking in the sunlight with its wings open flat. He most often found it in "an amphitheatre of foliage with tropical moisture;" in such places, he spent days watching it sailing majestically against the background of tropical verdure.

None of the other Jamaican butterflies is as spectacular as *homerus*, but they are interesting enough to the lepidopterist. In the lush rain forest of the Blue Mountains, *Ithomia* glasswing butterflies can be found floating above the fern-covered leaf litter. No ithomiids penetrate farther into the northern hemisphere than these. The equally rare Panton's patch *(Chlosyne panton)* also lives in the Cockpit Country. Gorgeous sulphurs and other pierids swarm about flowering vines throughout the island, and dancing swallowtails course along the sand beaches of the northern coast at the edge of the crystal waters.

Just before dusk begins to settle over the islands of Trinidad and Tobago, giant butterflies appear around clearings and along the beds of streams. These are the brassolids, none of their species particularly common but all of them sharing a preference for dark places. They tend to be rather localized, although the owl butterflies *(Caligo)* are spread through most parts of the islands.

The brassolids fly during the day in well-wooded areas but their favorite flight time is that one brief hour before dusk. To their secrecy and love of gloomy places is added their exceptional protective coloration—the undersides of their wings resemble the bark of the trees on which they frequently rest. The caligos have a simple large "owl" eye on the underside of the hindwing, which they flash to frighten a predator if their protective pattern fails to conceal them. Most of the brassolids feed ravenously on fruit and sap and thus may be easily baited by the collector.

Trinidad, which lies at the southern end of the Antillean chain, is perhaps the world's richest island environment for butterflies. The best time for seeing many of the 617 butterfly species is mid-May when the trade winds blow in from the southeast, laden with moisture from the Atlantic. It is humid until

Trinidad

211

early October or mid-November, when the "Petit Carême," a short, hot, dry spell, breaks the wet season. Then the rains begin under cooler conditions and continue until the dry season starts again after Christmas.

Malcolm Barcant, a noted lepidopterist who lives on Trinidad, has traced many of the life histories of the native butterflies. In his book *Butterflies of Trinidad and Tobago* his report on the scarce blue shoemaker *(Anaea eribotes)* is particularly interesting. This species, which also occurs in the Guianas and in the Amazon Basin, is extremely rare and localized in Trinidad. He found it in the dense Guayaguayare Forest of the southeastern part of the island, where a fifty-foot-high virgin growth virtually obscures the sun. Shafts of light break through the dense undergrowth along a narrow hunters' trail. Barcant reported that he saw the shoemaker daily for over three years, provided the sun was not clouded over. The period in which the butterflies appeared was precisely from 11 A.M. to 1 P.M. It was an uncanny display, according to Barcant, that seemed to correspond with the penetration of sunlight to the particular growth on which they liked to rest. One day in August 1962, without ever seeing more than two at a time, he took eleven during the two hours, after which they disappeared. By 1966 dense growth had covered the open break in the forest and the shoemaker seemed to have abandoned the area completely.

The butterflies of this region are most plentiful in May and June when, after a really "dry" dry season, heavy continual rain for several days signals instant hatching of most estivating butterflies, followed by abundant breeding. Collecting in the Central Range mountains or the forest reserves of southern Trinidad at this season yields many specimens. The twenty-four species of ringlets and wood nymphs love damp, shady surroundings. Cool areas of cocoa estates, forest clearings, and mountain trails are their natural habitat. With a slow, bouncing flight, the satyrs frequently settle on low vegetation or on the ground to rest or sip juices from rotting fruits, tree sap, or decaying vegetation. The predominantly brown colors displayed by nearly all species protect them well in these dark surroundings.

Inhabiting a somewhat higher level in the forest are the monarchs and tigers of the Danaidae, as well as the ithomiids and glasswings. These butterflies are a remarkable group of robust, broad-winged but lazy fliers, colored a vivid yellow and brown mixed with black. With the exception of Trinidad's one tiger butterfly, *Lycorea*, the family loves sunshine. A bad odor and an objectionable taste render them immune to predator attack, and the group can thus afford to be gaudy in color display and slow in flight. They are also physically tough; they can revive and fly away even after a severe pinch of the body by a bird's bill or human fingers.

Like the danaids, the ithomiids are found from a few feet to several dozen feet above the ground and are slow fliers. They prefer cool, well-shaded areas and their wing patterns blend with the quickly alternating sunshine and shade of their forest habitats. The glasswings have abandoned the colors of the tiger-striped species and have adopted transparency as a protective device.

Among the colorful names Barcant has given to many of the island's nymphalids are shoemakers or leaf-wings, crackers, daggerwings, preponas or king shoemakers, eunicas or purplewings, the dynamines or handkerchiefs, the anartias or biscuit and coolie, catonephile or Grecian shoemaker, victorina or bamboo page, and the street Arab. When at rest, the shoemakers or *Anaea* leafwings of the rain forests are distinctive in their resemblance to dried leaves. The undersides, although ranging from near black to light brown or yellow, display a sandy mottled effect which, when coupled with the unusual wing shape, provides a perfect imitation of the dried and decaying leaves in the forest. The leafwings are fast and solitary fliers that settle on foliage often high above the ground or on the bark of trees, and most are attracted to fruit juices and tree sap. One of the outstanding species of Trinidad, *Anaea fabius*, has a distinctive color pattern and resembles the danaids and tigers except for its longish tails.

The highly diversified nymphalids on Trinidad show well developed protective coloration in many species; in addition to recognizing mimicry, Barcant has found three associations of protective devices and feeding or perching behavior. The most striking aspect of the feeding behavior is a clear differentia-tion between the genera that suck nectar from flowers and those that feed on decaying fruit and the sap of trees.

The *Anaea, Prepona, Catonephile, Eunica,* and other fruit-and-sap-sucking butterflies have their undersides painted in ground colors of browns and grays. Even the colorful emperor morpho of Trinidad has a dull pattern on its underside. Such mottled patterns provide nearly perfect environmental camouflage when the butterflies settle on tree trunks to sip bleeding sap, or on fallen fruits among the leaf litter of the forest floor.

The tropical crescentspots, *Adelpha, Dynamine, Anartia,* and other nectar-sucking butterflies usually have a broken pattern of large white or translucent patches across the dull brown underside of their wings; this breaks up the wing shape and causes them to blend into the flowers on which they settle with folded wings. Although the camouflage is not by any means perfect, even to a human observer, it appears to be somewhat successful against natural enemies such as insectivorous birds.

The crackers or *Hamadryas* butterflies prefer to land on trees with light colored or gray trunks; after alighting with the head downward they spread their mottled wings out flat against the surface, blending perfectly with the tree bark. The king cracker *(Hamadryas amphinome)* is a very lovely butterfly with mottled iridescent blue across the upper wings and brick-red undersides. In July 1960, Barcant found an extraordinary brood of several hundred hatchings in perfect condition, flying in one small area in the Parry Lands district. Ripe fallen mangoes covered the ground and the king cracker abounded in the area, feeding on the fruit, resting on nearby tree trunks and filling the air with their strange cracking sounds as they fought each other. Curiously, Barcant reports that he never saw another brood in that area.

The great size of many Trinidad and Tobago butter-flies constantly surprises anyone who wanders through the islands, and the emperor *(Morpho peleides)* is most impressive of all. Unlike the skulking, gloom-loving brassolids, it is highly visible, showing its dazzling, iridescent blue sheen commonly throughout all hilly and forested parts of the islands. Males are often seen on trails or roads, while the females are more retiring and settle in low forest undergrowth for most of the day. It takes some eighty-five days for the butterfly to emerge after the egg is laid. The peculiar caterpillars have a thick bulge in the middle of their slender cylindrical bodies and short, forked tails. In the first three stages, the caterpillar is bright yellow and vermilion. Later, as it feeds on vines of the family Bignoniaceae, it becomes brown and rather barklike. The pupa is entirely green and hangs from leaves or stems like an unripe berry. Bright sunshine seems to influencé the movement of the morphos, particularly the males. As Barcant has observed:

"With remarkable precision cloud cover, bringing somber surroundings, leads within the minute to the seeking of shelter and prolonged settling of the male. As clouds disperse and valleys are again bathed in sunshine, flight is resumed with a deceptive and powerful dipping motion along the bed of some gorge or rivulet, the iridescent blue scintillating in the sun and painting on the land-scape one of nature's most beautiful pictures."

Some of the most colorful butterflies in Trinidad are the cattle hearts or aristolochias, and the kite swallowtails. Velvet black, orange, yellow, iridescent greens and blues are intermingled with white, red and magenta spots and patches across their broad, squarish wings. The tailless *Aristolochia* swallowtails are partial to shade and moisture, inhabiting the undergrowth of forest areas. They frequently settle on leaf edges, closing their wings as they do so. Males have an elaborate brushy set of scent scales, often white like cotton, within a fold along the inner margin of the hindwing. The true swallowtails usually have a well-developed tail on the hindwings and are generally orange, yellow, or black in color. Seekers of sunshine, these swallowtails have a swift and powerful flight, and when they settle, as at a flower or a mud puddle, they always land with a constant fluttering motion of the wings. They have a habit of flying for hours at great heights over the treetop canopy of mountain summits, but they will occasionally descend to drink water from moist sand.

The kite swallowtails are nearly square and much like the shape of a kite, with long thin tails. Their sparsely scaled wings look partially transparent. Most of the species are white, banded variously in black, and some have a greenish cast to their wings. They are forest species, but the onset of the rainy season may bring out numbers of males to drink from muddy pools in the open. The females are more reclusive, preferring to remain in the forest. While the adult swallowtails are highly visible in their gaudy and bold colors, most of the *Papilios* undoubtedly get some protection from their fast and nimble flight. The caterpillars of the *Aristolochia* swallowtails feed on poisonous forest vines, from which they get their strange Latin name (from the Greek words *aristas*, best, and *locheia*, parturition, for the supposed value of such a vine for childbirth). The slow-flying adults are apparently protected against enemies by the noxious chemicals retained in their bodies.

The whites and yellows are lovers of sunshine and flowers, and most of the twenty-seven resident species are well distributed throughout Trinidad. Flight in the medium-size species such as the *Phoebis* sulphurs is rapid, haphazard, and gay. In the more diminutive species, particularly the yellows of the genus *Eurema*, flight is slow and rather feeble, but as the pursuer soon learns, these butterflies are deceptive and readily weave in and out of the weedy growth as they fly low along the ground. Many pierids on Trinidad visit moist sand, and where this habit is coupled with swarming and migration behavior peculiar to some of the species, hundreds or even thousands of yellow butterflies can be seen sitting together in a crowded array on some wet sandy patch, enjoying a drink in the noontime sun.

Trinidad has the extraordinary distinction of having perhaps the densest concentration of metalmark species in the world. More than 107 species of these very small and brightly colored butterflies are known from the island. Nearly all are rare and usually localized to particular spots where their regular appearance year after year is almost a certainty. Hilly ridges exposed to sunlight and the edges of forest clearings are often their chosen habitats. Their flight is quite rapid, but they will usually circle and settle again in the same general location. Almost all members of the family hide by habitually resting on the undersurface of a leaf. Mimicry of protected groups of butterflies such as ithomiids is not rare, and some species show various forms of cryptic coloration such as resemblance to bird droppings. The showy, iridescent blue and green species apparently depend a great deal upon their speed and reclusive settling habits for protection. The blues and hairstreaks are found everywhere in the lowlands and mountains on Trinidad; although the great majority of the ninety-three known species are rather scarce, they may turn up almost anywhere on the island. Males are generally bright blue and iridescent, while females are less vivid or are dull brown. Their flight is fast, irregular and brief, with nearly all species settling for prolonged periods on leaves. The Trinidad lycaenids are not attracted to fruit or sap, but are lovers of flowers and moisture, and they may frequently be seen on wet leaves out in the sunlight immediately after a shower. As elsewhere in the tropics and temperate zones, many species enjoy a strange relationship with ants, the caterpillars attracting these normally predacious insects by the secretion of a sweet fluid from a dorsal gland.

Skippers form the largest family in Trinidad, with at least 230 known species. The "skipping" flight is very rapid, with long distances covered in one hop. They are voracious flower visitors; some drink moisture from wet ground or animal droppings. When settled on a leaf, the wings are spread flat, or the hindwings may be partially opened while the forewings are closed over the back. Like metalmarks, many forest species alight under the leaves. The richness of the Trinidad skipper population compared to that of other butterfly families is paralleled on the other Caribbean islands. Skippers, though nonmigrating, are strong fliers and robust travelers, and they appear to be well suited to successful crossing of open water to new islands when strong storms sweep over the mainland and oceanic archipelagoes.

Among the most spectacular butterflies in the world are the *Ornithoptera* birdwing swallowtails of the South Pacific. The male of the Queen Victoria's birdwing *(Ornithoptera victoriae regis)* has vivid iridescent green and gold uppersides with almost pure gold undersides. When John McGillivray shot down this butterfly in the 1880s, he had not collected the biggest or most exciting species in the area. The Queen Alexandra's birdwing *(Ornithoptera alexandrae)* is found in the same region and is one of the largest butterflies in the world. Some females reach a wingspread of eleven inches. This butterfly occurs only on southeastern Papua, and even there

The Islands of the South Pacific

it is rare. Although officially protected by the government, indiscriminate collecting on behalf of dealers and collectors has reduced the numbers of this magnificent creature, and the cutting of local forests is destroying the growth of its larval food plants, members of the pipevine family. The males are streaked with gorgeous broad bands of iridescent green and blue on a velvety black background, while the gigantic females have a more demure brown and black coloration.

The world of these great butterflies consists of many islands, set like huge emeralds in the South Pacific. The coral atolls and volcanic islands form a bewildering array of palm- and jungle-covered dots on the vast oceanic expanse. Starting from the north at the Tropic of Cancer and moving southwest across the equator to the Tropic of Capricorn in the Australian area, the three broad geographic groupings, based on native peoples, are: Polynesia (from Midway and the Hawaiian chain south through Samoa, the Tonga or Friendly Islands, the Society Islands including Moorea and Papeete, to Pitcairn Island and Easter Island south of the Tropic of Capricorn off Chile); Micronesia (including the Mariana Islands, Guam, Caroline Islands, and Gilbert Islands); and Melanesia (from the Bismarck Archipelago on the north side of New Guinea through the Solomon Islands, the New Hebrides, New Caledonia, and the Fiji Islands).

Most lepidopterists have worked in the rich Melanesian chains, which are closer to the source areas, Asia and Australia, from which butterflies come. These islands are largely volcanic and their varied topography provides a greater variety of habitats than the low, sandy or coral atolls. The Solomon Islands, for instance, form a nine-hundred-mile chain of volcanic islands with a combined land surface of over 11,500 square miles. The more remote islands such as the Hawaiian chain or Easter Island have quite poor butterfly populations, largely due to their distance from continental or other island source areas, their relatively recent origins (within the last few million years), and scant time to receive wind-blown immigrants or to evolve their own distinctive species.

The various beautiful races of King Priam's birdwing (*Ornithoptera priamus*), named after the unfortunate King Priam of Troy celebrated in the *Iliad*, range from gorgeous greens through deep blue. They are found on many of the South Pacific islands, and four races reach Queensland in eastern Australia. The stunning orange to golden green *Ornithoptera croesus* on the island of Bachan, just north of western Australia, managed to become the most famous of all butterflies through Alfred Russel Wallace's account—quoted in an earlier chapter—of his capture of the first specimen.

The strangest wing shapes among the birdwings

belong to the males of the Paradise birdwing (*Ornithoptera paradisea*). This butterfly possesses perhaps the most exquisite of butterfly designs, with bold iridescent green patches flung on deep black forewings and sharply plunging hindwings of gold and chartreuse that terminate in long, outward-curving tails. Now on the list of protected species, it has been heavily depleted by collectors in its northeastern New Guinea range. The diminutive *Ornithoptera meridionalis*, found in southeastern Papua and West Irian, resembles *paradisea* in its unique hindwing shape and has even longer, straight thin tails.

Many of the birdwing species and races are represented by only a few wild-caught specimens in museums and collections around the world, and yet a number of the life histories were worked out by the naturalist-explorers of the last century. When the larval food plants were identified, it became possible to rear perfect specimens of these magnificent butterflies, undamaged by any flight through their native forests. From Wallace's day to the present, most naturalists have agreed that the greatest possible thrill is to see one of these fantastic creatures free in the wild, and one can only hope that enough protected forest reserves will be established in their native islands to insure their survival.

New Zealand

Sir Joseph Banks, the brilliant naturalist who accompanied Captain James Cook in his circumnavigation of the world in 1769-70, was the first man to collect butterflies systematically in New Zealand. Banks was particularly impressed by the New Zealand red admiral (*Vanessa gonerilla*) and the common copper (*Lycaena salustius*), which are both unique to the New Zealand islands. He also discovered many new butterflies along the northern coast of Australia.

The gorgeous red admiral has a jet-black ground color belted with red on both forewings and hindwings. It flies everywhere, from remote hilltops and mountain slopes to gardens in the heart of the largest cities, and often shows a fondness for buddleia blossoms in the late summer, as does the English red admiral. Males have been observed drinking from wet moss and liverworts at the edge of a stream. The red admiral hibernates through the southern winter as an adult.

New Zealand is quite isolated. It lies more than 1200 miles east of Australia and consists of two main islands, North Island and South Island, as well as smaller coastal islets where such strange prehistoric animals as the tuatara lizard still survive. New Zealand is temperate in climate, and in contrast to the tropical Fiji group and Coral Sea islands such as the Solomons to the north, its butterfly species are very few in number. Only eighteen kinds are known, and two—the Australian blue tiger *(Danaus hamata)* and the Australian evening brown *(Melanitis leda)*—have been recorded only once in New Zealand. In the open country of the South and North islands, from sea level to perhaps 4000 feet, any of three local species of copper butterflies can be found. The common copper *(Lycaena salustius)* flashes its rich orange color across the countryside from late January to at least March during the southern summer. Darting in and out of dense bramble patches, it often alights on flowers along with the dark-banded copper *(Lycaena enysii)*, and spreads its wings in the sun. The small copper *(Lycaena boldenarum)* measures well under seven-eighths of an inch across the wings, and the male has a brilliant purplish reflection on the upper side. All of these coppers are related to the European and American *Lycaena* species, and their presence in the remote South Pacific is one of the mysteries that butterfly biogeographers must still solve.

The Hawaiian Islands

The lush and tropical Hawaiian Islands theoretically should be a paradise for butterflies, yet relatively few species flourish there. No doubt the reason for this is that many of the islands are new, at least in geological terms. They were thrust up from the floor of the sea as volcanoes and the largest islands, at the eastern end of the archipelago, are probably not much older than 700,000 years. In addition, vast stretches of ocean lie between the islands and the nearest source of immigrant butterflies.

The 6424 square miles of land in Hawaii were first inhabited by Polynesians who arrived between 500 and 900 A.D., bringing with them a variety of vegetables, fruits, and animals. The first butterflies, however, probably made the journey on their own. Two native butterflies—a nymphalid and a blue—occur in the Hawaiian fauna, and nine immigrant or introduced species, all from North America, are now established. Until 1970, no representative of the Hesperiidae was present, but in that year the fiery skipper *(Hylephila phyleus)*, a common California pest on lawn grasses, reached the islands. The only other butterfly families represented there are the Pieridae, Nymphalidae, Danaidae, and Lycaenidae.

The few butterflies that have, however, reached the islands have flourished there because the environment is almost perfect for them. The vegetation is lush, flowers are abundant and, except for the torrential rains of the higher mountains, the climate is ideal.

The populations are a mix of the species which somehow got to the islands "naturally" and those which have been introduced deliberately. The six North American species whose arrival was accidental but was probably associated with humans, perhaps by way of imported garden plants, include the cabbage white, monarch, painted lady, Virginia lady, red admiral, and the fiery skipper.

The bean butterfly *(Lampides boeticus)*, a tailed blue that is a common pest of beans and peas, is widespread from Africa across Europe to India, the Orient, and Australia, and reached Hawaii before 1882. Two blue-colored hairstreaks *Strymon bazochii gundlachianus* and *Strymon echion*, were introduced from Mexico by an entomologist in 1902 to aid in the control of lantana plants, which had become pests on the islands. The latter hairstreak has, unfortunately, also taken to attacking a number of garden crops in Hawaii.

The local nymphalid, called the Kamehameha butterfly *(Vanessa tameamea)*, and the local lycaenid, Blackburn's blue *(Vaga blackburni)*, have both come from the western Pacific, probably originally from the Bonin Islands south of Japan. Each of these butterflies has developed as a distinctive species in Hawaii but has apparently not had time to give rise to further species on the various islands. The blue is especially interesting because it has no specialized abdominal glands, which many other lycaenids use in their feeding associations with ants. There are no ants in Hawaii, and perhaps for this reason the caterpillars of Blackburn's blue have lost the honeydew glands. The Kamehameha butterfly was the first species of Lepidoptera to be described from the Hawaiian Islands, and can probably trace its origins to *Vanessa indica*, a great wanderer that ranges from the Atlantic coast of Spain to India, Burma, China, Korea, the Philippines, and the islands of the South Pacific. The Kamehameha is a forest dweller and is often seen on mountaintops and occasionally near beaches.

The Galapagos Islands

Since Charles Darwin's five-week visit in 1835, the Galapagos Islands have fascinated biologists as a natural laboratory for studies of evolutionary and ecological phenomena. The spectacular giant tortoises, Darwin's finches, and other strange animals that have evolved here attract thousands of visitors each year. This cluster of volcanic islands, located on the equator some 600 miles off the coast of Ecuador, presents unique biogeographical problems: the establishment of new forms of plants and animals is severely limited by the great distance from South America, strongly shifting oceanic and wind currents, and the harsh environment of the islands themselves. The lowland shores are desert, where only a few plants such as cacti grow and where flowing water in the form of streams or springs is nonexistent. In the highlands, which reach 5500 feet, daily cloud cover and drizzling rain is common. Only 600 species of plants have become established in the islands; and so the available habitats are not particularly hospitable to butterflies arriving as migrants from the mainland of South America.

The small number of butterflies found in the Galapagos, despite much scientific collecting in the past century and a half, is reflected in other insect populations as well. As of 1968, only 656 insect species were known from all the islands. The Lepidoptera are a major group, with ninety-seven species, including ten species of butterflies. No group of butterflies or moths has proceeded to evolve new species in the Galapagos; all groups now represented originated on the mainland, and relatively few butterflies have had sufficient time even to develop distinctive subspecies in the islands. Three butterflies are found only on these islands: the Galapagos gulf fritillary (*Agraulis vanillae galapagensis*), a dwarfed subspecies of a tropical American nymphalid, which occurs on nine of the islands; the sole native species, Wallengren's blue (*Leptotes parrhasioides*), which has been found on ten islands and is reasonably abundant at all seasons; and the Galapagos short-tailed skipper (*Urbanus dorantes galapagensis*), recorded from ten islands, which is a dwarfed race of a common mainland species of long-tailed skipper. The other seven species of butterflies found in the Galapagos have apparently become established through rare strays arriving on wind currents from the mainland. One of these, a large yellow sulphur, *Phoebis sennae*, is presently evolving a dwarfed race on several of the islands, with interesting rearrangements of the genetic material in its chromosomes accompanying the changes in wing size.

Scientific research on the adaptations, speciation and evolution of island butterflies is only just beginning. Studies of island butterflies that show major divergences from presumably ancestral populations on the mainland may prove as important as the theories of adaptive radiation of species that Darwin based on the finches and tortoises of the Galapagos. The problem of evolution in the spectacularly variable *Ornithoptera* swallowtails of the South Pacific is particularly challenging to biologists. But their story will only be a small part of the immense task of uncovering how butterflies colonized and evolved from a limited genetic stock in the many archipelagoes of both the Caribbean and the Pacific.

296. The lush tropical landscape of Moorea in the Society Islands of the South Pacific abound with spectacularly colored swallowtails as well as many danaids and satyrs. Other islands such as the Galapagos and many coral atolls are dry and desert-like, supporting few types of butterflies.

297.

298.

297-299. On Caribbean islands such as Trinidad and Tobago, which lie close to South America, many of the island populations originated as waifs blown over from the mainland. The satyrid Euptychia terrestris *(297) and other* Euptychia *species (298) are found all the way from eastern Ecuador across the Amazon basin and nine miles over the sea to Trinidad, while other deep-forested species such as the ithomiid* Godyris zavaletta *(299) seemingly cannot cross the water gap.*

300-315. Tropical swallowtails reach their peak of diversity on the islands of the South Pacific and Asia. The Ornithoptera *birdwings with their huge size and brilliant colors are the most spectacular (304-306). Delicate lycaenids and beautiful nymphs and skippers are also abundant on the islands of the world.*

*316. The red lacewing (*Cethosia chrysippe*) is a lovely nymphalid from Papua, in southeastern New Guinea.*

*317. The yellow migrant (*Catopsilia scylla gorgophone*), a common pierid in northern Australia, occasionally reaches New Guinea. One of its relatives, the lemon migrant (*Catopsilia pomona*), ranges from Australia through New Guinea and the Moluccas to the Solomon Islands. Both butterflies are prolific breeders and frequently make mass migrations, establishing new colonies.*

00. Papilio euchenor: *New Guinea*

304. Ornithoptera priamus poseidon: *New Guinea*

301. Troides oblongomaculatus: *New Guinea*

305. Troides amphrysus flavicollis: *Borneo*

302. Papilio polymnestor: *Ceylon*

306. Trogonoptera brookiana: *Borneo*

303. Papilio aegeus ormenus: *New Guinea*

307. Papilio ulysses autolycus: *New Guinea*

308. Pyrgus oileus: *West Indies*

312. Victorina steneles: *Trinidad*

309. Laxita damajanti: *Borneo*

313. Tenaris artemis: *New Guinea*

310. Megistanis baeotus: *Costa Rica*

314. Dryas julia: *West Indies*

311. Hypolycaena erylus: *Borneo*

315. Heliconius aliphera: *Trinidad*

Part Three

Butterflies and Man

An extraordinary English butterfly was discovered at Huntingdon in the Marshy Fens area in 1790, a creature of tropical splendor, far more colorful than most of the other butterflies of the British Isles. With its large wings shining like red-gold fire and its undersides bathed in a beautiful light blue, the large copper *(Lycaena dispar dispar)* quickly attracted collectors and then commercial interest. By the early 1800s, the butterfly had become valuable and was often offered for sale by dealers in London. The residents of the Fens learned that money could be made by collecting both butterflies and caterpillars from the leaves of the great water dock and selling them. The butterfly could not stand this hunting pressure. After the summer of 1849, the glorious large copper was no longer to be seen except in specimen cabinets.

Butterflies and man have been associated in peculiar and sometimes fascinating ways from the beginning of recorded history. Poets, musicians, artists, writers, collectors, dealers, merchants and scientists, have all sought inspiration, pleasure, meaning, facts and money from these fragile insects. Thus, butterflies have become an integral part of recorded history, legend, literature and lore.

More recently, however, butterflies have also become useful in the general sciences, particularly in biology, where evolution is being studied through the analysis of color variations in many individuals of a species collected in one locality. In their studies of butterfly life cycles, lepidopterists have also made interesting discoveries concerning the selection of food plants and the remarkable changes that take place during the metamorphosis from egg to adult.

By the 1940s, butterflies were being bred in captivity to study the inheritance of mimetic forms. Similarly, as more land is cleared for development and the natural habitats of many butterflies have been eliminated, scientists have turned to the study of the increasing number of extinct and vanishing species. A butterfly with a limited range and small population is vulnerable to any sudden change in climate; a series of unusually cold or dry years or a period of heavy storms may eliminate the species forever. Thus, Schaus's swallowtail *(Papilio aristodemus ponceanus)*, a large yellow and chocolate-colored butterfly resembling the giant swallowtail of the southern United States, was first described in 1911 from specimens collected in Brickell Hammock near Miami, Florida. As the city expanded the swallowtail was soon exterminated. Rediscovered on the hard-wood hammocks of the northern Florida Keys, it became celebrated as the rarest swallowtail in the United States, with as much as $150 being paid for a pair. The September 1938 hurricane that swept across the Keys was thought to have wiped out the last colony, but occasional captures of the swallowtail up through the 1960s showed that it was still surviving in a few of the hammocks. In 1972, two lepidopterists found that the butterfly was still living along nine miles of the northern part of Key Largo and on at least two of the islands in Biscayne National Monument, off the southern tip of Florida. Today, this swallowtail is again threatened— by developers who are clearing the hardwood forest for housing and commerce.

Florida, because of its explosive development over the last half century, has provided a series of case histories in the tragedy of man's impact on the natural world. Another great rarity in the state is the Atala butterfly (Eumaeus atala), a large tailless hairstreak with an orange abdomen, iridescent blue-green forewings, and shimmering spots on its jet-black hindwings. In the 1920s, it, too, was quite common in hardwood hammocks in the Miami area and on some of the southern Florida Keys. By 1933, however, only one mainland population was known; soon after that it apparently became extinct. Atala caterpillars fed on a fernlike cycad called "Coontie" (Zamia integrifolia), stands of which were devastated when rural areas were cleared for development. In February 1959, a small colony of Atala was rediscovered in southeastern Florida. George Rawson, a Floridian, made two attempts in the early 1960s to establish a new breeding colony in Everglades National Park by transferring seventy-five of the butterflies that had been reared from eggs laid in captivity. The first experiment was destroyed by a hurricane; in the second release, the butterflies failed to breed. At present the Atala butterflies continue their precarious existence outside the park.

Some butterflies, however, are rare for reasons other than man's works, usually because of extremely localized habitats, or the scarcity of a particular food plant. One of the rarest of all North American butterflies is Minor's swallowtail, a black subspecies of Papilio indra with narrow yellow bands across the wings, which was found in the 1930s in the wild mesa country of western Colorado. This race was named Papilio indra minori for its discoverer, Will C. Minor, a lepidopterist and sheepherder from Fruita, Colorado. Since that time, only several dozen adult specimens in good condition have been collected in the wild. In part, this results from the butterfly's occurrence in limited numbers and in rugged and inaccessible canyon country. A further factor is that the males of the species are extraordinarily belligerent and attack each other until their wings are battered and torn. Minor was once offered $25 each for pairs of perfect specimens, but on the day he and another collector went up to Black Ridge to get freshly emerged butterflies, they could only stand helplessly by and watch the valuable butterflies made worthless as pugnacious male pairs battled furiously above the edge of a cliff. When they finally netted a male, the wings had pieces missing,

and one leg and an antenna were gone.

My own field work in western Colorado since 1963, with my brother John F. Emmel, has uncovered other populations of Minor's swallowtail and revealed more details of its life history. Part of the reason for the rarity of the species may be the scarcity of its chosen food plant, Lomatium eastwoodae, a tiny member of the carrot family known only from the western mesa country of Colorado. Despite the fact that other, larger plants in this family grow in abundance on the same mesas, the butterfly prefers to feed on Lomatium.

The increasing interest and appreciation of butterflies has stimulated efforts not only to conserve habitats, but also to help spread rare butterflies into new ranges by artificial means. This procedure has provided a pleasant postscript to the extinction of the large copper in England. Because the main racial stock of the large copper is widespread on the European continent, several attempts were made to reintroduce the butterfly into England. A smaller and less colorful subspecies, rutilus, from Germany, France and parts of eastern Europe, was successfully established in southern Ireland when Captain E. B. Purefoy introduced about 400 fertile continental females in 1913 and 1914. Then, in 1915, English entomologists were excited to learn of the discovery of a new race of the large copper (Lycaena dispar batava) in the Netherlands. These Dutch "fire butterflies" closely resembled the extinct British large copper both in size and in the brilliance of their coloring. Using thirty-eight butterflies, a successful introduction of this Dutch race into England's Wood Walton Fen was completed in 1927, after extensive preparation of a bog site. Following a wet winter that flooded the Fen, the first large copper emerged June 29, 1928, and spread its brilliant wings in the sunshine of its new homeland. This colony has rapidly increased. One hundred pupae were sent back to Holland in 1931 to help restock a Dutch reserve that had been established to save Holland's large copper butterfly from extinction through overcollecting.

Other accounts of butterflies that have become extinct do not end so happily. Two well-known extinct butterflies were once inhabitants of the peninsula now occupied by the city of San Francisco. One, Boisduval's satyr (Cercyonis sthenele), a small brown butterfly with bold white markings and eye-spots on its undersides, was named by Boisduval, a famous French lepidopterist, in 1852 from material collected by a Gold Rush miner, Pierre Lorquin. According to contemporary accounts, it flew in fair abundance over the sand hills of the San Francisco peninsula. The rapid growth of the city destroyed much of its habitat, but oddly enough, it disappeared in about 1880 while open land still remained. Its decline and extinction happened so quickly that few specimens were preserved, and the largest series, in the California Academy of Sciences museum, was destroyed by fire after the 1906 earthquake. The early stages of its life history were never recorded. It probably fed on native grasses which were threatened by overgrazing and periodic fires as the city grew.

The other San Francisco butterfly exterminated by man's activities is the Xerces blue *(Glaucopsyche xerces)*. This beautifully spotted lycaenid persisted a little longer in the vacant lots of the Sunset District, the Lake Merced area, the Presidio and Fort Funston. The last known specimens were collected in 1941 from one surviving colony, in an area measuring 65 by 140 feet. Since then, numerous lepidopterists have searched unsuccessfully for other populations. Xerces would have made a unique tool for studies of the effects of population size and restricted geographical distribution on genetic variation. It was an incredibly variable species in its wing patterns and spotting, a condition that showed a remarkable level of genetic mutations in these populations. Described by Boisduval in 1852, Xerces was first reported to be extinct in 1884 by W. H. Edwards, an authority on North American butterflies. Apparently the forms with heavily black-centered white spots on the wings *("antiacis")* were then in the majority for the next thirty years. The white-spotted forms (true *"xerces"*) were extremely rare until about 1906. The white-spotted Xerces became relatively predominant again by 1911 and apparently was the more common form until the species disappeared thirty years later. The reasons for these rather dramatically rapid evolutionary changes in pattern are unknown.

Butterflies and Research

Since the days of the great nineteenth-century naturalists Darwin, Bates, and Wallace, butterflies have continued to provide the bulk of evidence for the action of natural selection in establishing mimicry complexes. Recently, two leading English geneticists, C. A. Clarke and P. M. Sheppard, worked out the genetic mechanisms that control patterns in Batesian and Müllerian complexes of butterflies, and developed wide-ranging principles of evolutionary mechanisms that can even be applied to man's evolution. Until the studies of two English biologists on certain satyr populations on the Isles of Scilly in the English Channel, it was not known that natural selection would remove more than a fraction of one percent of any animal population at a single generation. But these scientists found that changes caused by intense evolutionary selection removed 60 percent or more of butterflies with genes that produced particular spotting patterns on their wings.

In the United States, the leading population biologist and an outspoken advocate of human population control, Paul R. Ehrlich of Stanford University, has uncovered various principles of population regulation by studying wild butterfly populations in California and Colorado. His long-term studies have yielded conclusions of major importance to population ecology. Ehrlich and his students have been conducting research in Panama and Costa Rica on how tropical grasses protect themselves from butterflies and other insects, hoping to discover useful methods for reducing the impact of temperate zone pests on grain crops.

Butterflies have become valuable in studies of population biology and geographic distribution. They are large enough to be readily seen and handled in the field, and are easy to rear and study in the laboratory, mark, observe, and collect. Lately, the structure of their chromosomes is being studied for information on genetics. Current studies of species that can retain poisonous alkaloids in their bodies may enable man to find more efficient but ecologically harmless pesticides to use against destructive insects.

Commercial Collecting

In the nineteenth century, when collectors such as Bates and Wallace were sending back strange new butterflies from remote regions, at times risking their lives among savage tribes, enduring hazardous living conditions and primitive transportation, foreign butterflies fetched high prices from collectors. Butterfly auctions were held regularly in the famous sale center for natural history specimens, London's Covent Garden, from 1818 through the Second World War. Thousands of insects along with tens of thousands of English pounds changed hands under the auctioneer's gavel.

Many of those collectors were military men and administrators who had served in the colonies and later retired to their "cabinets of specimens." Others were clergymen and doctors who had sufficient money and leisure to devote themselves to their hobby, but were persuaded to sell their collections. Substantial prices have been paid for historic rarities, particularly for exceptional varieties of English species. Two marbled whites, one an entirely white insect and the other a black specimen, have been known to English buyers for more than a century. The albino was caught by Thomas Marshall in July 1843 on the cliffs between Dover and Walmer in Kent, and was sold for twenty pounds at auction in the same year. In a 1943 auction the specimen brought forty-nine pounds. The black butterfly was also taken in Kent on July 16, 1871, and its first auction sale netted forty-two pounds. A later purchase united these two unique specimens in one private collection. At the end of the Second World War, the pair was sold for more than one hundred pounds, or about four hundred and fifty dollars. In

1974 a perfect pair of the spectacular Alexandra birdwing, reared in captivity, was offered for sale at $184 by the Queensland Butterfly Company in Australia. But relatively few collectors make their living from selling butterflies today. Most of these enthusiasts prefer to collect their own specimens or trade material with other collectors in various parts of the world.

The commercialization of butterflies for decoration, however, has lately expanded greatly and now resembles the craze for using bird feathers on women's hats around the turn of this century. Most of the specimens now being sold in picture frames and shadow boxes in department stores and gift shops are imported in huge quantities from Brazil and Taiwan, and in smaller but significant numbers from Mexico, Hong Kong, Malaysia, and Singapore. Ordinary farmers and game hunters find that butterfly collecting can supplement their regular income, especially when they face a slack season. Sometimes collecting has its surprising aspects. Prisoners in the French penal colonies of Saint-Laurent in French Guiana were hired by guard officers to catch butterfly specimens for traders. The prisoners may not have been butterfly enthusiasts but collecting gave them great relief from the monotony of work parties and prison routines, and a chance for meaningful exercise. A few ingenious ones used collecting for another aim: escape. Collectors are only the first link in a commercial chain. In Brazil, specimens are stored in paper envelopes and then sold to a buyer who comes upriver from a larger town on regular purchasing trips. Eventually the butterflies reach small factories in Rio de Janeiro where the wings are usually removed from the delicate dried bodies and glued to an artificial body. The wings themselves are used in creating designs on trays, jewelry, and pictures. Some are sold in local shops, but great quantities are exported for sale in the United States. Similar techniques are used in Taiwan, Mexico, and other tropical countries where the butterflies are attractive and abundant. The impact of such massive collecting on local butterfly populations is considerable. One well-known dealer on Taiwan has advertised that she has more than twenty million specimens available. In Brazil and Peru, strict laws have been passed to control commercial collecting of morphos and other species, an act which has reduced the exploitation of wild populations and encouraged the development of butterfly farms and the breeding of butterflies used in art work.

Winston Churchill was fascinated by butterflies in his youth. His interest was rekindled in 1939 when he visited the famous Butterfly Farm in Kent, run since 1894 by Leonard Woods Newman and his son

Great Collectors and Famous Collections

L. Hugh Newman. After World War II, Churchill commissioned the Newmans to stock his garden at Chartwell with butterflies and their food plants. He even had a special butterfly house constructed in the garden for growing caterpillars and adults. A few years later, Churchill and Hugh Newman attempted to introduce the black-veined white from Europe at Churchill's Chartwell estate, but the experiment failed.

Churchill's interest in butterflies was very strong but it was that of an amateur, not a scientist. The first great student of butterfly classification was Carolus Linnaeus (1707-1778), the founder of systematic biology. He is famous for developing a scheme by which every animal and plant was assigned to a category—class, order, family, genus, species—a system later universally used in the scientific naming of plants and animals. He placed all butterflies in the world, from his native Sweden to tropical America, in the genus *Papilio*, a decision that was soon modified by other scientists. Another eighteenth-century scientist, Pierre André Latreille (1762-1833), described many new kinds of butterflies sent to him by collectors from around the world and has been called the "Prince of Entomologists." England's contribution to the ranks of great lepidopterists was John Obadiah Westwood (1805-1893).

In the United States, Samuel H. Scudder (1837-1911) became America's first widely recognized lepidopterist with the publication in 1889 of his three-volume work, *The Butterflies of Eastern North America and Canada*. Almost simultaneously, William Henry Edwards finished the serial publication of his *The Butterflies of North America*. Meticuously illustrated with color plates of life histories and adults, these books stimulated much interest in butterflies.

Andrew Carnegie, the American industrialist, was obsessed with the idea of expanding public knowledge through a network of libraries throughout the country. In 1895, the first part of his dream came true when the Carnegie Library was opened, later to become the Carnegie Institute. And by great good fortune, one of the best known and most distinguished lepidopterists in America, Dr. William J. Holland, was named the institute's first director. Holland's own butterfly collection, which became part of the institute's property, included William Henry Edwards's collection of butterflies of North America, an important grouping of the types of specimens illustrated in Edwards's three books. Holland, a minister in his earlier years, had persuaded a number of collectors and missionary acquaintances to collect extensively for him in Africa, Asia, the Himalaya, Burma, and South and Central America.

The work of these men, although often directed mainly at collecting, enriched modern knowledge of butterflies by the thoroughness with which the butterflies were collected, categorized, and brought together for the benefit of all men of science. André Avinoff, in particular, another famous Carnegie Museum director, made a great contribution to entomology and science in general by his systematic pursuit and study of butterflies. He was a Russian-born lepidopterist who was Gentleman-in-Waiting to Czar Nicholas before the Revolution of 1917. He built up one of the largest private collections of butterflies and moths in Europe, including 10,000 Apollos and 10,000 *Colias* sulphurs. His butterflies and moths were nationalized after the Revolution and now are in the Leningrad Academy of Science. The really notable feature of this collection was the huge numbers of specimens from remote and little-collected areas of Europe as well as the arctic and temperate areas of Asia. The son of a Russian general, Avinoff became interested in insects during a boyhood journey to Tashkent. He became a lawyer, but butterflies and moths were his passion, and starting in 1906 he financed forty collecting parties throughout Asia, and also hunted butterflies in India, Tibet, and Chinese Turkestan. He received many honors before his collections were seized during the Russian Revolution.

Harry K. Clench, who became Curator of Lepidoptera at the Carnegie Museum in the early 1950s continued to expand the worldwide holdings of the museum, and today Carnegie is noted for its peerless collections of lycaenids, metalmarks, and African butterflies.

Churchill represented the dilettante butterfly lover and Avinoff the true professional, but Vladimir Nabokov is another kind of lepidopterist, a man who became famous in both literature and the science of butterflies. For several years, he worked as Research Fellow in Entomology at Harvard and is the author of several scientific papers on the taxonomy of certain butterflies. Nabokov began collecting butterflies during his boyhood in Russia, and for six decades has chased and classified butterflies on both sides of the Atlantic. His devotion has been rewarded by his discovery—and naming—of several new species and subspecies in the western United States. The depth of that devotion is revealed in his book *Speak, Memory* when he says, "From the age of seven, everything I felt in connection with a rectangle of framed sunlight was dominated by a single passion. If my first glance of the morning was for the sun, my first thought was for the butterflies it would engender."

Nabokov's parents both studied Lepidoptera as a hobby and encouraged their son's interest with gifts of books and equipment. The intellectual delights of studying butterflies has stayed with him ever since.

At times his feelings transcended the worldly, reaching toward an almost mystical view of beauty. "This is ecstasy," he once wrote about the experience of standing alone in green woods among rare butterflies, "and behind the ecstasy is something else, which is hard to explain. It is like a momentary vacuum into which rushes all that I love. A sense of oneness with sun and stone. A thrill of gratitude to whom it may concern—to the contrapuntal genius of human fate or to tender ghosts humoring a lucky mortal."

Another butterfly lover was a famous athlete. The Australian long-distance runner, John Landy, the second man to run a four-minute mile, was, if nothing else, surely the fastest collector on earth. During the 1950s, he carried his net along on his daily practice runs and he credited his lifelong interest in the pursuit of butterflies with helping him develop into a champion miler.

In the United States, a distinctive feature of butterfly collecting has been the melding of private and public collections for the benefit of all. Donations from private collectors to nearly all the great public collections, particularly those in the National Museum at the Smithsonian Institution in Washington D.C., the American Museum of Natural History in New York, and the Allyn Museum of Entomology at Sarasota, Florida, have made them the biggest collections of species in the world.

One of the most splendid donations of a private collection came from Dr. William Barnes, a surgeon from Decatur, Illinois, who had many agents collecting for him around the world. His entire collection went to the National Museum. A lifelong enthusiast, he housed his hundreds of thousands of Lepidoptera in a specially constructed fireproof building with air-conditioning and humidity control. After his death in 1930, the United States Government bought his collection for $50,000, far less than its actual value, and moved it to the National Museum in a special railroad car. Two entomologists worked for fourteen days with 473,293 insect pins so that no valuable specimen would jar loose and be damaged in the move. The National Museum continues to receive major donations; in 1973 the Wilbur S. McAlpine Collection of over 12,000 specimens, primarily metalmarks, and the E. J. Newcomer collection of nearly 3000 Washington butterflies, particularly the *Speyeria* fritillaries of that area, came to the Smithsonian.

Each large collection has unique features. The American Museum of Natural History is noted for its many historic collections of North American butterflies. It has excellent coverage of the American tropics and its representation from other regions of the world is extremely large. One of the most complete collections of the giant skippers ever made—about 2353 specimens—came to the museum from H. A. Freeman of Texas in 1970.

Collecting for its own sake has no particular value in some fields, but it is invaluable in the study of butterflies. The greater the range of specimens, and species, the more readily scientists can work on minute variations and make refined comparisons. The Allyn Museum, which already has more than 500,000 butterflies from all areas of the world, is still rapidly expanding its collection. It was founded in 1969 by Arthur C. Allyn, a Chicago investment banker and the owner of a baseball team, with the aim of building up the best butterfly collection in the Americas. It often buys large private collections, and its acquisition of the fine collection in France of Eugene Le Moult was one of its triumphs. The museum also supports collectors and professional expeditions in little-studied portions of the tropics.

Abroad, the British Museum of Natural History has several million butterfly specimens, the largest collection in the world. Most of the great private insect collections accumulated by citizens of England and her former colonies, from Australia to Africa, have been deposited there. France's Muséum National d'Histoire Naturelle, in Paris, also has extensive collections of butterflies from all over the world. Other great national collections of butterflies are housed in Australia, Germany, South Africa, Kenya, India, Rhodesia, and Canada.

The merging of the work of amateur butterfly enthusiasts with that of professional entomologists continues apace. Although many collectors still simply catch butterflies and file them away like postage stamps in an album, increasing numbers are taking their hobbies a step further. They specialize in collecting only certain butterfly families, which eventually may be useful to science. Others specialize in working in previously unsurveyed wilderness areas. Other amateurs have made valuable studies of the complete life histories of single species and have thus become the first human beings to observe such a cycle. It is work that yields both satisfaction and excitement.

Such people may also be part of an important network of amateur cooperation with scientists. One of the most valuable of these has been a study of the migrating habits of monarchs, organized by Fred Urquhart of the Royal Ontario Museum. He devised an ingenious method of tagging butterflies in Canada and then persuaded hundreds of amateur collectors in the central and southern regions of the United States to hunt down these tagged specimens, as well as tag other monarchs, and report back to him. The result has been a fascinating contribution toward the solution of the mysteries of migration.

Observations of the social activities of butterflies, such as mud puddle groups, courtship displays, and mating habits, may be made by anyone with sufficient patience for quiet observation on a spring or summer day. Even studying butterflies and their caterpillars as they go about their daily movements, reacting to predators or parasites, laying eggs, or being attended by ants on their food plant may result in discoveries new to science.

Fossil Butterflies

It is astonishing that creatures as fragile as butterflies could have been preserved for millions of years as fossils, yet no fewer than seven species have been dug up from the 35-million-year-old shales at Florissant, Colorado. This is the greatest yield from any fossil bed and only two less than all those collected in European deposits. Five of the seven Florissant fossil butterflies belong to the family Nymphalidae, whereas only one European fossil is a nymphalid. One of the others belongs to the Pieridae, a family represented in European fossil deposits by three species. The seventh American species belongs to the small, nearly extinct snout butterfly family, the Libytheidae. The satyrs and the skippers each have two representatives in the European shales, while the swallowtails have a single fossil species—in the beds at Aix, France.
The most interesting fact about these fossil butterflies is that they are remarkably modern in general appearance even though considered to be species of extinct genera. Thus for over 35 million years the structural differences peculiar to most of the modern families were already in existence. This finding suggests that there was either great acceleration in evolutionary development when butterflies first appeared or that butterflies existed at a far earlier age than we know from fossil evidence.

The Useful and the Harmful

Although most butterflies are a pleasure to man, some species devastate crops and gardens. All Lepidoptera develop from plant-eating larvae and most of the great pests are moths, but some butterfly caterpillars are also harmful to gardens and crops. Foremost among these is the cabbage butterfly *(Pieris rapae)*, from the Old World temperate zone. It was accidentally introduced into North America in 1887, probably on imported plants, and rapidly spread across the continent. Reaching Australia in 1939, it spread from Victoria through the rest of the country in less than five years. The cabbage white's caterpillars eat crops of cabbage, cauliflower, and mustards, and even watercress and nasturtium.
Serious outbreaks of *Colias* sulphur butterflies strike clover and alfalfa fields in North and South America, as well as in South Africa. Several swallowtails around the world feed on citrus trees and occasionally become minor pests in Florida, South Africa, and Australia. The pine white *(Neophasia menapia)* of western North America is one of the few forest

butterflies that does economic damage, sometimes defoliating extensive areas of pines. A few of the hairstreaks and other butterflies eat ornamental garden plants, such as wisteria vines, and the long-tailed skipper *(Urbanus proteus)* is a minor pest on beans in the southern United States.

The skipper *Thymelicus lineola*, originally a native of Europe where it feeds on wild grasses, was accidentally introduced into Canada about 1910. Lacking its normal enemies in this new environment, it shortly became a major pest of hayfields and pastures, and has more recently spread into the United States. The fiery skipper *(Hylephila phyleus)* feeds on lawn grasses in California and is now causing concern in Hawaii, where, as noted earlier, it appeared in 1970.

On the positive side of the economic balance sheet, butterflies, together with bees and some flies, are extremely important pollinators of flowering plants. In some areas such as the Galapagos Islands, where only one species of bee occurs, butterflies are the only significant pollinators for many plants.

In tropical forests, adult butterflies are notable scavengers on fruit and droppings of many kinds and help to recycle the organic nutrients in these materials. Their caterpillars eat plant tissues, excreting nutrient-rich droppings that decompose into soil. Plant roots absorb the released nutrients and build new leaves, thus completing the recycling of the minerals.

Finally, all stages of the butterfly life cycle, particularly caterpillars and adults, form an important part of the diet of countless species of birds, lizards, fish, small mammals and predacious insects around the world.

Pesticides and Urban Expansion

The spraying of roadsides with herbicides and of crops with insecticides takes a tremendous toll of butterflies each year. In many areas of the north-eastern United States, lepidopterists have recorded ominous plunges in population levels, often associated with spraying, during the past ten years.

More dramatically, over 600 species of the rich and exotic butterfly fauna in Sikkim, an Indian state in the Himalaya, were nearly wiped out in a wide area because meadows and marshlands were sprayed a few years ago with DDT. The insecticide treatment temporarily reduces the number of malarial mosquitoes, and sometimes wipes them out, but its effect on all but the most hardy butterflies is catastrophic. Few butterfly species have become extinct in historic times but the chemical control of injurious insects promises to wipe out hundreds of species if the spraying is continued at its present level.

The world shortage of food means new agricultural areas are being mapped for development, which will result in further extensions of the insecticide and herbicide programs. The butterflies will, of course, suffer along with all the rest of the useful and harmful insects.

The expansion of the city of San Francisco is one example of urbanization that gives sobering evidence of the destructive nature of civilization on natural history. But in almost every area of the world, natural habitats are being lost to expanding cities and farms. The draining of bogs in Colorado, the damming and flooding of mountain canyons, the chopping and burning of butterfly food plants that grow along roadsides, all these add to the feeling that our world and that of the butterflies is inevitably changing for the worse.

In man's war against insect pests, butterflies are simply innocent casualties; nobody really wants to see them killed. It must by now be clear that the world of living butterflies is an important one, both for the benefit they bestow as plant pollinators and sources of food and for the matchless aesthetic pleasure they can give to us and our descendants. One might even say that a world safe for butterflies is a world safe for Man.

How to Collect Butterflies

Assembling a butterfly collection also provides a way to learn their classification and habits as well as many of the basic principles of biology. Irresponsible collecting, however, has contributed to the near extinction of some species of butterflies. Often more can be learned by carefully observing the butterfly in its natural surroundings, noting its food plants and keeping a record of its life history.

Equipment

To start a butterfly collection, the following basic equipment is necessary: net, killing bottles, forceps, envelopes, insect pins, spreading boards, and storage boxes for specimens. The forceps and insect pins must be purchased; the other items are also available from commercial supply houses, but they can be homemade. The preferred type of net has a relatively wide diameter, 15 to 18 inches, and a 36-inch handle. The net bag, about 30 inches deep, can be made of nylon, bobbinet, or even mosquito netting or cheesecloth, but the tougher materials last longer. It should be dyed a dull green or brown. At least one spare net bag is usually needed to replace inevitable losses from encounters with barbed wire or snags.

A killing jar is especially useful for dispatching small butterflies without damage to their scales, and it should also be used with "pinched" specimens.

A killing jar can be made by pouring half an inch of thick plaster of paris in the bottom of a wide-mouthed jar. After it dries, add a teaspoon of ethyl acetate (available at pharmacies) before departing on each field trip. Do not use carbon tetrachloride (its fumes cause liver damage in man) or chloroform or ether (they are too volatile and flammable). Commercially-made cyanide killing jars are available from supply houses; they last for several years and are quite effective, but are dangerous to children.

Stamp-collector tongs with broad flat tips are useful for handling specimens without damaging the wings. A pair that tapers to sharp, curved points can be used for holding antennae or legs.

Rectangular glassine envelopes from 2 to 5 inches in length are excellent for "papering" specimens in the field and storing them until they can be spread. These transparent envelopes (those without glue on the flaps are most useful) can be bought at any stamp and coin store. One can also fold triangles from various sizes of paper rectangles.

Use insect pins of standard length, with lacquer coating, firm heads, and a sharp point. They are inexpensive and are available from scientific supply houses. Size No. 3 is suitable for all but the bodies of the smallest butterflies; for the latter, No. 2 pins should be used.

Spreading boards are essential. The sloping side boards support the wings while the body is lodged in the center space. Balsa wood or soft pine are suitable materials, and boards of several sizes should be available to accommodate different sizes of butterflies.

Storage boxes must have tight-fitting lids and a bottom of cork or other material that will hold pins firmly but will not, like styrofoam, corrode them. Cigar boxes with two layers of cardboard in the bottom can serve as temporary housing, but it is best to invest in well-made wood boxes or glass-topped drawers. Unmounted specimens may be stored in glassine envelopes or triangles in a dry, tightly closed box until they are ready to be spread out. All specimens, spread or unspread, should be protected from insect pests and mold by means of a few paradichlorobenzene moth crystals or lumps placed in the storage box. Keeping specimens under glass on cotton is useful for special displays but not recommended for a general reference collection. It is too difficult to shift specimens safely in order to make room for additional species, whereas pinned specimens may be easily moved into new arrangements.

The two leading suppliers of insect-collecting equipment in the United States are: American Biological Supply Company, P.O. Box 3149, Baltimore, Maryland 21228; and Ward's Natural Science Establishment, P.O. Box 1712, Rochester, New York 14603. Either company will send a free catalog upon request. Many lepidopterists in Britain and Europe order supplies from Worldwide Butterflies Ltd., Compton, Sherborne, Dorset, England. This company also has superb offerings of living material from all over the world, and carries an excellent selection of recent books on butterflies.

Collecting Techniques

Many cartoons notwithstanding, a careful stalk and a rapid sweep of the net is almost always more successful than a wild chase after a specimen. Once the butterfly is in the net, a quick flip of the tip of the net over the rim will "lock in" the specimen and prevent its escape. When the butterfly has its wings over its back, it should, while it is still in the netting, be given a firm pinch at the base of the wings where they meet the thorax. This pressure will stun the specimen and, in fact, will kill medium or small butterflies immediately. Larger butterflies such as swallowtails may have to be pinched several times before they expire. However, with lycaenids and metalmarks the best results are achieved if a killing jar is put around the living insect and no attempt is made to handle or pinch these delicate forms. When the specimen has been dispatched, it should be gently dropped into a glassine envelope. A convenient carrying container for envelopes is a metal box with a leather loop attached to the back by small bolts. This may be worn on a belt or placed in a side bag, and will hold scores of butterfly envelopes.

Another collecting method calls for baiting the butterflies with rotting fruit, animal dung, or other odoriferous materials. Such bait attracts many species while the collector is searching elsewhere. When approaching a gathering of butterflies on the bait, many collectors suspend the inverted net bag over the assemblage, with the rim only an inch or two above the ground. Butterflies will crawl under the rim to get to the bait, and when finished feeding they invariably fly up and become trapped in the closed end of the net. Bait traps of this type can be left in the forest and checked daily.

Many lepidopterists have discovered that searching for the eggs or caterpillars of butterflies is quite rewarding because these can then be used to rear a perfect series of adults. This also allows the collector an opportunity to observe their life histories in close detail. One technique is to follow an egg-laying female and collect her eggs as they are deposited. It is important to be ecologically responsible and not collect so many specimens of a population as to endanger its continued existence at that site.

Spreading

Butterflies that have dried out by the time they are brought home, or that have been received in the mail from another collector, become brittle and must be treated before they can be spread. When the wings will not move, the body muscles can be relaxed by leaving the butterfly for several days in an airtight humid chamber such as a small glass baking dish. Place paper toweling over a layer of cotton in the bottom of the dish, pour in some paradichlorobenzene or napthalene to discourage mold, and wet the cotton thoroughly with hot water. Arrange the papered or dry specimens on a plastic screen to prevent direct contact with the dampness. After one or two days, when the humidity has thoroughly relaxed the muscles of the specimens and softened the wings, antennae, and legs so that they can be moved about without damage, the butterflies are ready to be mounted on the spreading board.

First, thrust the proper insect pin (usually size No. 3) through the center of the butterfly's mesothorax parallel to the sides of its body. Continue penetrating vertically until the head of the pin is only half an inch above the thorax. Now pin the specimen into the center groove of the spreading board.

Place a broad strip of paper next to each pair of wings on either side of the center groove. Holding the ends of one strip, push the wings under it down against the board and fasten the strip with a pin at both ends. Repeat with the pair of wings on the opposite side.

Then place pins on both sides of the abdomen in the center groove so that the body will not pivot during the next procedure. On the left-hand side, insert a fine insect pin (No. 0 or 1 size) behind one of the main veins along the front of the forewing and move the wing forward until the trailing edge is lined up at a

right angle (90°) with the body axis. Push the pin
gently into the board. Then move up the left hindwing
with a second pin in the same way until a "notch" is
opened between the outer adjoining edges of the two
wings. When both wings are properly positioned, pull
the paper strip tight and fasten it in place with pins
around the outside of each of the wings. Then remove
the fine pins originally used to move the wings into
place, and repeat the whole procedure with the right-
hand pair of wings.

When finished with the wings, pin the antennae into
place in front of the head, each between two crossed
pins. Use other pins, if needed, to untwist the head
and place it in a horizontal position. Pin the data
directly beneath each specimen in order to record all
pertinent details of where the butterfly was caught.
Store the drying specimens in a cabinet or other
place where rodents, cockroaches, and ants cannot
eat them. Leave the specimens on the boards for at
least several days until they are thoroughly dry
(the abdomen should not wiggle when touched).

Labeling

The value of a collection depends on how carefully the
specimens are prepared and preserved and whether
they are labeled with adequate data. The label should
be printed in India ink on a small white card or a
rectangle of heavy bond paper. It should include the
Latin and common name of the butterfly, exact
location of its capture (with a reference to the nearest
landmark or town, the county or province, the state
and country), the altitude if it has been collected in a
mountainous area, date of collection, and the collector's
name. If it was reared from an egg or caterpillar, that
information and the name of the host plant should
also be included.

On spread specimens, the labels are placed on the
body pin about half an inch below the butterfly. One
should never depend solely on code numbers on the
pinned label referring to notebook data; a detailed
specimen label is far more reliable. It is desirable,
however, to keep notebook records of collecting
places that can be correlated with dates on the
pinned specimen labels.

Clubs and Societies

The international organization known as the Lepidopterists' Society publishes a quarterly *Journal of the
Lepidopterists' Society*, which contains many articles
on field collecting, new species descriptions, life histories and behavioral studies. The society also publishes a bimonthly *News of the Lepidopterists'
Society*, which contains notices of meetings, books and
specimens for sale or exchange, and short articles on
butterflies. Members also receive a list of the worldwide society membership, including each member's
particular interests in Lepidoptera and whether the
member is willing to exchange, buy, or sell specimens.

How to Photograph Butterflies

Photographing butterflies provides probably the greatest challenge of any type of nature photography. The hobby requires investment in a good camera as well as time, patience, and much practice to achieve satisfactory results, but the rewards can be great. The remarkable pictures in this book were taken by students, amateur and professional lepidopterists, and a few professional wildlife and nature photographers. Even with years of experience, however, outstanding results may come in only one out of many shots. Much depends upon luck and perseverance.

Most photographers specializing in candid nature close-ups prefer the 35mm single-lens reflex camera because it allows the photographer to view and focus the exact area that will be exposed on the film at the release of the shutter. This is accomplished by means of a hinged 45° mirror in front of the film, which reflects the picture image seen directly through the lens onto a ground glass. The mirror snaps out of the way an instant before the shutter opens to expose the film. The camera should be equipped with contacts for electronic flash units, a range of shutter speeds (at least 1/2 second to 1/1000 second), and a "fast" lens—one capable of opening the diaphragm to at least F2 for shots in dim light.

Double-lens reflex cameras and the many cameras with indirect viewfinders (that is, separate from the lens itself) do not allow the photographer to see precisely what he is photographing; with an insect that moves frequently, this is a major disadvantage. Larger cameras tend to be unwieldy.

When buying a lens for candid close-up work the photographer has two choices. He can use the regular F2.8, F2, F1.8, F1.4, or other 50mm lens normally supplied with a camera, along with a set of hollow extension tubes. The tubes are inserted between the lens and camera body, and allow a considerable increase in the image size of the subject on the film. Alternately, the photographer can purchase a 50-100mm macro lens (preferably an F3.5 or F4), which can be extended a considerable distance from the camera body on its own built-in extension mechanism. The advantage of a macro lens is that it does not require frequent addition of extension tubes, yet makes it possible to focus on an object at any distance. A preset macro lens can focus as close as 2 inches, giving 1:1 image size on the film as maximum reproduction. An automatic macro lens normally focuses down to 3 inches, giving only a 1:2 image size on the film—that is, only half as much magnification as the preset lens. Some photographers prefer the convenience of the automatic lens, which allows them to focus with the camera's diaphragm wide open so that the object can be viewed with maximum light, and then closes down to the correct setting at the last split second. I prefer the preset lens because of its greater range of reproduction capability.

A newer type of lens is the macro-zoom telephoto,

which can focus at any range from infinity down to 3 inches and at any focal length from 70mm to 210mm. This lens has a remarkable versatility, allowing the butterfly photographer to frame and take pictures at almost any distance from the subject. The disadvantages are its increased weight (making it more difficult to hand-hold), the possibility of frightening the butterfly with the large lens and sunshade, and some difficulty in adjusting the lens settings to allow proper illumination by an electronic flash that may have to be placed as much as several feet from the butterfly. But this lens is unexcelled for taking pictures of wary butterflies in sunlight.

Using 35 mm film, I prefer Kodachrome (ASA 25) for all flash pictures and most natural-light pictures, although high-speed Ektachrome (AS 160) has proven quite useful and given excellent results in natural-light shots in the dark interior of tropical rain forests. Processing should be done only by the finest photographic laboratories, to insure good color and consistent processing results.

Outstanding butterfly pictures can be made with natural sunlight. Inevitably, though, the photographer will find himself in many situations where the butterfly is constantly in motion or where the lighting is marginal or even too dark for a good picture. After a few such experiences, some photographers have tried what has justifiably been called "nature faking." The extreme form of this is to kill the butterfly, place it on a sunlit flower in a lifelike pose, and snap the photograph. Other artificial efforts include refrigerating or anesthetizing the butterfly until it cannot move. This practice is about as satisfactory as photographing a pressed flower. The most effective way to eliminate lighting and motion problems, as well as to increase the depth-of-focus range in extreme close-ups, is by using an electronic flash. I particularly like the Vivitar 181 model because it takes about 160 pictures before needing recharging, a convenient feature for intensive photography in the field. There are also many good battery-powered electronic flash units. Use the first roll of film with a new flash to determine the F-stop settings that give the best results at various flash-to-subject and camera-to-subject distances. Shutter speed remains on a special electronic flash setting, which is generally around 1/50 of a second. A simple rule of thumb is as follows: For Kodachrome (ASA 25) film, when the flash unit is held at the same distance as the camera from the subject, a diaphragm setting between F11 and F22 will give excellent exposures and depth of field. At such small F-stop settings, the background behind the butterfly will be very dark or dramatically black.

As with any other skill, much depends on common sense, improvisation, and learning from experience. But the prime requirement, besides proper equipment, is patience. One has to be prepared to creep up on an aggregation of butterflies around a mud puddle only to see an explosion of whirling wings in the viewfinder just before the shutter is clicked. It may then take half an hour for the butterflies to return and allow another picture attempt. In the end, regardless of the difficulties, photographic trophies from this kind of chase will undoubtedly prove far more memorable than a butterfly captured and pinned as a specimen in a collector's cabinet.

Characteristics of the Butterfly Families

		Legs	Feet
Skippers	**The Skippers (Family Hesperiidae)**	Six fully developed legs; inner side of front leg's tibia bears the epiphysis, a movable lobe largely covered with scales.	The normal five segments, with claws at tip.
	The Giant Skippers (Family Megathymidae)	Six fully developed legs.	The normal five segments, with claws at tip.
True Butterflies	**The Swallowtails (Family Papilionidae)**	Six functional legs in both sexes; the tibia of the front leg bears a spur called an epiphysis.	Five segments; tarsal claws single and simple in structure.
	The Whites and Yellows (Family Pieridae)	Six functional legs in both sexes; no epiphysis.	Five segments; tarsal claws are bifid (split into two parts).
	The Ithomiids (Family Ithomiidae)	Four walking legs; front pair greatly reduced in size.	Males have only one or two nonfunctioning tarsal segments, and females have moderately clubbed tarsal foot (with four or five segments) on front legs.
	The Danaids (Family Danaidae)	Front legs greatly reduced.	Male with greatly reduced tarsus; female with four-segmented tarsus on front leg that ends in a peculiar spiny knob.
	The Browns and Satyrs (Family Satyridae)	Great reduction of forelegs in both sexes, more so in the male.	Reduced to several segments.
	The Nymphalids (Family Nymphalidae)	Four walking legs, greatly reduced forelegs, brush-like in appearance.	One elongate segment in male, five segments in female; lacks any claws.
	The Snout Butterflies (Family Libytheidae)	Four walking legs in male, six in female (forelegs much reduced in former, but fully developed in latter).	In male, tarsus is brush-like and composed of only one segment, without claws; female has tarsus with five segments and two normal claws.
	The Blues, Coppers, and Hairstreaks (Family Lycaenidae)	Four walking legs (forelegs somewhat reduced) in the male, six in the female. No epiphysis projecting from tibia in either sex.	Reduced to one segment and one tarsal claw in the male, fully developed and functional in the female with five segments and two terminal claws.
	The Metalmarks (Family Riodinidae)	Four walking legs (front legs greatly reduced) in males, six in females. Part of the first leg segment (coxa) extends notably beyond the joint of the next segment (trochanter) on the reduced male forelegs.	One tarsal segment with single claw in male, five tarsal segments with paired claws in female.

Antennae	Head	Wings	Larvae
Strongly curved or hooked at the tip.	Almost as wide as thorax. Palpi not noticeably small.	Relatively small; narrow. All veins arising from the center "cell" of the forewing are straight and unbranched.	Usually dull-colored, lack spines and other ornaments, thorax portion behind the head is so slender that it looks like a neck.
Clubbed; not hooked.	Only half the width of the thorax. Palpi noticeably small.	Large; proportionately narrow and pointed forewings. Venation similar to the other skippers.	Generally similar to other skippers, but with body much larger than head; whitish color with no ornamentation. These larvae bore into the stems of century plants and yuccas.
Clubbed; not curved.	As wide as thorax. Palpi short.	The central (or discoidal) wing cell formed between the veins in both the forewings and hindwings is completely closed (i.e., the veins are joined) at the cell end closest to the body.	Varied in appearance; often has enlarged thoracic region in the younger stages. Possesses a thoracic scent organ (the osmaterium) to spray noxious chemicals; not present in other families.
Clubbed; not curved.	Almost as wide as thorax. Palpi short.	Wing venation differs according to genera, but almost all have the first medial vein moved forward as a branch off a radial vein; in other butterflies, the three medial veins arise directly from the discal cell.	Smooth, slender, cylindrical in form, rarely with tiny spines.
A gradually tapering club; scales on shaft.	Very narrow; less than half the width of thorax. Palpi short.	Leathery, tough; quite rounded at tips of forewings.	Smooth or occasionally hairy, often with flattened fleshy lateral projections on each body segment.
Strongly clubbed; no scales on shaft.	Almost as wide as thorax. Palpi short.	Leathery, tough; forewings pointed as in most other butterflies except for the ithomiids and some riodinids.	Generally smooth and cylindrical, with two to four pairs of fleshy filament-like tubercles protruding from the top of the thorax.
Gradual club; scales always present (at least near the base of the shaft).	About two-thirds the width of thorax. Palpi short, often shaggy.	Cells of forewings and hindwings closed by tubular veins; one or more of the principal forewing veins broaden into noticeable swellings toward the base.	Forked tail, with two anal projections on the eleventh abdominal segment. Larva is spindle-shaped, thicker at the middle and tapering to the ends.
Clubbed; always scaled.	Almost as wide as thorax. Palpi short.	Cell in hindwing is never closed by a tubular vein; and the forewing cell is also usually open.	Usually bear many branched spines over the body.
Clubbed; scaled.	Almost as wide as thorax. Very long beak-like palpi stretching forward as a "snout."	The cell in forewings and hindwings is closed by a tubular vein.	Smooth, slender, cylindrical body.
Clubbed; scaled. Eyes notched around bases of antennae.	Very narrow. Palpi short.	Several radius veins lacking in forewing and no humeral vein in hindwing. Wings held vertically after landing.	Flattened and sluglike in most species.
Clubbed; scaled. Eyes slightly notched around the bases of the antennae.	Very narrow. Palpi quite short.	Wings held spread after landing. Humeral vein present in hindwing, in contrast to lycaenids.	Flattened and sluglike in most species.

Glossary

Aberration A butterfly strikingly different in appearance from the average individual in the population from which it was taken. Often called a "form."

Abdomen The last of the three major body divisions of a butterfly larva, pupa, or adult. It contains the digestive and reproductive organs.

Aedeagus The penis; the male intromittent organ.

Androconia Long scent scales on a male butterfly.

Antennae The pair of long-stalked, jointed sensory organs coming forward from the head, with an enlarged club at or near the tip.

Anterior Towards the head.

Apex The tip of the forewing.

Author The person who first described and named a species.

Batesian Mimicry The acquired resemblance of an edible butterfly species (the mimic) to a distasteful or poisonous butterfly species (the model) for protection from predators.

Bifid Forked or cleft, as a satyrid larval tail or an adult tarsal claw.

Binomial The Latin genus and species names of a butterfly.

Caudal Toward the tail.

Cell A space in the center of a wing enclosed by veins.

Cephalic Towards or situated on the head.

Chitin Horny material composing much of the external skeleton of a butterfly.

Chrysalis Butterfly pupa.

Claws The terminal hook or hooks at the end of the tarsus (foot).

Cline A gradual geographic change in coloration, size, or other feature in a species which occurs continuously throughout an area.

Communal Aggregating together as a group.

Compound Eye A group of hundreds of small eye units called ommatidia, each with its own lens and sensory cells.

Copulation The physical act of mating.

Courtship The behavioral sequence of male and female actions prior to copulation.

Coxa Basal segment of a leg, next to the body.

Cremaster An organ of attachment of the pupa, formed from the anal plate area of the last abdominal segment of the larva and often involving tiny hooks or spines to catch in the silk pupation pad.

Crepuscular Active at dawn or dusk.

Crochets Hooks on the ends of the prolegs of caterpillars.

Dentate With toothlike projections.

Diapause A resting state, such as estivation (over summer or a hot, dry period) and hibernation (over winter or a cold period).

Dimorphism Occurring in two forms.

Disjunct Distinctly separated, as the geographical ranges of two species.

Diurnal Active during the daytime.

Dorsal Upper surface

Emarginate Having a notched margin, e.g., the adult eye of a lycaenid around the base of the antennae.

Epiphysis A spur-like projection on the prothoracic (front-leg) tibia.

Ethiopian Region	The tropical areas of Africa.
Exoskeleton	The outside skeleton of an insect.
Facet	A single, six-sided unit in the butterfly's compound eye.
Family	A group of related genera, tribes, or subfamilies.
Femur	The third segment of an insect leg, often the longest. It is sturdy and undivided.
Food Plant	The host plant on which the larva of a butterfly feeds.
Frenulum	A long, strong bristle or bunch of bristles at the base of the leading margin of the hindwing of most moths and one Australian skipper; it locks onto the forewing and holds the wings together.
Genitalia	The external reproductive organs.
Genus (pl. Genera)	A group of related species or subgenera.
Geographic Races and Subspecies	Groups of geographically separated populations of the same species with somewhat different patterns, colors, sizes, or other physical evidence of adaptive response to differing environmental conditions.
Girdle	A silken thread spun around the thorax area of the larva and attached to an adjoining twig or other surface.
Ground Color	The color of the largest area of the wing.
Haustellum	A sucker-like part of the mouth of a sucking insect through which liquid is drawn into the gullet.
Head	The first of three major divisions of the butterfly body, bearing the eyes, antennae, and mouth parts.
Holarctic	The northern temperate and arctic parts of the world, including the Nearctic and Palearctic.
Hyaline	Semitransparent, as on wing areas devoid of scales.
Instar	The period between two larval molts.
Integument	Cuticle or exoskeleton, the outer covering of the butterfly's body.
Labial Palpus	A sensory appendage on the second maxilla or labium.
Labium	Lower lip on larval head.
Labrum	Upper lip on larval head.
Larva	Caterpillar.
Lateral	On the sides.
Maxillae	The functional mouth parts of a butterfly, including the sucking tube and its supporting structures.
Mesothorax	The middle thoracic segment which bears the forewings and the middle pair of legs.
Metamorphosis	The series of developmental stages through which a butterfly passes from the egg to larva to pupa to adult.
Metathorax	The posterior thoracic segment which bears the hindwings and the last pair of legs.
Micropyle	An opening in the top of an egg through which the sperm passes to fertilize the egg.
Migration	Periodic movement of individuals or groups between two geographic regions.
Mimicry	The resemblance of one individual to another or to a natural object, usually aiding in concealment.
Molting	Shedding the exoskeleton during growth.
Müllerian Mimicry	The acquired resemblance of several distasteful butterfly species to each other, all being avoided by predators.

Naked	Not covered with scales or hairs.
Nearctic Region	Temperate and Arctic North America (New World).
Neotropical Region	Tropical parts of North and South America (New World).
Nocturnal	Active at night.
Nomenclature	Scientific names applied in a classification system.
Ocellus	A colored spot (often with a white or black "pupil") surrounded by a ring of another color.
Ommatidia	The thousands of hexagonal eye units grouped in the compound eyes of a butterfly.
Osmaterium	A Y-shaped, fleshy organ that can be protruded from the top of the prothorax in swallowtail larvae and produces a penetrating odor.
Pad	Small body within the caterpillar that contains the adult body parts in rudimentary form.
Palearctic Region	The temperate and arctic areas of Europe, North Africa, and Asia (Old World).
Palp or Palpus	A three-segmented sensory organ (often hairy in appearance) projecting in front of the face.
Posterior	To the rear.
Proboscis	The sucking tube coiled under the adult face and used for drinking fluids.
Prolegs	Front pair of legs on a butterfly.
Protarsus	Tarsus (foot) of the prothoracic leg.
Prothorax	The anterior thoracic segment; it bears the first pair of legs.
Pupa	The chrysalis; an inactive, mummy-like stage with appendages tightly enclosed, where the larval structures are drastically reorganized into those of the adult.
Savanna	Open grassy plains with scattered trees.
Scales	Highly modified flattened hairs which form a shingle-like covering on the membranous wings.
Scent Pad or Patch	A compact patch of androconia, generally on the upperside of the forewing or hindwing.
Scent Tuft	A tuft of scent hairs displayed by some male ithomiids, nymphalids, and other butterflies during courtship.
Segment	A ringlike or tubular division of the body or of an appendage like a leg or antenna, bounded by sutures.
Sex Patch or Brand	A patch of androconia on the male.
Sexual Dimorphism	A striking difference in color and form between the males and females of a species.
Sibling Species	Species superficially very similar in appearance.
Silk Gland	A gland that passes silk threads out through a spinneret.
Simple Eye	A single eye on the head of caterpillars; composed of a lens and sensory units.
Species	Related organisms or populations capable of interbreeding.
Sphragus	A hard horny structure secreted by the male onto the abdomen of female *Parnassius* swallowtails during copulation; it prevents the female from mating with other males.
Spinneret	An internal tube ending in a pore from which issues a viscous fluid that hardens into a silky fiber. Used in spinning larval pads for pupation or in dropping from a leaf.
Spiracles	Respiratory openings in the sides of larvae, pupae, and adults.

Striated	Many fine transverse markings.
Subfamily	A group of related genera or tribes within a family.
Superfamily	A group of related families. There are two superfamilies of butterflies, the Hesperoidea (skippers) and the Papilionoidea (true butterflies).
Sympatric	Occurring in the same area.
Tail	A slender, scale-covered, membranous projection from the posterior lateral edge of the hindwing, found in certain swallowtails, hairstreaks, pierids, nymphalids, and hesperiids.
Tarsus	The fifth division or foot part of the leg; it usually consists of five subdivisions and a terminal pair of claws.
Thorax	The second of the three major divisions of the butterfly body, bearing the six legs and four wings.
Tibia	Fourth segment of a leg, between the femur and tarsus. It is usually long and slender, and is undivided.
Trachea	A thin-walled respiratory tube in insects.
Tribe	A group of related genera or subtribes.
Trochanter	Second segment of a leg between the coxa and femur, usually short and ball-like.
Truncated	Cut off squarely at the tip, as the forewings of the snout butterflies.
Tubercle	A small projection on the skin of a caterpillar or the surfac of an egg; often with spines.
Urea	A nitrogenous waste product which can be used by pierid butterflies to make white, yellow, and orange pigments.
Ventral	Lower surface.

Bibliography

Listed here are some oustanding books on butterflies of various regions of the world. For the most part, only books in print or readily available are included, but in a few instances rare works are listed for areas not covered by other material.

Africa

Williams, John G.
A Field Guide to the Butterflies of Africa
London: Collins, 1969, 238 pp.

Australia and the South Pacific

Common, I.F.B. and D.F. Waterhouse
Butterflies of Australia
Sydney: Angus and Robertson, 1972, 498 pp.

D'Abrera, Bernard
Butterflies of the Australian Region
Melbourne: Lansdowne Press, 1971, 415 pp.

McCubbin, Charles
Australian Butterflies
Melbourne: Thomas Nelson Ltd., 1971, 206 pp.

Canada

Hooper, Ronald R.
The Butterflies of Saskatchewan
Regina, Saskatchewan: Museum of Natural History, 1973, 216 pp.

Ceylon

Woodhouse, L.G.O.
The Butterfly Fauna of Ceylon
Colombo, Ceylon: The Colombo Apothecaries' Co., 1950, 231 pp.

England and Europe

Forster, Walter
Biologie der Schmetterlinge
Stuttgart, Germany: Franckh'sche Verlagshandlung, 1954,
Vol. 1, 202 pp. Vol. 2, 126 pp.

Higgins, L.G. and N.D. Riley
A Field Guide to the Butterflies of Britain and Europe
London: Collins, 1970, 380 pp.

Howarth, T.G.
South's British Butterflies
London: Frederick Warne & Co., 1973, 210 pp.

Manley, W.B.L. and H.G. Allcard
A Field Guide to the Butterflies and Burnets of Spain
Faringdon, England: E. W. Classey Ltd., 1970, 192 pp.

Mansell, Ernest and L. Hugh Newman
The Complete British Butterflies in Colour
London: George Rainbird Ltd., 1968, 144 pp.

Hong Kong and China

Marsh, J.C.S.
Hong Kong Butterflies
Hong Kong: Shell Company of Hong Kong Ltd., 1960, 113 pp.

India

Wynter-Blyth, M.A.
Butterflies of the Indian Region
Bombay Natural History Society, 1957, 523 pp.

Iraq

Wiltshire, E.P.
The Lepidoptera of Iraq
London: Nicholas Kaye Ltd., 1957, 176 pp.

Jamaica

Brown, F. Martin and Bernard Heineman
Jamaica and Its Butterflies
Faringdon, England: E. W. Classey Ltd., 1972, 478 pp.

Japan

Esaki, Teiso and Mitsuo Yokoyama
Coloured Illustrations of the Butterflies of Japan
Osaka: Hoikusha, 1955, 136 pp. (Text in Japanese, names in Latin.)

Shirozu, Takashi and Akira Hara
Early Stages of Japanese Butterflies in Colour
Osaka: Hoikusha Publishing Co., 1962, Vol. 1, 142 pp.
Vol. 2, 139 pp. (Text in Japanese, names in Latin.)

Lebanon and the Middle East

Larson, Torben
Butterflies of Lebanon
Beirut: The National Council for Scientific Research, 1975, 255 pp.

Liberia	Fox, Richard M.; Arthur W. Lindsey, Jr.; Harry K. Clench; and Lee D. Miller "The Butterflies of Liberia," Memoirs of the American Entomological Society Philadelphia: Academy of Natural Sciences, 1965, 438 pp.
Malawi	Gifford, David Butterflies of Malawi Blantyre, Malawi: The Society of Malawi, 1965, 151 pp.
Malaya	Corbett, A.S. and H.M. Pendlebury The Butterflies of the Malay Peninsula London: Oliver and Boyd, 1957, 537 pp.
New Zealand	Laidlaw, W.B.R. Butterflies of New Zealand Auckland: Collins, 1970, 48 pp.
Southern Africa	Clarke, Gowan C. and C.G.C. Dickson Life Histories of the South African Lycaenid Butterflies Cape Town: Purnell, 1971, 272 pp. Pinhey, Elliot Butterflies of Southern Africa Cape Town: Nelson, 1965, 240 pp. Swanepoel, D.A. Butterflies of Southern Africa Cape Town: Maskey Miller Ltd., 1953, 320 pp. VanSon, G. The Butterflies of Southern Africa Pretoria: Transvaal Museum, 3 volumes: 1949, 1955, 1963
Trinidad and Tropical America	Barcant, Malcolm Butterflies of Trinidad and Tobago London: Collins, 1970, 314 pp.
Venezuela	Schmid, Michael and Bradford M. Endicott Mariposas de Venezuela, Spanish-English edition Caracas: Calproven C.A., 1968, 67 pp.
United States of America	Ehrlich, Paul R. and Anne H. Ehrlich How to Know the Butterflies Dubuque: W.C. Brown, 1961, 262 pp. Klots, Alexander B. A Field Guide to the Butterflies of North America, East of the Great Plains Boston: Houghton Mifflin, 1951, 349 pp.
California	Comstock, John Adams Butterflies of California Los Angeles: privately published, 1927, 334 pp. Emmel, Thomas C. and John F. Emmel The Butterflies of Southern California Los Angeles: Natural History Museum of Los Angeles County, 1973, 148 pp.
Colorado	Brown, F. Martin; Donald Eff; and Bernard Rotger Colorado Butterflies Denver: Denver Museum of Natural History, 1957, 368 pp.
District of Columbia	Clark, Austin H. "The Butterflies of the District of Columbia and Vicinity," United States National Museum Bulletin No. 157 Washington, D.C., 1932, 337 pp.
Florida	Kimball, Charles P. The Lepidoptera of Florida: An Annotated Checklist Gainesville: Florida Department of Agriculture, 1965, 363 pp.
Georgia	Harris, Lucien, Jr. Butterflies of Georgia Norman: University of Oklahoma Press, 1972, 326 pp.
Illinois	Irwin, Roderick R. and John C. Downey "Annotated Check List of the Butterflies of Illinois," Illinois Natural History Survey, Biological Notes Vol. 81 Decatur: University of Illinois, 1973, 60 pp.

Kansas	*Field, William D.* "A Manual of the Butterflies and Skippers of Kansas (Lepidoptera, Rhopalocera)", Bulletin University of Kansas Vol. 39 *Lawrence: University of Kansas, 1940, 327 pp.*
Minnesota	*Macy Ralph W. and Harold H. Shepard* Butterflies, A Handbook of the Butterflies of the United States, Complete for the Region North of the Potomac and Ohio Rivers and East of the Dakotas *Minneapolis: University of Minnesota Press, 1941, 247 pp.*
New York	*Forbes, William T.* "Lepidoptera of New York and Neighboring States, Agaristidae through Nymphalidae, Including Butterflies, Part IV" *Cornell University Agriculture Experiment Station Memoir, No. 371, 1960, 188 pp.*
North Dakota	*Puckering, D. Lovell and Richard L. Post* Butterflies of North Dakota *Fargo: North Dakota State University, 1960, 32 pp.*
Pennsylvania	*Tietz, Harrison Morton* The Lepidoptera of Pennsylvania: A Manual *Agricultural Experiment Station, University State Park, Pennsylvania, 1952, 194 pp.*
Virginia	*Clark, Austin H. and Leila F. Clark* "The Butterflies of Virginia" *Smithsonian Miscellaneous Collections, 1951, 116, 239 pp.*
Washington	*Pyle, Robert Michael* Watching Washington Butterflies *Seattle: Seattle Audubon Society, 1974, 109 pp.*
Wyoming	*Ferris, Clifford D.* "An Annotated Checklist of the Rhopalocera of Wyoming," *Agriculture Experiment Station, University of Wyoming, Science Monograph, No. 23, 1971, 75 pp.*

Index

Numbers in italic refer to illustrations.

Credits

Note: The numbers refer to the photographs.

1-10, Maria Zorn
11-16, Othmar Danesch
17, L.A. Williamson/Natural History Photographic Agency
18, Edward S. Ross
19, Boyce A. Drummond III
20, Edward S. Ross
21, Kjell B. Sandved
22, John F. Emmel
23, Edward S. Ross
24, D.C.H. Plowes
25, Boyce A. Drummond III
26, Edward S. Ross
27, Keith S. Brown, Jr.
28, Thomas C. Emmel
29, Edward S. Ross
30, John F. Emmel
31, Edward R. Degginger
32, Peter Ward /Kirrin Lodge
33, Thomas W. Davies
34, Anthony Bannister/Natural History Photographic Agency
35-37, Othmar Danesch
38, Stephen Dalton/Natural History Photographic Agency
39, Edward R. Degginger
40-44, Gayle Strickland
45-48, L.A. Williamson/Natural History Photographic Agency
49-54, Kjell B. Sandved
55, Othmar Danesch
55-66, Kjell B. Sandved
67, Othmar Danesch
68, Thomas C. Emmel
69-79, Boyce A. Drummond III,
80, 81, Edward S. Ross
82, James H. Carmichael, Jr.
83, 84, Edward S. Ross
85, Larry West
86, Edward S. Ross
87, H. Vannoy Davis
88, James H. Carmichael, Jr.
89, Edward S. Ross
90, Thomas C. Emmel
91, Edward S. Ross
92, 93, Thomas C. Emmel
94, Robin Fletcher/Natural Science Photos
95, Keith M. Spencer
96, Boyce A. Drummond III
97, Peter Ward/Natural Science Photos
98-102, Edward S. Ross
103, Sonja Bullaty and Angelo Lomeo
104, Thomas W. Davies
105, Sonja Bullaty and Angelo Lomeo
106, Boyce A. Drummond III
107, 108, Edward S. Ross
109, 110, Larry West
111, Edward S. Ross
112, C. W. Perkins
113, Edward S. Ross
114, Thomas W. Davies
115, Larry West
116, Edward S. Ross;
117, S.K. Ong/Natural History Photographic Agency
118, Thomas W. Davies
119, Hermann Eisenbeiss
120, Robert Goodden/Worldwide Butterflies Ltd.
121, Larry West
122, Anthony Bannister/Natural History Photographic Agency
123, Edward R. Degginger
124, Stephen Dalton/Natural History Photographic Agency
125, 126, Thomas C. Emmel
127, Edward S. Ross
128, Peter Ward/Natural Science Photos
129, Keith M. Spencer

130, Robin Fletcher/Natural Science Photos
131, Thomas W. Davies
132, Keith M. Spencer
133, Boyce A. Drummond III
134, N.A. Callow/Natural History Photographic Agency
135, Boyce A. Drummond III
136-138, Edward S. Ross
139, Werner Zepf/Natural History Photographic Agency
140, Edward R. Degginger
141, Hermann Eisenbeiss
142, Larry West
143, Gayle Strickland
144, H. Vannoy Davis
145, Stephen Dalton/Natural History Photographic Agency
146, P.H. Ward/Natural Science Photos
147, 148, Edward S. Ross
149, Robert Goodden/Worldwide Butterflies Ltd.
150, Edward S. Ross
151, L. Hamilton
152, Nicholas Brown/J. Allan Cash, Ltd.
153, Werner Zepf/Natural History Photographic Agency
154, H. Vannoy Davis
155, Edward S. Ross
156, Paul Burnham/Kirrin Lodge
157, Werner Zepf/Natural History Photographic Agency
158, 159, Larry West
160, Gayle Strickland
161, Larry West
162, Edward S. Ross
163, Max Berger/Natural Science Photos
164, 165, Werner Zepf/Natural History Photographic Agency
166, Edward S. Ross
167, Boyce A. Drummond III
168-170, Edward S. Ross
171, Boyce A. Drummond III
172, Edward S. Ross
173, 174, D.C.H. Plowes
175-177, Thomas W. Davies
178, Thomas C. Emmel
179, 180, Keith S. Brown, Jr.
181, Boyce A. Drummond III
182, 183, Keith S. Brown, Jr.
184, Thomas C. Emmel
185, Othmar Danesch
186-188, Thomas C. Emmel
189, Keith M. Spencer
190, Boyce A. Drummond III
191, Keith M. Spencer
192, 193, Edward S. Ross
194, Keith M. Spencer
195, Peter Ward/Kirrin Lodge
196-198, Edward S. Ross
199, Thomas W. Davies
200, Keith S. Brown, Jr.
201, Othmar Danesch
202, Edward S. Ross
203, Peter Ward/Kirrin Lodge
204, Edward S. Ross
205, H. Vannoy Davis
206, Edward S. Ross
207, Thomas C. Emmel
208, Keith S. Brown, Jr.
209, 210, Edward S. Ross
211, Boyce A. Drummond III
212, 213, Thomas C. Emmel
214, Edward S. Ross
215, Ivan Sazima
216, David Muench
217, Thomas W. Davies
218, 219, Edward R. Degginger
220, 221, Thomas C. Emmel
222, 223, Edward S. Ross
224, William A. Bake, Jr.
225, Edward R. Degginger
226, Stephen Dalton/Natural History Photographic Agency
227, David Cavagnaro
228, M. Chinery/Natural Science Photos

229, Alois Bilek
230, Larry West
231, P.H. Ward/Natural Science Photos
232, Larry West
233, Gayle Strickland
234, P.H. Ward/Natural Science Photos
235, 236, Larry West
237, Betty Randall
238, Robin Fletcher/Natural Science Photos
239, Larry West
240, Edward S. Ross
241, Larry West
242, Edward S. Ross
243, Stephen Dalton/Natural History Photographic Agency
244, Thomas C. Emmel
245, Keith M. Spencer
246, Alois Bilek
247, C.W. Perkins
248, Alois Bilek
249, P.H. Ward/Natural Science Photos
250, Stephen Dalton/Natural History Photographic Agency
251, P.H. Ward/Natural Science Photos
252, 253, Edward S. Ross
254, Stephen Dalton/Natural History Photographic Agency
255, Robin Fletcher/Natural Science Photos
256, Larry West
257, C.W. Perkins
258, Othmar Danesch
259, Edward R. Degginger
260, Thomas C. Emmel
261, Alois Bilek
262, Edward S. Ross
263, F.G.H. Allen
264, Edward S. Ross
265, Alois Bilek
266, 267, Larry West
268, Robin Fletcher/Natural Science Photos
269, Nicholas Brown/J. Allen Cash Ltd.
270, 271, P.H. Ward/Natural Science Photos
272, Stephen Dalton/Natural History Photographic Agency
273, Robin Fletcher/Natural Science Photos
274, Gayle Strickland
275, Larry West
276, Edward S. Ross
277, Larry West
278, R.C. Revels/Natural Science Photos
279, M.W.F. Tweedie/Natural History Photographic Agency
280, David Muench
281, Robert J. Long
282, Edward S. Ross
283, David Cavagnaro
284, Robert Goodden/Worldwide Butterflies Ltd.
285, Larry West
286, 287, Werner Zepf/Natural History Photographic Agency
288, Thomas C. Emmel
289, Larry West
290, J. Shaw/Bruce Coleman, Inc.
291, Thomas C. Emmel
292, Stephen Dalton/Natural History Photographic Agency
293, 294, D. Overcash/Bruce Coleman, Inc.
295, M.F.W. Tweedie/Natural History Photographic Agency
296, Allen Keast
297, Keith M. Spencer
298, Boyce A. Drummond III
299, Keith M. Spencer
300, Thomas W. Davies
301, Bernard d'Abrera
302, Robert Goodden/Worldwide

Butterflies Ltd.
303-306, Thomas W. Davies
307, Bernard d'Abrera
308, M.W.F. Tweedie/Natural History Photographic Agency
309, M.P.L. Fogden/Bruce Coleman, Inc.
310, Thomas C. Emmel
311, M.P.L. Fogden/Bruce Coleman, Inc.
312, Carl W. Rettenmeyer
313, Bernard d'Abrera
314, Larry West
315, Edward S. Ross
316, Bernard d'Abrera
317, Robert Goodden/Worldwide Butterflies Ltd.

Map page 108-109, Howard Friedman.